In 1988, David Mason joined the French Foreign Legion. He stayed for five years and served in the Legion's elite Parachute Regiment. In 1998, alone with three camels, he walked across Australia at its widest point, carrying out the first recorded solo east-to-west crossing of the Simpson Desert. For this expedition he was awarded the Gold Medal of the Australian Geographic Society. He wrote a book of this journey titled, *Walk Across Australia: The First Solo Crossing.* For a decade David was Counsel, International Law in the Department of Defence. He was Senior Adviser to Australia's Defence Minister and later, National Security Adviser to the Attorney-General of Australia. David left the Attorney's office to pursue a Doctorate in Law at the Australian National University's College of Law. His doctoral thesis deals with the status of mercenaries in international armed conflict. David has deployed on operations eight times and is the only person to have served as a Legionnaire, Australian Defence Civilian on Bougainville and in Iraq, Private Contractor in Iraq, and as an Australian Defence Force Officer in Afghanistan.

HACHETTE MILITARY COLLECTION

MARCHING WITH THE DEVIL

LEGENDS, GLORY AND LIES IN THE FRENCH FOREIGN LEGION

DAVID MASON

hachette
AUSTRALIA

Author's note

For nearly two centuries men have joined the French Foreign Legion. Men in its ranks have died, deserted or served their time with honour. Each man has a story of the things he saw, did and felt. This story is mine.

First published in Australia and New Zealand in 2010
by Hachette Australia
(an imprint of Hachette Australia Pty Limited)
Level 17, 207 Kent Street, Sydney NSW 2000
www.hachette.com.au

Second edition published in 2011

This edition published in 2017

10 9 8

The authorised representative
in the EEA is
Hachette Ireland
8 Castlecourt Centre
Dublin 15, D15 XTP3, Ireland
(email: info@hbgi.ie)

National Library of Australia
Cataloguing-in-Publication data:

Mason, David, author.

Marching with the devil: legends, glory and lies in the French Foreign Legion/David Mason.

ISBN: 978 0 7336 3913 5 (paperback)

Mason, David.
France. Armée de terre. Légion étrangère – History.
Soldiers – Australia – Diaries.
Soldiers – Australia – Biography.

355.359094

Cover design and illustration by Luke Causby, Blue Cork Design
Cover image courtesy of AdobeStock
Map on page vii © 1992 Magellan Geographix/Corbis
Text design by Bookhouse, Sydney
Typeset in Simoncini Garamond by Bookhouse, Sydney
Printed and bound in Great Britain by Clays Ltd, Elcograf S.p.A.

*This book is dedicated to my friend Brett Duthie,
who helped me out of many tight spots when a lesser
man would not; to those few good men in the Legion;
and to those too few good men who stay.*

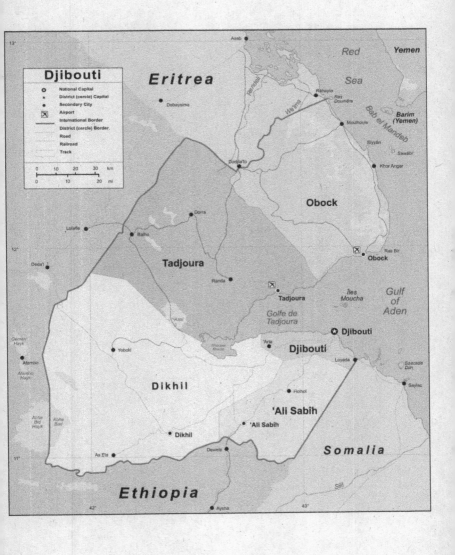

CONTENTS

PREFACE

If a man tells you he has never dreamed of joining the French Foreign Legion he is a liar, has no imagination, or both. The Legion is a place of fierce passion, fears, fighting and fucking. In short, it is the perfect home for a young man who needs to test himself somewhere unforgiving, uncaring and uncompromising.

In 1894 a French Foreign Legion general told his troops, 'Légionnaires, vous êtes faits pour mourir, je vous envoie là où on meurt' – which translates as: Legionnaires, you are made for dying, I will send you where you can die.

In my mid teens, while living in suburban Canberra, reading and dreaming about adventures in far-off places, those words were powerful and confronting. Rather than fatalistic or focused solely on death, I read them as a challenge and an invitation to live. The words, and the feelings they evoked, remained deep inside me; I would always be someone who needed to test himself.

By the time I eventually joined the Legion in Paris and began a five-year contract of service, I was twenty-seven. After six years of study, I'd graduated from the Australian National University in Canberra. I had spent a year as an associate to a Supreme Court judge in Darwin in the Northern Territory. It was the late 1980s and, on the face of it, with an Honours degree, a Law degree and a good first job, I was on my way to a promising career at the bar.

But it seemed to me then, as it does now, that there had to be more to life. I watched my friends sucking cancer into their lungs, growing fat and grey before my eyes, and I knew that their lives of mixed portfolios, new cars and big houses was not for me. I had other ideas.

I spent a childhood on Canberra's suburban fringe, among the golden paddocks, the muddy dams and the dry eucalypt bush of Black Mountain. I spent weekends with my brothers, trapping rabbits and yabbying, playing cricket in summer and football in winter. Bloody knees and ripped shirts from playing British Bulldog in primary school were tended to by my mother with stinging solution and needle. I broke my arms and wrists so many times falling from trees my mother asked a doctor if I had soft bones. He looked at her, then me, and said it was more likely I had a soft head. School was seldom a bore and I did well; sometimes very well. Perhaps I did too well, too easily, and had too much time to dream.

Even from my middle teens, I saw my life as being made up of a number of parts. I knew I had to have an education; it would give me choices as I grew older. I wanted military experience and to serve my country, to learn to live among men. Finally, I wanted to do something that was unique – perhaps write a poem or create a painting that moved people to tears or song, or even climb a mountain. These were things that I understood I wanted to try to do, and I challenged myself to ensure that I did get them done.

I embraced these life challenges because in my world, the industrialised, middle-class western world, there are few measures of worth other than consumption and the possession of things. Unless you seek it out, there is no rite of passage, nothing to temper or define you. A man can hide, passive and complacent, in a large organisation and never really be exposed; forever fearful of challenge and change. Me, I wanted to be tested, so I looked for things against which I could measure myself and learn.

During my years at Canberra High School I left home to hitchhike around the country. I loved the sunrises, the open plains and the far horizons that I found. I loved, too, the frank conversations of men. I worked at an open-cut coalmine in central Queensland and, later, down shafts mining opal in Lightning Ridge.

At university I was elected President of College, played all the sport I could fit into a week and trained myself until I was lean and hard. I boxed, relished the fear of entering a ring and was an Australian Intervarsity runner-up. I parachuted, ran up mountains and sometimes ran for twenty-four hours without sleep. Neglecting any studies I did not like, I excelled in what interested me and told too many lies to too many young women I did like.

Still, this was not enough. I wasn't satisfied, no matter what I achieved; and even when I failed, it didn't seem to touch me.

There was something missing – a meaning, a thing truly significant. But if not sport, sex or drinking until I fell over, what was it to be? The answer had to be something that went to the core of me. I wanted something powerful, yet I didn't know where to look. No one I asked could guide me.

I looked to the men I knew and sought inspiration. But there was nothing in their lives that moved me. Instead, when

I watched my father and other men, it was as if they were insubstantial, as if the shadows they cast were indistinct. So, if they were not my role models, where to look? Sport, acting or politics – there seemed little that appealed.

The great explorers and travellers did strike a chord with me, though. They risked everything in their pursuit of what they wanted to achieve. In driving themselves they sometimes had to abandon their home, their country and their security. I imagined that many of them were lonely and felt exposed. This appealed to me because I could relate to such aloneness; I felt alone in a world that seemed to value things that I did not.

I needed adventure, an experience that exposed me – raw and hurting. I wanted to see the hurt, and wonder and worry at the feeling it left, like at a scab on a wound. No one I knew seemed to understand this. My parents certainly didn't. I was not long a teenager when I first took off alone to hitchhike the countryside. My father ignored me. My mother gently shook her head and told her friends I would grow out of whatever it was that drove me. She was wrong. I never did and I would leave home, for weeks or months at a time, with little warning.

Was I reacting to something? Was there emotional hurt or neglect? It did not feel so then. There was a hellion inside me. It told me I was surrounded by banality; empty, fruitless, meaningless life that had little value beyond its existence. The question was not so much one of escape from a world I did not like. Rather, it was a need to reach out and become much more than I was. I wanted – no, I needed – to feel my heart soar, to sob at things that moved me. There was no finding that in peak-hour traffic, standing in line for a lunchtime salad roll or negotiating a mortgage with a bank.

So I looked beyond the world of university and law. My adventure had to be unique and difficult. It was to be my crucible, and if it were anything less, it would be too easy and therefore of no value to me.

I knew I had to leave my hometown, my own shores, to have a great adventure. I embraced the hellion and the fire that drove me from the prospect of an easy life. I knew then, as I know now, there are many who feel like me. The difference is in actually doing something about it, in using the fire as a fuel to do extraordinary things.

I joined the French Foreign Legion but I could have attempted to climb Mount Everest – both are extraordinary things. I chose the Legion because no one I knew had been there or could tell me anything about it. The Legion was remote, alien, intimidating and far removed from my own life, and so all the more attractive. Films and books told me it was full of men who were violent, who whored, drank and fought like demons among themselves and against their enemies. I liked the sound of that.

After its creation by King Louis-Philippe of France, on 10 March 1831, the Legion was sent to Algeria, in North Africa, where it would see a great deal of fighting over more than a century. In fact, the Legion has fought all over the world: in Spain, Morocco, Mexico, Madagascar, Turkey, Europe, Indochina, Syria, Congo, Chad, Djibouti and more. I read that one of the Legion mottos was 'Marche ou crève' (March or die). I loved the sound of that, too. It was unambiguous, uncompromising.

Along with the idea of a military life, the Legion's appeal was its reputation as one of the world's elite units. It was supposedly well trained, had good equipment and its men were said to be well led and honed lean. In the Army Reserve, I had been in Norforce, one of Australia's northern surveillance units, and as an infantry lieutenant later, I'd relished being outside, leading others when the going got tough – when it was wet, when we were tired, when more was asked of us than we thought we could give. In those six years as a Reservist I came first in a number of courses and considered I'd been well trained by some of the best infantry and Special Forces soldiers in the world. I could read a map, knew about weapons and was trained to lead an infantry platoon in an attack. But while the Australian Army Reserve was all great fun, we would never be deployed or go to war. I wanted more than endless exercises.

From all that I had been able to research, the Legion's men had created for themselves, for *la Légion* and for France, an unsurpassed history of pain, grief and glory. I *really* liked the sound of that. Surely joining the Legion was the extraordinary adventure, the crucible I'd been searching for. It was just the place for me.

I've waited almost two decades to tell my story. Why? Because I needed that time to put my service in the Foreign Legion into context and to judge some of the men I met against many I've met since. In the ensuing years, I walked alone across Australia with three camels. Later I tried to walk across one of the world's largest salt lakes and nearly died. I served overseas as a civilian adviser on Bougainville in Papua New Guinea, and then three times in Iraq. The Australian, French and United States governments have decorated me.

Eventually, I collected my thoughts on the Legion, on the men I met and the things I did up until the end of my contract in May 1993. Not much about my experiences while a Legionnaire gladdens my heart. On the contrary, most of them diminished me in various ways. My sense of self was challenged and, at least in part, corrupted.

Some aspects of my service in the Legion made me stronger and since my contract concluded I have been gentler with myself. More than anything, I know I am able to endure the difficult, the hurtful, the heartbreaking.

And now, it is time to tell my story.

1

ENLISTMENT

Voilà la Légion.
(There goes the Legion.)

On Friday, 20 May 1988, I left the Paris Métro at Château de Vincennes and walked along the footpath on a spring morning of crisp air and newly opened flowers. I mounted the cobblestone slope to Fort de Nogent, where I was greeted by a red and green sign screwed into the stone blocks of the fort's wall. The panel of white letters read: *Légion Étrangère: Recrutement.*

My heart beat faster and my throat seemed to swell. I had travelled across the world to do something that the average lawyer would never consider doing. In fact, if I wanted to ruin my career, along with committing rape, murder or robbery, this was probably one of the ways to really cut it short. But I wanted more than a career. I wanted to join the force that told the world its standards were high and exacting; that expected excellence and did not tolerate those unwilling to give their best. I wanted to be with others who sought a military life and who demanded to be outstanding.

So I rapped on the nail-embossed heavy wooden doors until a grille slid back to reveal a shadowed face. The shadow was topped by a *képi blanc*, the iconic hat of the Legionnaire. From the shadow came a one-syllable word that was more a challenge than a question: '*Oui!*'

Then, having for years silently rehearsed the words, I said, 'I want to join the French Foreign Legion.' After a brief pause to study me, and the bag in my hand, he demanded, '*Passeport!*'

I pushed my passport through the grille and the citadel's door opened just enough to allow me to step across the threshold into the darkness within. As I did, a curious feeling swept over me. It was as if, for a moment, time eddied around me. I felt part of that file of thousands of men who had done, or would do, what I had just done and crossed the divide into the French Foreign Legion. At that moment, I was part of the great succession of young men looking for something beyond themselves.

From the half-light of the covered way where a portcullis would once have stood, I could see bright whitewashed façades around a square dominated by a green grassy mound that was bisected by a long-disused carriageway. The Legionnaire who had opened the door, wearing a skin-tight dark green uniform and buckled black boots, indicated with a horizontal wave of his hand that I should move to my left, and I passed through another doorway into a small windowless room. That first Legionnaire I met I never got to know; not his name, his past nor his future. He would forever be remembered as a shadow.

The room had a concrete floor, four metal-grey chairs lined along one of the equally grey walls, and a poster penned in black of a severe-faced Legionnaire looking into the distance. The air was stale with old cigarette smoke and a door too long closed. Like the chairs, the walls were smooth with many coats of paint. I sat, looked at the ceiling, waited, and looked at the poster again. My watch told me I waited fifteen minutes.

Abruptly, a plump fellow bustled through the doorway. He wore a green uniform stretched tight across his belly, with silver metal wings on his chest and two medal ribbons over his heart. The three coloured stripes on a green velcro tab over his diaphragm – two green and one gold – signified he held the rank of *caporal-chef* or senior corporal.

'Australian,' he declared. 'Good. *Allons-y.*'

This last made no impression on me, as I spoke little or no French at all. He laughed and said, 'Come. Yes, come with me.'

I picked up my bag, threw it across my left shoulder, and followed him out the door to the carriageway and then into the spring sunshine of the main square. We passed to the left of the grassy mound and climbed some steps up to the entrance of one of the bright white façades.

Inside, a bitter antiseptic scent hung in the air as if the place were a recently cleaned latrine. On the first floor I followed the Legionnaire with the green and gold stripes along a corridor with a wooden floor buffed to a glassy sheen. He pointed me into another small room, containing only a narrow desk that looked to belong to some minor functionary. Gesturing to the bag I carried, he said, 'Empty.'

As I did so, another man walked into the room. He wore two green stripes on the velcro tab on his chest – a *caporal*, or corporal – and was carrying a clipboard.

'I hear you're an Aussie,' he said, in an accent that was pure East London.

'That's right. What's he doing?' I asked, nodding towards the Frenchman.

He put hands on his hips and smiled. 'Just checking your kit for knives and shit. No worries.'

The *caporal-chef* was quickly making inroads into my bag. Pockets of blue jeans and shirts were closely scrutinised. Various items were placed at the end of the table. These included my camera, Swiss Army knife, a pewter flask of whiskey, my address book, wallet with 850 French francs and a large envelope containing my biographical details and personal documents.

The English *caporal* made an inventory of everything I had. Jeans, leather bomber-jacket, new trainers, T-shirts, shaving gear and the rest. At the bottom of his list he drew a line, under which he began detailing the objects that had been separated.

'The stuff we've got here we keep in a safe,' he explained. 'The rest of your shit, including the gear you've got on, apart from your shaving kit and two pairs of jocks, put back in the bag . . . Oh yeah. Is that flask full?' He was pointing to the pewter container.

It was and I nodded. 'Drink it all now,' he continued. 'Because if you don't, some other bastard sure as hell will.'

So I drank the wonderful liquid while being relieved of my bag and most of my gear. The *caporal* departed with the bag over his shoulder and a few final words of reassurance for me: 'You'll be all right. We'll look after this stuff till you leave here.'

I was led by the plump *caporal-chef* to yet another room, where he told me to strip and gave me a cursory medical examination. He directed me onto some scales and recorded where the arrow peaked, took my height, made me open my mouth, checked me for scars and tattoos, and then checked that I had two balls and an arsehole. Over the next few months my arse got looked at more often than it had in my entire life.

He inscribed the results on another sheet of paper. 'Okay,' he said finally. '*C'est bon.*'

I pulled on my boxer shorts and again followed the *caporal-chef* back out into the empty corridor. He cried out, '*Gamelin, viens là!*'

I supposed it was Gamelin who appeared from a distant doorway. He ran towards the *caporal-chef,* came to attention, arms by his sides, palms seemingly gripping his thighs, his chin elevated. This man was in his early twenties, slight, with black hair, dark eyes and small bat-like ears. He wore a brown-stained, ill-fitting dark green tracksuit and canvas tennis shoes that might once have been white, but were now snot-blotched dirty grey.

Indicating to me with an inclination of his head, the *caporal-chef* addressed himself to the brown stain in dirty green, and said something about a '*tenue de sport*'. With shaving kit and spare underwear in hand, I followed Gamelin to draw my very first Legion uniform. Like his, mine was a stained green tracksuit and dirty canvas tennis shoes. This I gathered was the *tenue de sport*, or sport uniform.

After slipping into my not-so-new clothing, and still with my gear under one arm, I followed Gamelin to my bunk. The sleeping quarters was a high-ceilinged, grey-walled utilitarian space, filled with double bunks and with tall windows along one wall. A quick scan around the room told me it could hold more than forty prospective Legionnaires.

In my dirty green tracksuit, inexplicably sticky around the thighs, I was left alone for a moment on the bunk I'd been allocated. It was not long before two men wearing similarly dirty green *tenues de sport* introduced themselves. According to Tom's tattoo he was an ex-Royal Marine. Benny was from Denmark, barrel-chested and sporting a golden beard. 'Just call me Hagar,' he said. And I did.

A few minutes later, at midday precisely, there was a shrill whistle blast and a cry of '*Soupe!*'

'Lunch,' Tom translated.

We jogged out the door, the rubber soles of our canvas shoes slapping on the shiny wooden surface of the corridor, down the stairs and outside, where we joined other men who were forming up in two columns. We were counted by the English *caporal,* who then gave our number to the generous-bellied *caporal-chef* I'd also met earlier. Marking this number on a piece of paper, the Frenchman declared, '*C'est bon. Allons-y, les engagés gamelle!*' And like dirty green ducks we followed in his wake.

Later I asked Tom for a translation of the *caporal-chef*'s parting remark and learned that *les engagés gamelle* meant 'mess-tin enlistees'; in other words, to the unimpressed Frenchman, we'd all enlisted solely for the food. As Tom put it: 'The Frenchies think we're shit. Why else would we want to join up but to be fed?' Looking around the mess hall and viewing some of the skinny, sunken-faced specimens from whom the green tracksuits hung too loosely, I couldn't help thinking that could well have been the case.

Lunch came on large communal steel platters. There were six pieces of chicken swimming in sauce and beans. On the wooden tables, colour-bleached and corners worn from years of scrubbing, were long sticks of bread with hard crusts and interiors of little substance. If you didn't like the look of the main dish, you could always try to fill up on the bread. Many did.

As steel forks and spoons clattered against the metal trays, and the chatter of many languages filled the room, I had to lean in to hear Tom, who had already formed a rather poor view of our fellow aspiring Legionnaires. 'I can't believe these bastards,' he offered. 'You'd think they hadn't eaten for days. Bloody pigs.'

Most of the green tracksuits were Frenchmen, with a few 'Brits' (that is, anyone from the British Isles, South Africa or indeed the Commonwealth – in fact, anyone who said the word 'fuck'), along with some West Germans, Yugoslavs and others. There was even a hopeful from the Ivory Coast, whose skin was as shiny and black as an oil slick. He spoke melodious French and smiled with pleasure and surprise when I introduced myself and shook his hand. We had all crossed the divide and were to live, sleep and eat together, perhaps for as long as five years.

That day was a Friday and it seemed we had an uneventful weekend ahead of us. Usually on Sunday nights, potential recruits from Fort de Nogent in Paris caught the train to Aubagne, the Foreign Legion's administrative headquarters in the south of France, near the historic Mediterranean port of Marseilles. Unfortunately for me, the Monday after I enlisted was a holiday, so it turned out we'd have to stay an extra week before leaving for the south.

We waited and were wasteful with our time. We spent most of it under the watchful eye of a *caporal* in a smoke-filled room, feigning interest in the flickering images on television. Our number grew to about forty Legion hopefuls, many of whom sat on the plastic chairs, smoked, clapped and laughed at their own farts, and scratched at their balls through their tracksuit pants.

The tedium of waiting was interrupted by two events. The first was my presentation before an officer, a *colonel,* who spoke to me in French and had me sign and countersign a number of pages. '*Tous ça c'est normale*,' he told me. There was no translation into English but the Cockney *caporal* had told me what to expect. It was the Legion's contract of engagement. It meant I would be a Legionnaire for five years. The authorities in Aubagne could break this contract if I did not meet their requirements or those of the recruit course. I have a copy of the contract still.

The second interruption was a visit to a hospital for tests that included checking my blood pressure, knee-bending, eye tests and an abrupt and unnecessarily exploratory rectal examination. Neither well-greased nor gentle, it brought tears to my eyes.

That evening, after the hospital visit and before lights out at ten o'clock, the English *caporal* took me aside in the hallway to give me some free advice. With hands on hips and lips close to my ear he said, 'Listen mate, you've got to get yourself out of the shit as soon as you can. My advice to you is to get yourself promoted fast – otherwise you'll go fucking mad. This place is shit and full of people who are shit.' He was no longer conspiratorial; he was angry.

I must have looked puzzled, so he went on. 'This place is not like what you or the world thinks it is, but you'll find that out soon enough.' He was silent then. Shrugging his shoulders, he walked away into the shadows at the end of the corridor, the buckles of his boots clinking gently in time with his footfall on the wooden boards.

I soon learned that from the moment we arrived the selection process had already begun. Before the week was out, the fellow from the Ivory Coast, a Yugoslav and a couple of dark-haired, rat-eyed Frenchmen had all retrieved their gear and been escorted to the front gate, never to be seen again.

On my final night at Fort de Nogent, I lay in my bottom bunk thinking about the move to Aubagne the next day. In preparation for the grand event, we had been issued our second Legion uniform. Like the tracksuit, this was also second-hand. It comprised stained French Army combat greens, a pair of boots with the usual buckles, and a beret, seemingly large and flat enough to land a helicopter on top of it. I did not feel the least bit military, but I supposed this was hardly the point.

Our money was taken from us and we carried no identification. We were different now, separated from all others. We were in an in-between place: not soldiers, not civilians. To the NCOs around us, at least, we were the lowest forms of life. We were not even recruits yet, merely enlistees, hopefuls – little more than flesh and bone to be processed. No one listened to what we said. No one looked us in the face.

I felt vulnerable. I knew little of what lay ahead but I was relatively untroubled, as already I knew that life and love were like that. What was significant to me was that I had no control over what was to come. I had willingly thrown myself into a world that was not my own, a crucible of my own choosing, and was already being tested.

I thought about the nights I'd spent camped out in Australia's remote places, watching the stars and dreaming of adventures in other places among different people. I was finally where I wanted to be – in an extraordinary adventure.

Tom stirred in the bed above mine, breaking my train of thought. Looking up to the mesh of his bunk, I watched the thin mattress squeeze through the triangles of wire. I thought for a moment of a girlfriend's warm thigh inside black mesh stockings. I supposed there would be no pleasures of the flesh here, certainly not for months. My sigh at that recognition joined the nocturnal sounds of groans, moans and farts of the others on their squeaking, creaking beds.

In keeping with decades of Legion process and routine, late the next afternoon – Sunday, 29 May – after echoed yelling in long halls and enclosed courtyards, a hurried lunch and five rollcalls, a Legion bus spat us out at the Gare de Lyon, the main railway station for trains to the south of France. As we stepped off, there was no 'Bonne chance' from the driver. Instead, just a hiss as the door shut. We were merely the latest of thousands.

The well-practised *caporal-chef* lined us up in two long columns. He had a thick wad of documents in a briefcase in his left hand, and he waved us towards the overnight mail train to Marseilles with his right. As we snaked through the station, green duffel bags across our shoulders, trying to keep the ridiculous berets on our heads with free hands, not one person looked directly at us. Instead, there were quick, oblique glances and the shaking of heads. I even heard a muttered '*Voilà la Légion*' (There goes the Legion). For some reason the *caporal-chef* was in very good humour. He nodded to the passing civilians and murmured things to them in reassuring tones. Then he indicated us with his thumb and laughed.

We soon found ourselves in economy class compartments with facing bench seats. I realised that unless I secured a window seat my chances of sleep would be very slim. I got myself one, with Hagar opposite. Before settling in I went off to the toilet at the end of the carriage, only to return and discover that a Frenchman named Becker had claimed my place. I thought for a moment and realised I didn't want to start off on the wrong foot.

'Get the fuck out of my seat!' I shouted.

Becker moved, not looking at me, and bleated something in French to others in the compartment. Among the words I heard him say '*les mad fuckings*', as I was to learn, a label applied to me and anyone else who spoke English and stood up for themsleves.

What did I care? Like most of the others, Becker stood all night. There was no room to move and after another rollcall, the *caporal-chef* locked us in the compartment. In the close, stifling heat, just before I dozed off, I wondered why it was so necessary to isolate us from the world.

2

THE LEGION'S HOME

Montrez vos culs!
(Show your arses!)

Arriving at the Gare Saint-Charles in Marseilles just after 7 am, how could we be anything but tired, apprehensive and uncertain as to what the future would hold? Hustled by the *caporal-chef* into two dirty, crumpled, twisting green lines, we headed outside to a bus sent to collect us new arrivals. As we climbed in, the driver, another *caporal*, looked at us with an open sneer and the disdain of someone who had seen it all before.

We headed north-east and inland along the autoroute for some 15 kilometres to the small town of Aubagne and Legion headquarters. Passing through the gates between the walls into Quartier Viénot, the guard, in parade dress of *képi blanc*, red epaulettes and a wide blue band of cloth around his belly, presented arms. This is the base for the *1er Régiment Étranger*, or 1 RE.

The first thing I saw, at some 250 metres across the parade ground, was the *Monument aux Morts*, the memorial to the

Legion's dead. Looking like a square marble tomb, it has a bronze globe on top and is guarded by four armed Legionnaires from different eras in Legion history, also in bronze, at each corner. This was the Legion's most significant monument, brought to France from Sidi-Bel-Abbes in Algeria, the Legion's former headquarters, in 1962. The bus turned to the left and climbed a small rise as we passed the *foyer du Légionnaire*, a two-storey white building that housed a bar and shop and was the nearest thing here to an other ranks' club. The *caporal-chef* laughed again, saying, '*Voilà, beaucoup de bières!*' (Lots of beer there!) Another left and we passed through a second gate into the *Section Engagés Volontaires*, a compound surrounded by a 4-metre-high cyclone fence. As before, we were kept from the view of others and the world was kept from us: we were in a compound within a cage.

But at least we'd arrived. Disembarking, we took our duffel bags, which contained our returned personal items, and single-filed into the building marked *Réception*. There were green-clad Legionnaires to the left and right of our line, urging us along and shepherding us inside. We headed down some stairs and into a large windowless room, lit by ceiling-mounted fluorescent lighting encased in iron grilles.

In the unnatural light, away from the morning sun, everything seemed to lose its glow and become monochromatic – just shades of grey and black and white. Along one end of the room was a long, low counter behind which stood men with the familiar stripes of *caporal* or *caporal-chef* on their chests. Above the low hum of uncertain voices came an order: '*Deshabillez-vous!*' I looked left and right to see men forming up before the counter and taking off their combat greens.

Once we'd all stripped, we stood there, forty young hopefuls, with clothes in small bundles at our ankles and, for those without underwear, balls in their hands. And we waited. Legionnaires behind the counter smirked, laughed and pointed at the naked men before them. It was humiliating and I felt sick at my own powerlessness, only made endurable because so many others were in the same position as me.

I heard what sounded like an order: '*Demi-tour droite!*'

Beside me men turned around, their backs now to the counter. So there we were, tired, disorientated and without breakfast, when another voice barked, '*Baissez vos culottes!*'

Men around me who still had underwear on let it fall to their ankles. I followed suit. The voice then ordered, '*Montrez vos culs!*' Men bent over. I now had a translation for that particular French phrase: Show your arses!

I stopped momentarily and heard what I thought was 'What is this bullshit?', followed shortly afterwards by the sound of a fist on flesh and a moan. We waited too long while low-toned discussions took place behind the counter. The order came at last: '*Levez vos culottes!*'

Turning around, we again faced sneers and derision from the Legionnaires on the other side of the counter, while fellows in the familiar greasy-green Legion tracksuits collected our cast-off uniforms. Standing there in underwear that varied from nothing to baggy boxers, we were called in alphabetical order to the counter, where our belongings were searched.

As I waited for someone to call out my name, I glanced around at my fellow hopefuls. A few looked at their feet, as though they were ashamed of something. Others looked at the ceiling, perhaps to remind themselves where they were. It seemed to me that this Legion process had little to do with treating men with respect; it was closer to dehumanising them. I didn't understand why it was being done and I certainly didn't like it.

Before long, the sound of my name filled the room. I turned out the contents of my duffel bag onto the benchtop before an examining *caporal-chef*. Of particular interest to him were my leather bomber-jacket, running shoes and Swiss Army knife. He compared the inventory made in Paris with what he now had before him. My flask was missing. He muttered something and shrugged his shoulders. He then took up the only book I had brought with me – an anthology of nineteenth-century English literature.

'Ah, intellectual, non? Here, French only,' he said, and smiled. He then watched my face as, wetting his lower lip with his tongue, he began ripping pages from the book, letting them fall to the floor. 'I am your friend. *La Légion* no place for intellectuals.'

I looked into his narrow, dark eyes and decided that, in some circles anyway, it certainly was not.

He went through the pockets of my jeans and jacket with a dexterity that indicated experience and had me fill out a docket with my name written at the top. This docket was attached to a duffel bag into which all my remaining belongings were stuffed. He told me that if I was rejected or failed to finish instruction, I would have them all returned to me. If I did stay, he continued, my belongings would go to the Red Cross. He then had me sign another form and waved me away with a disdainful swish of his wrist.

At the conclusion of the search, we new arrivals each had nothing save the underwear in which we stood (if we had any), as well as a pair of socks, a towel and shaving kit. Quickly issued with another green tracksuit and more tennis shoes, we were led off to our *chambres*. These were rooms of off-white walls and white-tiled floors, eight beds, mattresses, sheets and long round pillows. Hagar, Tom and I secured adjoining beds.

It was becoming clear to me that to survive in this place I needed two things: a disposition that did not take to heart every little humiliation and a couple of mates upon whom I could rely. We were hungry and had no idea of what was to happen next. We stayed in our rooms and waited. No one spoke much; we sat on our beds, each thinking through the events of the morning.

And so the hours passed. After an afternoon of whistle blasts and yelling, of being lined up and counted, our names called too many times to remember, and an evening of sandwiches and, later, tears and nightmares for some of the younger would-be recruits, we made it through our first night in Aubagne.

At 0630 hours the next day, after more blowing of whistles, shouting and counting of bodies, we were escorted the 200 metres or so over to the regimental *infirmerie*. For the second day in a row we had no breakfast.

Ordered to strip again, we sat on hard wooden benches, bare feet on cool tiled floors, waiting. In alphabetical order, we were then called to another room. We learned from those who were first that we had to give blood; this much was obvious from the cotton swabs they held to their arms and the fact that their faces looked very pale.

'I just don't believe this shit,' said Tom.

'Fucking crap, man,' agreed Hagar.

Then it was my turn.

I have never enjoyed having steel pointy things being stuck into me. To distract myself from the inevitable, I said hello to the medic, who wore a white T-shirt and a white coat to his knees that was spattered with blood. I nodded to the *caporal* who had escorted us from the holding centre. After waiting until the white plastic-covered bench, coloured with streaks of red, was wiped down with a bloody towel, I lay down and extended my right arm. Then I became very interested in the procedure.

This fellow in blood-spattered white wore no gloves as he prepared to stick into me a rather large-calibre needle attached to a clear, semi-flaccid tube. Having tied the tourniquet, he held a test tube in one hand and, with the other, slipped the needle into my vein. I could only hope the needle wasn't the same as the one he had used on the others.

Blood flowed down the plastic tube, turning it red. Then it flowed into the glass test tube. The medic had to exercise some dexterity to ensure my blood dripped into the glass tube, but gradually the deep red liquid flowed up its sides.

The floor was greasy with blood, I noticed, leaving me to suppose that some of my predecessors had been very generous or the medic less than coordinated. Then I felt the snap at the tourniquet release and sensed, rather than saw, the removal of the needle. The medic placed cotton wool on the puncture and folded my arm over as he waved me off the bench and outside the room. I slid from the bench, stepped onto the floor and nearly slipped on the thick, dark red blood. My feet smeared it across the tiles and red footprints followed me outside.

'This has got to be the fucking nineteenth century!' I declared once I'd made it beyond the door. I was appalled, and couldn't help needing to share my thoughts. 'Gentlemen,' I said to a room of mostly near-naked young men, the majority of whom did not understand a word of English, 'either France does not care about the AIDS virus or it's a third world country. Which is it?'

'Fuck knows,' replied Tom. Hagar just looked very unhappy and shook his head.

The morning disappeared with more waiting, this time to have our height and weight measured. After heading back to our compound and lunch, we were then brought back to the *infirmerie* for the afternoon.

Later that day, a dentist examined me. I walked through the door into his surgery and he indicated for me to open my mouth. He said, 'Okay, *ça va*,' and I was waved away as he called for the next man. I never even sat down.

The last activity of the day was a visit before a tribunal of three medical personnel. In English, they asked if I had ever been in hospital, had any physical problems or currently took any medication. To these questions I replied as well as I could, telling them about my allergy to penicillin and that I had joined for adventure and the possibility of action.

'Okay Mason, *c'est bon*,' said a beribboned *officier* with three gold horizontal stripes on his chest. 'You can go.'

On our third morning at Aubagne, we had what passed in the Legion for 'intelligence tests'. A short, plump, almost breathless *caporal-chef* went out of his way to impress upon us the importance of doing well. He said that if we performed our best, there would be much opportunity for us in the Legion. Anything to give myself a chance, I figured, so I tried my best to answer the multiple-choice tests on mathematics and logic.

Unfortunately, my educational achievements were of little help. The English was of a type I had never encountered before; it was imprecise, the meanings opaque and obscure. Looking around the room, I could see I wasn't the only English speaker having problems. Tom happened to look up and, meeting my gaze, he lifted his eyes to the heavens, shook his head and mouthed, 'Bullshit . . .'

After an hour on one paper, we were given a short break before the next. A young Hungarian was given a paper in

Romanian because there were no remaining tests in his own language. I hoped for his sake he was bilingual. Not that speaking the right language had helped me much, of course.

After a morning of exams, we were bussed off to spend the afternoon at Lavéran, the military hospital in northern Marseilles, to wait for a chest X-ray. The hospital was a place of greasy floors and walls, dirt, cigarette smoke and apathetic staff. The patients looked pallid and sickly – not unusual for a hospital, but made worse no doubt by all the chocolate they seemed to eat and their ever-present cigarettes. Looking around, I hoped I would never end up there. In contrast, even the blood-soaked *infirmerie* didn't look too bad.

At the end of that third day I'd had enough of waiting around for health checks and intelligence tests. I was fed up with being passive, looking forward instead to regaining some control, to experiencing some physical challenges. But I had no idea when that would begin.

There was no life to the Legion legend. Not yet anyway.

3

GESTAPO

Vous êtes Légionnaires. Nix boom-boom!
(You are Legionnaires. No fighting!)

The following day, Thursday, 2 June, I presented myself to Legion security – colloquially known as 'the Gestapo' – at the curiously named *Bureau des Statistiques de la Légion Étrangère*, or BSLE. The Gestapo were housed on the second floor of the administration building, located just outside our compound within Quartier Viénot. I was unprepared for the reception I received there.

An Englishman with pale blue eyes like ice, a bleached freckled face and close-cropped ginger hair met me at the door and waved me into his office. A jacket hung on the wall to one side of his desk. Above the left breast pocket was a red and blue ribbon, below it a metallic brevet, similar to that worn on the tunics of German soldiers in the Second World War. In letters about the circumference, it said *Commando Guyane*. On the desk sat a small plaque that read 'Westway'. His rank was sergeant, or as the French say, *sergent*.

Looking at me, *Sergent* Westway said, 'I'm the guy charged with finding out if you are full of shit or not. Have a seat.' He opened an envelope that I saw contained my passport and driver's licence together with the biographical details I had brought along with me to France. The two sheets of information took a couple of minutes for him to read.

When he'd finished, he looked up from his papers. 'I don't believe this,' he said with genuine disbelief. 'What the fuck are you doing here, Mason? You should be at home laying the foundation for a successful career in law. Get out of my office now. Go and pick up your kit, if there's anything the thieving bastards out there have left – and go home. You're wasting my time. You don't belong here.'

I was sure this harangue was merely part of the screening process. He was testing my resolve. The *sergent* met my eyes and demanded, 'Well, what are you waiting for?'

I gave him a measured, truthful reply. 'I've come a long way to join the Legion and that is what I intend to do.'

He sighed, put his hands behind his head and leaned back in his chair. 'Jesus Christ, you're a fuckwit . . . Okay, very commendable. Listen, I was at university myself, in England, then at the Sorbonne. And I'm telling you, this is no place for you. Have you looked around at the kind of people who are here? I'm telling you that we wouldn't piss on 90 per cent of them if they were on fire. And you already know I'm right.'

After a short pause, he shifted hmself forward, put his elbows on the desk and crossed his arms, preparing for a different tack. 'Let me tell you something. You might think this is melodramatic, but hear me out. I see your life as a Rolls-Royce parked in the driveway. All you have to do is open the door, start it up and drive away. What do you say to that?'

I looked square into his icy-blue eyes. 'You're right. I could go back home and do just as you say, but that would be too easy. That's not what life is all about.'

There was another pause, during which I reminded myself that I had come to look for something I could never know at home. I wanted fear and uncertainty. To play it safe was to die a death in life. People were lining up to climb Everest, had crossed deserts and reached the North and South Poles. For me, the French Foreign Legion was the place to look for a part of myself. Even though I was becoming aware that the Legion was going to be difficult for reasons other than I'd expected, I wanted to join.

Westway broke the silence with another sigh. 'Fuck me, a thinker in search of himself . . . Most people in this world would call you a bloody idiot, but I'll do the best I can for you. How well did you do in your exams here?' I shook my head and replied that I had no idea.

The *sergent* told me to wait there in his office. He was gone for almost five minutes and during this time I watched the other voluntary enlistees, or *engagés volontaires* (EVs), through the office window, which happened to look out over the EVs' compound. I knew my own reasons but I pondered what had brought them to this place. In Paris and during the few days at Aubagne, I had learned that many came because it was their last chance to do something with their lives, or rebuild their lives. They were often failures, and the Legion was, for most of them, the failure's choice. For men like this the Legion was a refuge; a chance to rehabilitate their self-worth through self-sacrifice to a myth and an idea greater than themselves. Even better, the myth and the idea were things of which they could become a part.

While I knew these were generalisations, there were common themes among the groups that joined. As far as I could make out, the Western Europeans – Germans, Scandinavians and others – the assorted Brits and those from the United States were, like me, looking for a military life that challenged them. Many had either left their own militaries because they were dissatisfied with peacetime service, or they had been shown the door for excessive drinking. For some, the former led to the latter.

For the French, who formed the majority of those who joined – though they were often enlisted as Belgians, Monegasques or Canadians (after all, the Legion was *Étrangère*) – they appeared to fit into that category of men whose lives had been punctuated by failure. They were usually directionless. Certainly, there were those who had served in the French Army, but most of these had been national servicemen, and that hardly counted. The Frenchmen told me they were searching for *la gloire*, something more than themselves – which sounded familiar. Joining the Legion also had the advantage, they said, of feeding you regularly and giving you a uniform that the whole world respected.

As for many of the others, including Eastern Europeans and North Africans, it seemed that being fed and having a roof over their heads were the main motivations. For these men, French citizenship after five years (which meant access to social security), and a pension granted by the French government after fifteen years' service, was very attractive.

Importantly, the common thing that brought all these men together was the one step that so many others did not take: they took the chance, crossed the threshold, and embarked on the journey that is the Legion. Whatever I thought or would come to think of these men, there was courage at least in that first step.

Sergent Westway returned and interrupted my thinking. 'The first thing we do is change your name,' he announced as he came through the door. I asked why it was necessary and with a sly smile he simply said, 'Believe me, it's the done thing.'

He paused for a moment before going on. 'Then again if you'd rather not, that's fine. We do this to protect you from enquiries from the outside world. Or,' he added, looking out the window towards the compound, 'keeping you from the world so that you can learn to love us.'

The principle of the *anonymat*, being anonymous to the world, may indeed protect Legionnaires from wives, bankers and governments, but there were at least two other elements to the principle, one of which came to me sooner than the other. Once a man's name is changed, he is prohibited from having contact with the outside world. In many ways, he is a voluntary prisoner. Few EVs understood the implications when they agreed to have their name changed. I had nothing to hide; I would keep my name.

'Okay, not a problem. I have here your test results – excellent. So I'm going to recommend that if your recruit results are reasonable, you pass on to the rapid promotion stream. That will get you quickly promoted to *caporal*, and get you out of the shit.'

It was an echo of what I had heard at Fort de Nogent, and it didn't seem a bad idea at all. Besides, I could always turn it down if it wasn't what I wanted. 'Sounds like a very good idea,' I replied.

He sat behind his desk, rocked back in his chair and crossed his arms over his chest. 'For me this is easy. You're the one who'll have to work for it. Nothing comes easy in the Legion except for getting pissed and catching the pox.'

Again, neither of us spoke, and I looked into those pale eyes of his once more.

Westway shifted forward in his seat, shuffled some papers and said, 'Now to administrative matters. Your passport, you will not see for five years, nor your driver's licence, or anything else. In a way, you become a non-person. I don't believe you can understand what this means. So let me tell you: it is shit. You will be treated like a moron, as if nothing you say is important. French officers are very different from what you are used to. Do not have high expectations of them.'

I noticed he had begun to perspire slightly and then he said, 'I know I'm not wasting my breath, so fucking well watch out. And I don't want to see you back here squealing to be released from your contract.'

'I won't be,' I assured him and he watched me for a moment without saying a word.

'Right, now I can tell you that you're in. The French are not going to reject someone like you. It's too late for you to go to Castelnaudary this Saturday, so enjoy your time scrubbing pots and pans.'

I was in – and I was delighted. Even years after that meeting I remember the thrill of hearing those words. So, too, do I remember his warning. Surely it had to be his job to overdramatise things, to test the resolve of newcomers.

The ginger-haired Englishman had certainly made an impression on me during that first meeting. When I saw him again the next day, *Sergent* Westway had little to say though, as he took me before a tribunal of officers, or *officiers*, all wearing horizontal yellow stripes on their uniform to signify their rank. The three men, with serious faces, were placed intimidatingly along the far side of a long wooden table. Behind them, hung on the wall, was a framed black and white print of a Legion officer with a neatly trimmed beard, perhaps in his fifties, kepi on his head and many decorations on his chest. It was the only adornment to a room that was otherwise grey and clean.

One of the *officiers* motioned me to sit down on a chair and then asked, 'Why do you want to join the Legion?' He held his chin between his right forefinger and thumb and waited for my reply.

'Adventure,' I responded.

There was a murmur from the three and I could sense, rather than hear, *Sergent* Westway shuffling near the door behind me. 'Yes,' said one *officier*, 'but five years is a long time, do you not think?'

'Yes, five years may be long, but you have my background details before you. Once started, once committed, I've never given up.'

There was a nodding of heads and the *officier* in the middle of the three called me forward. On the tabletop, I saw a form. 'Sign here,' he said, indicating with his ballpoint a line at the bottom of the page. I did.

I was now through to the next stage of incorporation into the French Foreign Legion. But if I'd thought I would now be told what was to happen next, or even the structure of my days, I was sadly mistaken.

For reasons not explained to newcomers, that Saturday we were trucked into Marseilles again and taken to the *Centre des Permissionaires de la Légion Étrangère Malmousque* (CPLEM), or simply, Malmousque. This Legion 'holiday camp' is not far from the spectacular coastal road known as the Grand Corniche, and sits perched on a small headland just a few metres from a 5-metre drop to the Mediterranean. This is the place where

Legionnaires may stay and spend their leave because it costs them nothing. From the rooms you could watch small open fishing boats, luxury yachts and ferries entering and leaving Marseilles' Old Port, the main shipping lanes of which pass right by the headland. You could also rest your gaze on the Château d'If, a few kilometres out to the west, the now abandoned island prison where many had languished, and reflect on hope, fear, and time lost and perhaps wasted. Malmousque is a location for dreamers.

On the right of the entrance to Malmousque was a recruiting office, a *Poste d'Information de la Légion Étrangère* (PILE), where hopefuls often presented themselves. There was also the ubiquitous flagpole upon which the French *tricolore* fluttered and snapped in the morning breeze.

On entering the main building, despite the profusion of light, the air was stale, laden with the twin Legion fragrances of beer and tobacco smoke. To the left were the cigarette and beer vending machines. A *caporal* took charge of us and formed us up in *binomes* (or pairs), one French speaker partnered with a non-francophone, and we were then issued with equipment of rakes and small shovels. I was becoming used to the unexpected, and under close observation we spent the rest of the day weeding, collecting rubbish and watching or trying to speak to *les anciens* – those who had been in the Legion for more than five minutes.

I managed to catch the attention of one, an American named Joe. 'Listen,' he said, 'you only have to look around you to see what the Legion is like . . . Jesus, where else would you find a beer machine except among a bunch of alcoholics and social cripples? I'll have done my five years in two weeks and, believe me, I'm going to be one happy camper when I walk out of those gates at Aubagne.

'The only people who do more than five years are those people with fuck-all to do in civilian life. And you know what that means – the guys who stay are generally the shit. Some are okay, but the French are fucking hopeless. Some would kick my ass if they knew I was telling you this. So just look out and never trust a Frenchman. Have a nice day.'

Joe, from Virginia, seemed very, very pissed off, but his words and what I'd seen so far made me question the basis on which the Legion's reputation survived. Was it a fraud? Surely there had to be some substance to the Legion's fame?

Back in Aubagne that night, just before sleep, it troubled me that the negativity I'd encountered in such a short time was so consistent and from sources that seemed reliable. Even so, these shadows did not diminish my intent. I was keen to be a part of the Legion and there was a long way to go.

Sundays were usually easy days in the French Foreign Legion. As usual in Aubagne, ours began with a whistle blast at 0630 and an escort to breakfast for a bowl of chocolate and a croissant. There was another shrill blast to leave the *ordinaire* (other ranks' mess hall), and one more calling us to *corvée quartier* – area cleaning. This last activity was something of a way of life in the Legion.

We would stand in one long line and advance very slowly, with heads bent in deep scrutiny of the ground, searching for cigarette butts and other offensive objects. *Caporals* trailed behind, watching to ensure that we picked up every remnant. I'm not sure why Frenchmen attach such an inordinate importance to the pursuit of butts. Was it because it was one of the few things anyone could measure? For whatever reason, *corvée quartier* was something I did nearly three times a day, nearly every single day I was in the French Foreign Legion.

Here at Aubagne, we were corralled inside the enclosure that included our accommodation block. When we had nothing to do, we sat about outside the block talking and taking in the sun. Here it was possible to watch the traffic barrelling along the autoroute on its way to Marseilles or do chin-ups on the bar provided. Mostly we talked, in our national or linguistic groupings, and watched the other groups. In my group there was Billy, an African-American, undecided as to whether he should stay. He had recently left the US Army and was looking for action. Tom and Hagar had made it through the initial phase of recruitment also and, like Billy, they wondered about their futures with the Legion.

I understood their doubts. We were treated like cattle. We had little idea of what would happen to us. I think being in a state of total ignorance is even more stressful than the possibility of rejection. Forbidden to contact the outside world, read papers or watch the news, we became dumb, ignorant things. We were no longer part of society. So we talked and talked, about life lived and love lost. Some were less keen to discuss themselves and their feelings. Perhaps they were shy, or perhaps they were prudent. We were generally open with each other – some were probably telling the truth, while others were creating a truth for their future in the Legion.

There was a Brit who said he was a bank robber intent on keeping low. 'The bloody coppers will never find me here,' he said. 'All you do is give the Frenchies a dodgy name and it takes 'em two weeks to find out it's bollocks. It's all right 'cause in two weeks the filth will have moved on to another poor geezer.' A German said he had been involved in a fight where knives were drawn. It wasn't his fault someone had been killed. A Frenchman told us how his lover was a countess who betrayed him to her husband in a fit of regret. Anonymity from the world meant he could be safe from the attentions of the Count's hitmen.

These stories led me to understand the other element of the *anonymat*. Not only could a man hide and the Legion keep him close; a man could also join the Legion and be whatever he wanted to be. In joining the Legion, a man could create a new past, a new present and a new future. It was a way for a man to be rid of a past life of mistakes, failure or loss and be reborn. In a practical sense, a man could have a new identity with a new French passport. As I was later to learn, in a psychological sense, men also adopted those parts of the Legion mystique they required for their own needs, to underpin their new identities and reinforce their perceptions of themselves.

When we grew tired of talking, we played soccer on the sloping ground behind the accommodation block. The teams formed up as anglophones versus the rest. The 'rest' included Frenchmen, Algerians, Poles, Yugoslavs and an Italian. The games became very physical very quickly, and on this particular Sunday, just as I set myself to kick a goal, an Algerian tripped me up and I fell. Enraged, I got to my feet and grabbed him by his dirty green tracksuit. In my dislocation, anger and ludicrous sense of superiority, I was going to put his teeth through the back of his head.

From beyond the sidelines a French *caporal-chef* appeared and dragged us apart. '*Vous êtes Légionnaires. Nix boom-boom!*' he said, which I took to mean: You are Legionnaires. No fighting!

'What a wanker,' spat Tom. 'And that little Arab bastard isn't much better.'

A former Royal Marine, Tom didn't have much time for Frenchmen in the Legion and I wondered if he ever would. As for me, I took each man as I found him, no matter his past, his colour or his country. Even so, if anyone tried to trip me I would give plenty in return, which I was to do at some cost further down the line.

Later that day, I dared ask one of the English-speaking *caporal-chefs* if I could have my camera and Swiss Army knife back. This request caused a great amount of bent-headed consternation, whispering and grunts. Apparently, once things were collected by the Legion they very rarely made it back to their owner.

After the *rassemblement,* or parade, at 0730 the next morning, along with Hagar and Tom, I was allocated to the *ordinaire*, to do the washing-up. We three were responsible for washing up all the pots and pans of two day's cooking for hundreds of men. *La plonge* was not a difficult job in itself but was complicated by three factors. First, there was no detergent to speak of. Second, given the preference for grease and fat in the food, there was always an oily film coating everything.

The third factor was the cockroaches. Only in the tropical jungle of south Queensland had I seen bastards as big as these. They were not shy either. Rather than scuttle away, they fearlessly held their positions, until high-pressure water treatment blew their bodies to pieces and smeared whatever was left of them into the grease.

In the afternoon, instead of going back to *la plonge* with Tom and Hagar, I was called out of parade and taken to a small office. There, I discovered three *caporal-chefs* were waiting for me, along with a *sergent-chef* – or senior sergeant, distinguishable by the three angled gold stripes on the velcro tab on his chest. As soon as I entered the room, one of the *caporal-chef*s began to yell at me, the red tongue in his mouth a fat slippery slug, and the thick black monobrow above his nose seeming to bristle as he ranted. He was dark-faced and his complexion grew even swarthier as his monologue continued.

I had no idea what he was talking about. Listening to him, I figured I must have been guilty of some heinous crime. At last, in broken English, the *sergent-chef* told me that once the Legion had one's gear, it was not customary to ask for any of it back. All this noise was about my request.

I was surprised when, for whatever reason, the *sergent-chef* agreed to allow me access to my bag. Against the protestations of the others in the room, and in the company of a *caporal-chef*, I went down to the basement where the sacs were stacked, one atop the other. There was no order to the arrangement and it took me almost fifteen minutes to find mine. Someone had already been through its contents. My leather jacket and Swiss Army knife were gone, but the camera remained.

It seemed that new Legionnaires were required to give up most of what we had, and what we were, without comment or complaint. I didn't like it, and I wondered if what we were to receive from the Legion would make up for what we had surrendered.

4
GOING *ROUGE*

Vous êtes l'avenir.
(You are the future.)

That same afternoon, those of us who had passed the next step to *instruction*, or recruit course, handed back our dirty-green tracksuits and in their place were issued old army greens, a large floppy green beret, second-hand boots and a small band of red material that was to slide over our left epaulette. We had, as the Legion called it, gone '*rouge*' and at the end of the week we would be heading off to join the recruit training regiment at Castelnaudary, in south-western France.

To mark our success our heads were shaved; not attractive, but practical. Some of those who had gone up a rung attempted to lord it over those still in tracksuits, the very latest arrivals. It was childish, and passively condoned by *les anciens*, those kepi-wearing Legionnaires who supervised everything we new recruits did. I was quickly learning that our socialisation as Legionnaires was built on a dislocation from the world, focused on time in service and, too often, exploiting each other's weaknesses.

Despite us all having gone *rouge*, the next day Tom, Hagar and I were again called to work in the mess hall with the cockroaches. During the break for lunch, there was a cry from *les chiottes* (the latrine), where Teabag, another Brit, was working some menial *corvée* – unblocking a squat toilet using a coat hanger, or shoving his hand down the pipe. It was not an uncommon task.

Shortly after his shouted cry, Teabag stormed into the *ordinaire* and exclaimed, 'There's a fuckin' faggot in the shitters! He pulled his dick out an' all. I thumped him one . . . Jesus, I hate Frogs!'

Two Legionnaires, who worked as cooks, rushed to the latrine. They soon reappeared, carrying the alleged offender, a *caporal*, between them, his feet dragging, his face twisted in pain – or was it humiliation or thwarted lust? His appearance before the assembled EVs was met with silence by all except Teabag. The Brit stood up, raised his arm and pointed to the stumbling man: 'Fucking *pédé*!' Teabag learned basic French fast.

Other than Teabag's outburst, the silence continued until the *caporal* was dragged out of the hall. When he was gone, there was a general murmur from those seated and a few slaps on the back, cries of 'Well done, Teabag', and 'Fucking good job, mate' from Teabag's fellow Brits. Apart from that, no one else said or did anything. There was no comment, not even a raised eyebrow from an *ancien* or anyone with rank. No inquiry, no official allegations – no repercussions at all.

The same *caporal* who had tried to solicit Teabag was back at work later that afternoon. I was surprised. Was this how the Legion dealt with accusations of homosexual assault? Was it up to the individual to protect himself? Fine by me; I'm an ugly bastard who can look after myself. But I wondered what happened to those too small or otherwise incapable of dealing with unwanted advances. As I was to find out, in the Legion you looked after yourself as best you could, and sometimes it was not enough.

After a couple of days in old baggy army greens, those on their way to Castelnaudary were measured up for their kit on the Wednesday. So with Teabag, Tom, Hagar and some twenty-five others, I was escorted to *habillement* (clothing), where old *caporal-chef*s went out of their way to measure our inside legs for the new uniforms. Why there was such a need for these guys to handle some of the younger recruits for so long was beyond me. Maybe, like the *caporal* in the latrine, these men who worked in tailoring liked other men, but it puzzled me that, like him, they should be so forward, so aggressive.

Despite the time taken measuring and the noting of numbers, it became clear that for some of us a well-fitted uniform was going to prove rather elusive. Because I had a narrow waist and long legs, I was informed that I was '*taille d'une femme*' (shaped like a woman) and that the tailors did not have uniforms in my size. In English and to no one in particular, I voiced a view that if the Legion's own depot did not have uniforms for its recruits, maybe someone was selling them. A puce-faced, well-bellied *caporal* breathed rancid red wine in my face and warned me that it would be better if I shut up. I did.

He wasn't the only one who gave me advice. On Thursday morning, I found myself allocated to the Legion's newspaper, *Képi Blanc*, where an English fellow told me I was mad. 'Get the hell out of here while you have the chance. I'm telling you, you're wasting your time.'

He went out of his way to point out the *sous-officiers* – senior non-commissioned officers such as *sergents*, *sergent-chefs* and *adjudants* – who were useless for anything other than the consumption of beer and wine. 'The men who remain in the Legion have no other alternative but to stay,' he insisted. 'There's no place outside the Legion for them.' He turned to me, sighed and concluded: 'Get out before it kills your spirit and your soul.'

This all struck me as rather dramatic, and I told him so. He just shook his head and said how delighted he was that he had only nine months left to do of his contract. He made it sound like a prison sentence.

It seemed odd to me, a new recruit, that rather being intimidated by stories of violence, battle and death – something that one would almost expect from a world-class fighting unit with such a proud tradition – everything I was hearing and seeing was so negative. 'Believe me, the *officiers* are shit and they don't give a fuck about you or anyone else' was a common example; others challenged the very professionalism of France's *corps élite*: 'In five years I've yet to hear of the Legion go into anything resembling a military defensive position', or 'The Legion isn't an army, it's a dressed-up Boy Scout group.' It was hardly surprising that this didn't fill me with great confidence in the organisation.

That afternoon, when we were issued our *paquetage,* or kit, the Legion again did not meet expectations. We lined up in alphabetical order and were told to strip. Singly, we approached a bench and received three pairs of *tenue de combat*, vest and pants. Unfortunately, these were rarely of the same size, especially if one found oneself towards the end of the alphabet. Other items included a woollen jumper (too small) and a greatcoat (second-hand), the last of which was more suited to a native of the Ituri Forest in the Congo than a tall person like me. Fellow recruits tried to work exchanges, shook their heads and muttered.

Once we'd been given the one pair of new greens that fitted, boots, socks and beret with the Legion badge, we packed everything else away in brand-new *sacs marine* (duffel bags). We wrote our names on the base of our respective *sacs* and then stacked these in a pile, the flat bottom of the bags visible so we could read each name.

Next up, we were told, was an opportunity to revel in the glorious tradition, the myth, of the French Foreign Legion. It was something I, for one, sorely needed.

The Legion museum is not simply a museum. It is a shrine to a legend; a legend built upon the death of Legionnaires in wild, remote and sometimes unforgiving places. It is an extraordinary place. Outside the building are cannons, carved stones that marked the sites of Legion camps in Algeria and Indochina, a tank, and an amphibious vehicle from the Indochina War.

There are two entrances to the museum. The main entrance faces, and is some 20 metres from, the *Monument aux Morts*. We new recruits were escorted – it seemed we could never be trusted to be left alone – through the side door. There, we were handed over to an *adjudant-chef* (France's equivalent of a senior warrant officer), recognisable, as usual, by the velcro patch on his chest: in this case, a single yellow band with a fine red line through it.

The *adjudant-chef* spoke only in French, which was a shame because the enthusiasm for his subject was clear, and I would've liked to understand the words behind the passion. He stood before us and regaled us with stories, bringing the tips of his fingers to his thumbs and balancing them before his chest for added emphasis. With brand-new berets in hands, we followed him up the stairs to the first-floor display area. Here were stored the relics and souvenirs of Legion campaigns, from Mexico in the 1860s to Lebanon and Chad in the 1980s.

Glass cases containing the decorations, uniforms and rifles of past campaigns brought home the idea of the Legion as a force that had fought throughout the world and left many men dead on foreign soil. A force, too, that despite the disparate nature of its constituents, fought as one.

After going back down the stairs, we turned left into the *salle d'honneur*. This room was dominated by a large table in its centre. On its walls were paintings of the major heroes and historical figures of the Legion. As interesting as it all certainly was, my attention was drawn to the far end of the room, where a handful of steps descended into a crypt.

No remains lay in this crypt. However, to look at the illuminated cross, the dome that allowed in only subdued natural light, the various *drapeaux* (flags), the names of *officiers* killed on campaign listed by country and year, and the wooden left hand of *Capitaine* Jean Danjou in its glass case, I was under no misapprehension that this was a very special place.

My heart beat faster; I felt colour flushing my cheeks and the palms of my hands moisten with excitement. I sought this – a place that acknowledged honour could be had in battle, where actions could be respected and men remembered for what they had done.

On 30 April 1863 in southern Mexico, *Capitaine* Danjou, with two other *officiers* and sixty-two Legionnaires, was trapped in a small farmhouse called Hacienda de la Trinidad – not unlike the Alamo in Texas – some two hundred meters east of the small village of Camarón. They were besieged by thousands of Mexicans. The battle raged most of the day, the heat was oppressive, and the men were without food or water. Danjou was killed early in the battle and by late afternoon, there were only five men left standing: *Sous-Lieutenant* Maudet, *Caporal* Maine, and Legionnaires Catteau, Constantin and Wenzel. At six o'clock, the men had only one round each and at the *lieutenant's* command, they fired.

According to *Caporal* Maine's account of the Battle of Camerone:

We discharged our five rifles and, he [Lieutenant Maudet] in front, we jumped forward with fixed bayonets. We were met by a formidable volley. Catteau threw himself in front of his Officer to make a rampart with his body and was struck with 19 bullets. Despite this devotion, the Lieutenant was hit with two bullets. Wenzel also fell, wounded in the shoulder, but he got up immediately. Three of us were still on our feet . . . but the Mexicans surrounded us with their bayonets at our chests. We thought we had breathed our last, when a senior Officer . . . ordered them to stop and with a brusque movement of his sabre raised their bayonets which threatened us: 'Surrender!' he told us. 'We will surrender,' I replied, 'if you will leave us our arms and treat our Lieutenant who is wounded.' He agreed. He offered me his arm, gave the other to the wounded Wenzel and they brought a stretcher for the Lieutenant. We arrived behind a small rise where Colonel Milan [the Mexican Commander] waited. 'Is this all that is left?' he asked when he saw us. And when told yes he said, 'These are not men. They are demons.'

Having taken us on the tour to show us our past, the *adjudant-chef* formed us up in the *salle d'honneur*. He put his hands on his hips and regarded each one of us in turn. His right arm shot out and his index finger seemed to challenge each of us, as did his next few words: '*Vous êtes l'avenir*' (You are the future).

There was no mistaking the tone of his voice. We were the future of the Legion and we had much to live up to.

When I think back to our time in the museum, three things come to mind. Firstly, if I ever wanted to win people over and have them identify with my cause, I could not think of a better way of doing it. Here were combined ideas of honour, glory and sacrifice for others. Secondly, there was not one mention of France. There was reference solely to *la Légion*. Finally, the *adjudant-chef* was one hell of a good salesman, despite the fact I understood very little of what he said. He won me.

He won me because he was able to convey what the Legion was, or at least what the Legion said it was. When I looked around the room at my fellow recruits, I wanted to know what was it about the Legion in particular that made these men choose to join its ranks? What was it that made them decide to devote themselves to something more than themselves so that they might share in the glory? I wanted to find out because, in finding out, perhaps I could learn more about myself.

The Legion won me then with that reference to 'demons', for I had one of those in me. I had found it. This, finally, was what I had been looking for.

That night, the thirty or so of us who were destined for Castelnaudary the next day went on guard duty for the first time. In new *tenues de combat*, we were to guard the EVs' compound. I did my two hours with a bilingual Frenchman named LeCoq – a useful guy to know as he could explain what the hell was going on. Besides, I thought that if we were going to do recruit training together, we might as well get to know each other.

I had been in the Legion for three weeks and I was yet to hear anyone laugh. Of course, I'd heard angry laughs or laughs intending to humiliate or belittle, but nothing to indicate someone having a genuinely good time. I raised this with LeCoq, who said that in the army people did not laugh. I wondered how long it would take to find out why.

5

WELCOME TO CASTEL

Personne se branle dans les chiottes.
(It is forbidden to wank in the latrine.)

Friday, 10 June, had arrived at last, although there seemed little urgency to the proceedings at first. After being woken up at 0400 hours, we found ourselves standing about idly inside the EVs' compound, waiting for something to happen. At 0630, once they'd had their breakfast, the *sergent* and the *caporal* who were to escort us to Castelnaudary finally showed up. Even then, the truck for our kit was still missing.

It turned up hours after it was due, along with a bus and the relevant paperwork. We embarked for the Gare Saint-Charles in Marseilles and from there caught a train bound for Toulouse. During the course of the next few hours, our journey took us through the spectacular scenery of the Languedoc-Roussillon region and a host of French towns steeped in history – Montpellier, Sète, Béziers and Narbonne among them – roughly following an arc parallel to the coast, before we headed due west and inland for Carcassonne, with its fairy-tale medieval castle, and

Castelnaudary. The latter's twin claims to fame, I learned, were the Foreign Legion base and its standing as the world capital for a traditional culinary dish known as *cassoulet.*

It was shortly before midday when we finally arrived at our destination. Shepherded onto the ubiquitous waiting bus, we skirted the town centre and headed straight to the camp, named Quartier Capitaine Danjou, after the hero of Camerone. Located a kilometre or so south-east of town, between the Route de Pexiora and the Canal du Midi, Quartier Danjou was (and remains so today) the home of the Legion's Training Regiment, the *4ème Régiment Étranger,* 4 REI.

I liked the look of the camp. Not only was it new, but it was spacious and well set out. On entering Quartier Danjou, our bus passed under a red and white-striped boom raised by a Legionnaire on duty, who then presented arms. Ahead, and roughly to the north, was the large red-tarmac parade ground, or *place d'armes.* At each of the *place d'armes'* four corners, an L-shaped, two-storey block served as home to one of the regiment's companies – the three *compagnies d'instruction,* and the *compagnie de commandement et de service.* Set back from the parade square on all sides bar the south, and separated from it by a ring road, were various utility buildings, including the regimental headquarters, to the north, and the *infirmerie,* to the east.

Once clear of the sentry post, the bus followed the road around to the western side of the parade ground. On our left now, we saw a large building containing the *sous-officiers'* mess and our *ordinaire,* while opposite this were the L-blocks housing two of the regiment's companies. All the buildings were off-white, almost a bleached pink, like sunrise across Tangier, capped with terracotta tiles.

The bus stopped in front of the entrance to the *ordinaire* and immediately we were barked at to descend from the vehicle and form up on the road in two groups. Someone had divided our detachment into two on language grounds. The downside of this was that I found myself separated from Hagar, Tom and Teabag. The only Brits in my group, in fact, were a bloke called Northam and the brothers Blacke, the last of whose names were changed to 'Blacker' and 'Blackest'.

Northam seemed like a good lad. Almost six feet tall, he wore glasses and had a benign, affable face. Perhaps it was part of a scheme to win people over, but I didn't think so. Although not an extrovert, he was reliable and trustworthy. He said he had served in the Light Infantry in England and this did not surprise me at all.

On the other hand, there were the brothers Blacke. Both had red hair, were short in height and on brains, with eyes set very close together. Both men were very loud and, I was sure, rather stupid. I thought they were trouble and I was right.

So, one half of our detachment of thirty trainee Legionnaires was sent off to join *2ème Compagnie* (2nd Company), and the half of which I was a part, to *1ère Compagnie* (1st Company), on the other side of the square. We humped our *sacs marine* over our shoulders and formed up in single file behind a *sergent*, who then led us, continuing our clockwise journey along the ring road, towards our new barracks.

After swinging around the north-west corner, the headquarters building came into view, to our left; and, directly opposite it, positioned between the parade ground's top two L-shaped blocks, we soon passed the regimental flagpole. Beyond the fluttering *tricolore*, cradling the north-east corner, was *1ère Compagnie's* block.

In the middle of the road, a *caporal* appeared to be waiting for us. He was smoking, and as we arrived he dropped the butt to his boot and crushed it. After saluting one another, our NCO escort handed us over to the *caporal,* whose velcro nametag proclaimed him 'Dober'.

Caporal Dober spoke to us in French. There was no translation into English, or any other language, so I had no idea what he was talking about. Then he came to attention and again saluted in the manner characteristic to the French Army. His arm described a wide arc – longest way up and longest way down – the arm staying rigid till it was parallel to his shoulder; at which point the forearm bent, describing a short arc to his beret, and then, after a two second pause, descending in a wide arc to a thwack of open palm on thigh. After this performance, with a hitch of his thumb, he indicated that we were to go inside and up to the first-floor corridor. I did what I was to do for the rest of the day, indeed for the weeks and months to come: I followed everyone else.

Arriving in the white-tiled *couloir* (corridor), the fifteen of us waited, with our backs to the wall, for Dober's arrival. He counted off the number of recruits necessary to fill bunks in the various rooms that ran off from the corridor. I placed my *sac marine* beside the bunk I'd been allocated. Then it was '*Tout le monde dehors*' (Everybody out), and we formed up again in the hallway. Here we joined the rest of the *section* that had been awaiting our arrival. Dober began an intense and emphatic dialogue, none of which I followed. Instead I just looked at him.

Caporal Dober was of medium height, very lean, with pointy ears set flat against his head and the colouring and cheekbones of a Mongolian horseman. His monologue ended with a glance at his watch and the barked '*Execution!*'

Although his words had offered me no clue, it became clear from the others that we were to clean our rooms before going off to lunch. And we were to go nowhere without permission from a *caporal*. Most important was the emphatic '*Personne se branle dans les chiottes!*' (It is forbidden to wank in the latrines!)

That I was enlightened on this last point was thanks to a Canadian named Canuk. Rather than being one of the many Frenchman who had changed his nationality to Canadian, to give the fiction that he was a foreigner, Canuk was the real deal. With silver-blond hair and very blue eyes, he looked like apple pie. He'd been at 'Castel' for one week already, with the previous detachment from Aubagne, and had done nothing but scrub and polish lockers, floors, windows and latrines all that time. No wonder he was delighted to see us. For Canuk, our arrival meant a change in routine. We were the second half of his new *section*.

Another blast from a whistle was followed by a cry of '*Soupe!*', which saw everyone drop their cloth rags and bound out to the corridor in an instant. There, Dober greeted us with the words '*Tout le monde en position*', and everyone duly got into position – for pushups.

When you have boots and backsides in your face, pushups become a challenge, especially if you have to do fifty of the things.

'*Debout, bande de clochards,*' Dober shouted next. '*Dehors!*' (Get up, you bunch of tramps. Outside!)

The new guys and the those who had waited our arrival joined the rest of *1ère Compagnie* outside the barracks. Here, we all formed up in *sections* of around thirty men, the French military's equivalent of an Australian or British platoon, and presented to the duty sergeant, the *sergent de semaine*. He was the senior NCO who, with a *caporal*, had company duty for one week; each *section* in its turn having to provide a *sergent* and a *caporal*. The pair slept in the company office, the *bureau de semaine*, and except for mealtimes, rarely got outside. Their responsibilities included the allocation of *corvées*, the direction of Legionnaires to the *infirmerie* and, most importantly, the constant counting of Legionnaires.

The *sergent de semaine* noted the number of personnel in each *section* in a small notebook. We formed up as a company, and marched to the *ordinaire:* long columns of green, the new recruits at the rear. Before many paces, the *sergent* ordered us all to sing.

Someone within the ranks gave a bar or two of the chant, while marching, so that the chant was in time with the marching cadence. A couple of paces, and the *sergent* yelled, '*Trois, quatre!*', so that the chant commenced on the left foot. We marched slowly – very slowly – at the Legion's eighty-eight paces a minute. This was just over two-thirds of the pace of a normal infantry unit in the United States, Britain, Australia or even France. It took some getting used to.

The song they sang that day meant almost nothing to us new arrivals, and even less to those of us who spoke little French, but it was one with which I was to become very familiar: '*Dans la Brume la Rocaille*' ('In the Mist the Rocks'). The English translation is as follows:

> *In the mist the rocks*
> *Legionnaire, you combat*
> *Despite the enemy, the machine gun*
> *Legionnaire, you will overcome.*

> *You fight for France*
> *Under the Legion flame*
> *You will fall for the defence*
> *Of all its traditions.*

Veteran, you that rest
Look and remember,
That the 1st Company has
The same strength as you.

Simple stuff really, but when sung by nearly one hundred men it sent a shiver down my spine. It had all the Legion ingredients: no matter where you are, be prepared to die under the Legion's flame, the seven-flamed grenade that is the Legion's symbol; and never forget, the past is watching and you have a lot to live up to.

That first day at Castelnaudary, I supposed this singing was intended to lift the hearts and souls of Legionnaires within the ranks, but as I discreetly looked about me, not one of the fellows appeared exhilarated. They looked tired and bored. Maybe they were just acting completely pissed off.

As it was, from that day forth I never really minded singing Legion songs. It was something outside me, and something greater than me, to which we all contributed. The sound of a *section*, or a *compagnie*, left boots striking the ground, singing in time with the slow cadence, some with a high tone, others low, will bristle the hairs on anyone's neck, no matter how recently they've been shorn. The feeling was one of history and subdued passion, not forgotten, but controlled. This was at least part of what I was looking for.

Lunch – a couple of cold cuts of sausage followed by crumbed composite beef, boiled beans, potatoes and plenty of bread – was a hurried affair terminated by Dober's cry, '*Troisième Section dehors!*' We in *3ème Section* immediately finished eating, took our platters to some benches where Legionnaires were attacking *la plonge,* and quickly filed out. Outside, we formed up as one *section*, and for the first time, according to height.

We found ourselves in four columns. Layman, a Belgian, was the tallest at the head of the right-hand column. My place was at the head of the second column from the left, with Colonol, a Frenchman, to my right and Schmidt, a German, to my left.

Having thus formed up, Dober began to play games. He would walk some 20 metres away with Layman, and we would all have to sprint the same distance to stay in formation; then he'd go and do the very same thing again, but 50 metres away – and so on. It was very tedious. I assumed this was Dober's way of hinting that we shouldn't eat too much, and a way of exercising control. Even so, it was no way to treat grown men.

We spent the afternoon cleaning everything again and meeting our *section* leader, *Lieutenant* Hildebrandt in his office. Going before the *lieutenant* – or even presenting oneself to a *caporal*, for that matter – was a highly formal, structured affair. Before entering the office, one man at a time, Dober instructed us on how to present ourselves and what to say, down to the finest detail. At least, as well as he could to the non-francophones among us.

On entering the room, as stipulated by the *caporal*, I stopped two paces from the *officier*'s desk. There was no pounding of the foot as there is in the Australian Army, but rather, a neat shuffle. I saluted with palm open, held it for a two-second count of '*Trois, quatre*', the descent concluding with a satisfactory thwack on the thigh. (I'd already noticed that a few of the new recruits had found some paper, folded it tight and slipped it into the right outside pocket of their pants, to ensure the quality of the thwack.)

With my left hand, I removed my beret and kept it firmly in hand, close to my left thigh. Then, all the while at attention, or *gardez-vous*, I presented myself and repeated Dober's spiel, the English version of which would be as follows:

'Legionnaire Mason.

One month of service.

First Company,

Lieutenant Hildebrandt's *section*.

At your orders, *Lieutenant*.'

I remained at attention until the *lieutenant*, after an appropriate pregnant pause, declared '*Tu peux te mettre au repos*' (You can go to a position of stand at ease). To which I replied, '*Je me mets au repos, à vos ordres, mon Lieutenant.*' I then went into an at-ease position, legs shoulder-width apart.

So far, so good.

At this point the *lieutenant* discussed something in French. Most of what he said was lost on me, but I took the gist to be that as a Legionnaire I had entered a brotherhood. It was up to me to be true to that brotherhood.

At the conclusion of the one-way homily, he sat up straight and said, '*Tu peux disposer*' (You can go), to which I responded by coming to attention, setting the beret back on my head and declaring, '*Je peux disposer, à vos ordres, mon Lieutenant.*' I then saluted – not forgetting the slap on the thigh – and did a *demi-tour droite*, an about-turn, to leave the room.

There were a couple of interesting things about this encounter. One was *Lieutenant* Hildebrandt himself: blond hair, very pale blue eyes and very, very plump. He was not my idea of a Foreign Legion *officier* at all, which was sparse of frame and lean of face, with a sharply defined jaw. Instead, my *section* leader had the air of a benevolent badger.

The other point concerned the structured formality that surrounded every meeting with an *officier*. Separated as they often were by the language barrier, how was the *officier* to work the vaunted bond between himself and his men if he kept himself so distant? Why was there such an emphasis on form rather than understanding what the meeting was supposed to achieve?

A few minutes later I heard from the *section* office a loud shout of '*Correct, on a trouvé!*' (That's right, we've found one!) After asking LeCoq what had happened, I learned that one of the recruits, a Frenchman named Millard, had been appointed *popottier*, the apparently very important post of cook to the *lieutenant* and the *sous-officiers* whenever the *section* was away from Quartier Danjou. Why this was so important, I was soon to learn.

At 2130, having cleaned the rooms, latrines and offices, we formed up in the *couloir* of white tiles like the floor of a butcher's shop, from the window overlooking the flagpole and the *place d'armes,* down to the entrance to *les chiottes*. On command, we dropped to the tiles and did pushups, in our boots and new greens, while the *caporal* chanted the up/down cadence: '*Au haut . . . en bas . . .*' Writhing, groaning and grunting, we were like green geckos on hot sand; nearly forty young men, moving up and down, while Dober stood over us and sneered at those too weak to carry on. Bodies sweated and we cursed under our breaths for almost half an hour until *appel* (rollcall).

At 2155, a whistle blast from the company office and the cry '*En place pour l'appel!*' found us at attention and being counted. I heard the same sound across the parade ground from the other *compagnies*. As the count moved from left to right along the single rank we each had to shout out our number. This was difficult for non-francophones, and at every mistake, the individual at fault was loudly informed he was a moron and received a thump of encouragement in the chest from Dober, before the count was restarted.

At last the *sergent* arrived to hear the *appel*. Dober, as the *section's caporal du jour*, and thus responsible for our safekeeping for the day, ordered us to *gardez-vous*, then saluted and presented us in what became the ritual evening chant of my next five years:

'Third *Section* ready for rollcall.

Effective total, thirty-seven Legionnaires;

Effective present, thirty-seven Legionnaires.

Nothing to report.

Materiel complete.

At your orders, Sergeant!'

Dober then handed him the *billet d'appel*, the written record of what he had just shouted. The *sergent*, apparently not satisfied, also went along the line thumping and counting chests. It soon became clear that all this frequent counting was meant to deter if possible – and detect early if not – anyone from choosing to desert.

With Dober's *billet d'appel* in his fist, the NCO bid us good night with, '*Bonne nuit, mes enfants*' (Good night, my children). As one we shouted, '*Bonne nuit, Sergent!*'

It was true, the *sergent* treated us as if we were children. When he'd thumped my chest earlier and exhaled, I caught the scent of wine on his breath.

The following day we had our photographs taken, in civilian and military clothing. Later we learned how the Legion liked to have all kit folded into squares of 30 centimetres and placed into lockers. This was not very practical as everything was in one tall pile, meaning that to get one thing out you often had to refold everything. To ensure that lockers were clean and things folded *carre comme carre* (in a perfect square), as Dober had said, he and the two other *caporals*, Kronk the Frenchman, and Malvina the Argentinian, were very enthusiastic in their reviews of our efforts. They believed they were stamping their authority over us.

Caporal Dober entered our room, we jumped to *gardez-vous*, and he began a meticulous examination of our lockers. Rooting around behind Lebeck's socks and jocks, he found a pair of soiled underpants and was thus inspired to lecture us all on the importance of hygiene. Dober then ripped the cotton garment into bite-size pieces. Lebeck perspired and dry retched as the *caporal* stretched open his mouth and stuffed the cloth inside.

Dober was almost beside himself with zeal. It was this zeal, so clearly written in his glittering eyes, which probably set LeCoq off sniggering. It was contagious, and I began to snigger too – not at Lebeck's discomfort, but at the stupidity of what was happening. Dober was outraged. He came over to me with Kronk, looked away to distract me, and then gave me a tremendous elbow in the guts. I was winded and collapsed to the white-tiled floor with a slap of skin and a thud of body. Placing his booted foot on my throat, Dober then lectured everyone again in passionate French before eventually leaving our *chambre*.

As I lay choking and gagging, spit running down my chin, I knew I would have to exercise better self-control. I knew, too, that I would have to keep a careful eye on Dober and not give him another opportunity to humiliate me.

It was an important lesson for survival on this recruit course, and no less important was the choice of *binome*, and next day each non-francophone teamed with a French speaker. Like many things over the next few months, this took place in the corridor outside our rooms. The Frenchmen stood with their backs to the wall along one side of the *couloir*, the rest of us on the other. Dober got the non-francophones to choose their *binome*. It was like being ten years old and picking a girl for a dance, although this was for months rather than minutes.

Despite a couple of the other Frenchmen pulling on my arm, I chose LeCoq because, of all his compatriots in *3ème Section*, he spoke the best English. I wanted to know what was going on. I knew that a basic tenet to any soldiering was knowledge and anticipation, yet I could already see my fellow recruits becoming passive, waiting to see what would happen next. Therefore, LeCoq became my *binome*. He and I shared the same double bunk and over the next fourteen weeks we were, during course activity at least and therefore for the most part, inseparable.

While Sundays for those not in the Legion's Training Regiment was ordinarily a day of rest, we ran. As part of a physical test, we had to run around a synthetic track behind the *ordinaire*. The track was 400 metres in circumference and we had twelve minutes in which to do as many laps as we could. Unfortunately, we only had our recently issued flat-bottomed canvas tennis shoes and none of us had run for weeks.

We ran in two groups. The *binome* of one counted the times his partner made it around the track. LeCoq ran first and did almost eight turns. I managed eight-and-a-half circuits, which turned out to be the best performance of the entire *section*.

Even *Sergent* Romett, the only English *sous-officier* in *3ème Section*, was enthused. His narrow, pinched face hiding rows of crooked teeth nodded in appreciation. The Brits generally helped each other out with information or equipment, but Romett was different. In fact, when Northam tried to have a short chat with him, the *sergent* simply told him to fuck off. This was unfortunate – we craved insights into the Legion from anyone who had been in longer than us.

For the next couple of days there more locker reviews, more cleaning of things like bed frames, walls and toilets; lots of scrubbing toilets. LeCoq told me we were to go to the *compagnie* farm, Bel Air, on Wednesday for a period of three weeks or so. Apparently, this was where we'd get into some serious training, which would certainly make a useful change from the endless *corvées* we had endured thus far. All of us were yet to have a lesson, see a rifle or even be instructed on how to march properly. We just got yelled at for being stupid.

We were issued more kit, including *épaulettes de tradition*, the Legion's standard red and green shoulder boards, and a *ceinturon bleu*, a metre-and-a-half length of blue woollen material that one wound about the waist. Reportedly a legacy of war in North Africa, the latter item was designed to keep the kidneys warm and so ward off dysentery. How these *ceinturons bleu* were relevant today was beside the point; they were symbols of our heritage and marked us out as Legionnaires.

Later we were also issued sports kit from the foyer, like that in Aubagne, where you could buy beer and essential items like shaving gear and T-shirts, located in the same building as the *ordinaire*. At last a reasonable tracksuit, and cheap (though far better than those we'd had at Aubagne) runners. Through LeCoq I learned that we were not issued this gear at all, strictly speaking. Rather, we had purchased it ourselves. One of the many forms that we had to sign gave Hildebrandt the power to deduct these and other costs from our monthly *solde,* or pay, of 1200 francs. I wouldn't have minded having to pay, because we needed good running shoes; but why did our *section's* Algerian *sergent-chef* – the equivalent of a British or Australian platoon sergeant – *Sergent-Chef* Mahmood, not tell us or explain? According to LeCoq, even the Frenchmen in our *section* had no idea what was going on half the time. Maybe he was just trying to reassure me.

LeCoq, my *binome*, was some 170 centimetres tall, of middle build with elephantine protruding ears. His character was harder to pin down, however. He would be happy and moderate one minute, then prepared to beat the shit out of someone the next. In moments of ire, he used to roll his shoulders forward and frown, his huge ears flushing red and giving his face a very brutish look. I figured that these great emotional highs and lows could have been due, in part at least, to his background. According to LeCoq, his father used to beat him unconscious, things getting so bad that a church group had to rescue him and place him with another family when he was sixteen. His family background might have been true, but I didn't believe it completely accounted for his erratic behaviour. There was something else.

We lived, if living it was, in a *chambre* at the end of the corridor on the top floor of the *1ère Compagnie* block, sharing with the *binomes* of Stein and Fekler, Millard and Locolo, and Lebeck and Contein. Each pairing occupied a double bunk, LeCoq taking the top one in our case.

Connected to the room was its own *salle de bain*, a bathroom of one shower and two washbasins. The latrine was down the corridor. At night, Dober waited in one of the cubicles to catch out masturbators.

6

THE FARM

Dépêche-toi, ou je vais t'encul à sec!
(Hurry up, or I'll arse-fuck you without lubrication!)

As LeCoq had predicted, *3ème Section* left for the farm on Wednesday, 15 June. We marched some 15 kilometres to Bel Air, known to all as simply 'the farm', set in the southern French countryside. On our backs we wore musettes, similar to the canvas packs used by the British Army during the Second World War, inside of which we all carried identical items: a chunk of bread, a can of sardines, a spare pair of socks and jocks, and a plastic jacket called a K-Way.

Even on such a relatively short march, a couple of the recruits had trouble making the distance. Chief among these was Locolo, who pointed with a flourish to his feet and declared in a thick Spanish accent, *'Pieds pas bons'* (Feet no good). For a former Spanish Foreign Legionnaire, which Locolo assured us he was, he was not at all impressive. Maybe the *Legión Española* didn't march very often. But more significantly, why had nothing been done for the huge warts on his feet? Little wonder he found it so painful to walk.

Any hardship some might have felt was cerainly worth the effort. Bel Air was a pastoral pleasure, a location surrounded by green rolling farmland with copses of trees, some almost amounting to small forests. We marched through farmyards with dogs barking and farm smells of chickens, pigs and fresh cooking. I was reminded of local history when we passed by stone memorials, mounted with wrought-iron crosses, to Frenchmen killed in ambushes by the Germans in 1944.

Each of the training companies, the *compagnies d'instruction*, had its own farm. They brought their newest recruits to these farms to be 'formed' into Legionnaires, over a period of three to four weeks, by the *section* staff – the Legion's *anciens*. For us, the *anciens* were *Lieutenant* Hildebrandt, *Sergent-Chef* Mahmood, *Sergents* Romett and Bronski, and the three *caporals*, Dober, Kronk and Malvina.

After a chunk of bread and a slippery sardine each, we placed our musettes against the stone wall of the farm and did some Legion drill. *Sergent* Bronski, whom I had taken for a fairly reasonable fellow, took great delight in giving contradictory or confusing orders that made us look stupid. On a simple turn for example, he would give the order '*À gauche droite*' (Left . . . right) instead of '*À gauche gauche*'. I found it tedious. It was our first drill lesson.

Next, we unloaded the truck that had brought our gear and put it upstairs in what was to be our accommodation for almost a month. It started to rain, and because the roof leaked and water ran down the walls, *Caporal* Kronk turned off the electricity. He didn't want anyone electrocuted on his watch. If our first prepared meal at the farm was inauspicious – beans and corn from a can, with a lump of gristled fat and a chunk of bread – it set the standard for what would follow.

Not long after sunrise the next day we went on what was to become an almost daily activity: a long morning run. I ran with the *première groupe*, having performed so well on the run back at Danjou, with *Sergent-Chef* Mahmood, a veteran of the Legion's famed Parachute Regiment, as our leader. In the fresh June morning we ran some 8 kilometres, a truly liberating experience. It was exhilarating to be able to feel the power in my legs and fill my lungs and my senses with the countryside around me. After the desiccated eucalypt bush of Australia, this land was filled with dark green. Everything we ran by looked fat – the cattle, the sheep, the geese; even the blades of grass seemed to be swollen with goodness and moisture. Australia's air, golden with dust and pollen, was a distant memory. Within running distance around the farm at least, the air was clear and crisp. After a final sprint up the short, sharp hairpin bend into the grounds of the farm, we did pull-ups and situps until we choked and burned.

I loved the physicality of these mornings, to feel my muscles and tendons stretch, my heart thumping and sweat rolling down my cheeks. More than anything, I loved leaving the closed spaces of Quartier Danjou and Bel Air, where everything we did was scrutinised, then mocked or condemned.

Unfortunately, LeCoq and I were allocated *les gamelles* twice that day. This meant that rather than looking after my own kit, I was scrubbing large battered pots. As usual, there was no detergent and we scrubbed with steel wool, dirt and small stones. Despite all our efforts, the permanent fine layer of grease remained. The kitchen was a primitive affair: a bench, a hand-wound can opener and four large gas rings set above bricks, presided over by whoever had been tasked with food preparation. The blackening of the pot bases from these gas rings was the focus of much attention when the *caporals* reviewed our work. There was also a refrigerator for food, although we recruits never received any fresh fruit or vegetables, just pickled things out of a can.

There was more to the farm experience than drill, running and the usual *corvées*. At the opposite end of the stone farm-house from where we slept, there was a small, concrete-floored classroom into which the entire *section* crammed for a lecture. In this low-roofed, soon-stuffy room, *Sergent* Bronski educated us on the different regiments within the Legion. During the course of his discussion on the regiment stationed on Mururoa Atoll in the southern Pacific, he made a number of jokes about Greenpeace and the sinking of its flagship, the *Rainbow Warrior*, back in July 1985. From the tenor of his remarks, and thanks to LeCoq's translation, I gathered that most Frenchmen viewed DGSE agent Dominique Prieur and her bomber accomplices as nothing short of heroes – and good for them that they'd been able to escape the clutches of a very naive New Zealand government. It came as no surprise to hear this, but the arrogance underpinning Bronski's comments, not to mention the elbowing and smirking among the other Frenchmen in the room, was tough to tolerate.

Next morning, just before dawn, I waited for Kronk to open the door to our room so that I could use the latrine. Every night the thirty-odd of us in *3ème Section* were locked in our room at Bel Air, as the staff appeared certain that someone would try to desert. It was not clear to me why anyone needed to desert. Sure, there was the odd punch, kick or thump dealt out to us, but to have joined the Legion and not expect some intense physical encouragement . . . Well, you'd have to be very ill-informed, if not naïve. I had read accounts written by former Legionnaires, mainly British, all of whom made it very clear that violence demanding adherence to orders was a fundamental aspect of life in the French Foreign Legion. It was simple really: either you demonstrated conformity to the will of the organisation or the organisation did not want you.

The trouble for the Legion was finding the right balance, getting the mix just so; not too violent, nor too soft. After all, when you had such a wide variety of people enlisting, how was it possible to get the mix right every time? Besides, if those candid anciens I'd spoken to back in Paris, Aubagne and Malmousque were to be believed – and so far, little of what I had seen personally contradicted their assessment, it has to be said – the Legion might have told the world it was all about professionalism, but it certainly didn't seem to attract or keep many who were professional. Maybe the really good ones were in the regiments, away from Castelnaudary. I had to hope so.

There was no question of balance when it came to the Legion's grand marching song, 'Le Boudin', which we were introduced to by *Sergent-Chef* Mahmood that evening. The way we stood and sang reminded me of old black and white footage of the Hitler Youth standing around roaring fires at night, singing their hymns to the Fatherland. We were taught the words only in French, as an aid to learning the language. 'Le Boudin' was always sung while at *gardez-vous* and today remains the most important song in the Legion.

First, a none-too-subtle introduction sets the tone, the English translation of which is:

> *Another pretty boy fucked*
> *In the tent of the padre*

And then it's straight into the song's chrous, the French word *boudin* meaning a type of sausage:

> *Tiens, voilà du boudin, voilà du boudin, voilà du boudin,*
> *Pour les Alsaciens, les Suisses et les Lorrains,*
> *Pour les Belges, y en a plus, pour les Belges, y en a plus,*
> *Ce sont des tireurs au cul.*

> *[Look, here is the sausage, here is the sausage, here is the sausage,*
> *For the Alsaciens, the Swiss and the Lorrains,*
> *For the Belgians have not any, for the Belgians have not any,*
> *They are arse-fuckers.]*

The last two lines are reprised for maximum offence towards France's northern neighbours.

The Legion has both a public face and a very private one. There's no hiding the fact that '*Le Boudin*' is a highly provocative, bawdy song sung by men, many of whom are affected by alcohol when they belt out the words. They know what the words mean, just as surely as they sneer in derision when other, saccharine words are published by the Legion or the French Army – the public face – and consumed by an unknowing, ignorant public.

While tapping our plastic shavers into a shared tin washbasin before dawn on Saturday, Blacker confided to me that he was fixed on leaving. The red-headed Englishman was pigeon-toed and could not run or march. As such, he was an indictment of the Legion's screening process. He and his idiot brother Blackest talked about getting themselves to Canada. How they thought they might do so, nobody knew; but they talked about it long enough to irritate the rest of us.

If they wanted out they had to desert. There was no walking away before the end of recruit training at least, but even then, there was some confusion regarding this last point. According to Mahmood, no one would be granted permission to leave. 'Once you sign it's for five years, yes?' the Algerian said in his broken English. If his words were designed to stop people from thinking about quitting, they had the opposite effect.

At 0600 the next day, a quick coffee, bread with a smear of jam, the raising of the flag and we were off running. We ran in our blue *1ère Compagnie* T-shirt, white shorts and white socks with Legion stripes of red and green. While we had to keep in close with the *sergent-chef*, it didn't trouble me, as mentally, I was already a long way away. I often did that: just let the body do its work and let the mind travel away, to places I had been and places I wanted to go. It was a way of resting emotionally and putting things into perspective. It helped that I had always run a lot, at university especially, and more recently I'd even won Army Reserve regimental awards for running.

Back at the farm afterwards, and while standing under the prostate-troubled dripping showerhead, a tearful LeCoq punched the air and told me he too was leaving. He'd been demoted to the second running group for some reason and then bashed by *Sergent* Bronski for making some insolent comment. The evidence was a swollen left eye.

After his shower, LeCoq saw the *lieutenant*. According to LeCoq, he was told he could not leave until the end of fourteen weeks' instruction. This was news to me and everyone else, and quite different from Mahmood's comments only the day before. It was quite typical, though; we rarely got straight answers to questions, if we got answers at all.

In any event, LeCoq remained most unhappy, so I gently asked if he had some sort of medical problem contributing to his inability to cope. His response was a straightforward 'Go fucking away and leave me alone.' I thought it was his sugar levels. He was always at his most lucid after a meal.

It wasn't long before I found my own resolve being severely tested. That same Sunday, with most of the *section* staff in town drinking, Dober, as *caporal du jour*, thought he'd keep us occupied by having us weed the lawn in front of Bel Air. The only tools at our disposal were our fingers. As I twisted weeds between my thumb and forefinger, I realised that these would be hours of my life I had wasted. I squatted, twisted and pulled at the weeds, all the while feeling Dober's hot eyes on my back.

I hated wasting time. And I hated Dober's imperious walk and the demeaning way he spoke to the men in his charge. I wanted to stand in front of him and scream in his face that we were men who simply wanted to learn, not chattels for his pathetic amusement. But I did not. I kept my own counsel.

The incident from day two at Castel was fresh in my mind – Dober's boot on my throat and the realisation that I'd need great reserves of self-control around him – and I reminded myself that if I felt this way, at least it meant I was still alive, still passionate. And I allowed myself to admit what I had been suspecting, that this treatment of us could in itself be a form of instruction. As far as the Legion knew or cared, we were worthless, we knew nothing – so weeding was a task that suited us well. I gritted my teeth, twisted and pulled for all I was worth.

Even then, I had to hope that our enthusiasm and willingness to submit would not be wasted. When would those who knew better actually use us and grow us into Legionnaires, as soldiers in their elite force? It was too much to expect complicated instruction; we all recognised language as the major barrier. Besides, any person who had been through or read up about military recruit courses expected to be treated as if he were an ignorant thing. In time though, and certainly as basic instruction progressed, things changed for the new recruit: having endured and proved his worth, he began to be treated better as he was integrated and indoctrinated into the army. I wondered when this would happen to us.

The following week, the *première groupe* of runners was down to six from our original twelve. One day's run along the Canal du Midi for almost two hours was a heartbreaker for many. But me, I was never giving up. As the lone Australian in *3ème Section*, I would never give in to pain. It was this, I think – the knowledge that we were representatives of our respective nations – that drove many of us beyond what we thought possible. Often we were referred to by our country of origin, as the Australian, the Brit, or the German. So who wanted to be the Australian, the Brit or the German who gave up? I made a commitment to myself that it would never be me.

One morning, without any indication or warning that we were to do so, we suddenly found ourselves doing that most soldierly of things: handling weapons. It was Wednesday, 21 June when, after the usual morning run, we were loaded into trucks and headed off to a small rifle range called Burnell, some 5 kilometres west of Quartier Danjou. There, finally, we'd be firing the French Army's rifle, the FAMAS, the assault rifle manufactured at Saint-Étienne in central France.

The weapon is a bull-pup design; it is short, compact and neat, fires a 5.56 mm round, and weighs some 3.5 kilograms. One can fire one round, three rounds or an unlimited burst that can empty the twenty-round magazine in a matter of seconds.

If I thought there was a ritual surrounding presenting to a *caporal*, it was nothing compared to firing a rifle in the Foreign

Legion. Inspected by *Lieutenant* Hildebrandt, we formed up 100 metres from our targets. We placed our weapons down, supported on their bipods, and stood at *repos* (at ease), each man behind his weapon.

When all was ready, with three rounds placed by a *caporal* on the ground next to each rifle, Hildebrandt declared: '*Pour les tireurs – gardez-vous! Numérotez-vous!*' (Firers – attention! Number yourselves!)

Then, from left to right, we responded. In my case, as the first in line: '*Tireur numéro un, prêt. À vos ordres, mon Lieutenant!*' (Firer number one, ready. At your orders, *Lieutenant*!)

At the conclusion of numbering, Hildebrandt declared, '*En position!*' So we went to ground.

'*Graillez vos chargeurs!*' So we loaded the rounds into our magazines.

'*Approvisionnez!*' We loaded the magazine onto the weapon.

'*Armez!*' We cocked the weapon, loading a round into the breach.

'*Selecteur de tir au coup par coup!*' Using the selector lever, we set the FAMAS to single round by single round. By squeezing the trigger, we could now fire the weapon.

At last the order came to fire when ready: '*Des que vous êtes prêt n feu!*'

I don't know who it was, but someone moved their *selecteur de tir* to the wrong position. They fired their three rounds in one burst. The three rounds of what were meant to be aimed shots weren't too well aimed at all.

Above the firing I could hear our plump *lieutenant* screaming, '*Crétin! Mongol! Tête de noeud!!*'

It was hardly the environment for concentrating on firing a rifle, but fire the rifles we did. When I'd finished I gave the appropriate response; I stood up, went to *gardez-vous* and yelled, '*Tireur numéro un, tir terminé. À vos ordres, mon Lieutenant!*'

Then I waited for more rounds.

But that was it – there were no more. Those three rounds were all we were to fire. I waited, disbelieving, until pushed away by one of the *caporals*.

Hildebrandt had his right hand on the holster of his 9 mm pistol, I noticed. Was it a valid concern that someone would go berserk? Maybe it was – perhaps it had happened in the past. We picked up the brass casings and surrendered them to Kronk, who counted them. Malvina then re-counted and Dober verified the number of brass casings to make sure all were present.

So much for firing the FAMAS, and we still hadn't learned how to take it to pieces. Only later, back at Bel Air that afternoon, on the grassy oval next to the farmhouse, did we get to clean the rifles. Those who didn't know how to strip the weapon joined those who did. I knelt on the grass next to LeCoq and watched.

A *caporal* stood in front of the long rank of us and demonstrated how to take it apart. He did so quickly, without explaining how, what or why. Then one of the *binome* had to strip the weapon in its entirety. If you got something wrong, a *caporal* patrolling behind the rank would *baffe* (punch or slap) you in the back of the head and call you a moron. It was an afternoon punctuated with expletives and groans. But no matter what – we'd finally seen a weapon, after four weeks in the French Foreign Legion.

Next day we were trucked to the *parcours du combattant*, the assault or combat course, next to Burnell range. This was not like an Australian or British combat course. Everything in this place was concreted; there was no water, no dirt and no mud. We did little but watch the *caporals* cross obstacles, none of which looked too difficult. I figured that if the *caporals* could do something, it couldn't have been hard.

Following the combat course and a lunch of bread and a smear of pâté, we threw practise grenades on the field beside the farmhouse. This was nothing to do with accuracy, just distance. I threw the furthest, over 50 metres, and smiled at what a lifetime of cricket will do.

My success upset LeCoq – which delighted me. I was becoming very tired of his complaining and his sense of superiority. 'After all,' he'd say, 'haven't you and the other fuckings come from all over the world to join our army? Why would you join if it wasn't the best or you had nowhere to go?' As Tom, the ex-Royal Marine, had first noted back in Fort de Nogent, this uncomplicated and apparent truism was shared by so many Frenchman that it was almost universal.

But I'd selected LeCoq as my binome, so there was no escaping the man. The Legion *section* is divided into three groups, or *groupes,* and a command *groupe.* In our group the commander, or *chef de groupe*, was *Sergent* Bronski, supported by *Caporal* Kronk. Bronski was a blond-haired, blue-eyed Frenchman. As an *ancien* of the Legion's Parachute Regiment, *2ème Régiment Étranger de Parachutistes* (2 REP), he wore silver wings on the right side of his chest. He also drove a two-door BMW. He seemed arrogant, tolerably intelligent, but ignorant of much of the world outside France. Disturbingly, his teeth were all false, the rear set being of stainless steel, so that when he opened his mouth he reminded me of Jaws in the James Bond movie *Moonraker.*

Kronk was a Frenchman with what I assumed was an Austrian background. A likeable-looking fellow, he was missing his left eye tooth. Some 165 centimetres and of slim build, he was a cross between a pixie and a very angry quasimodo. He had a forced laugh, which was a little like a Father Christmas but a lot more throaty, and very irritating. When he laughed, it was a comment to himself on our performance, and to demonstrate to us his derision of our efforts, of course. He was from *2ème Régiment Étranger d'Infantrie* (2 REI), the Legion's Infantry Regiment at Nîmes.

As for the other recruits in the group, they were the same characters, the same binome pairings, as those LeCoq and I had been rooming with at Quartier Danjou. Stein, a blond Austrian, who looked startlingly like the eagle out of *The Muppet Show*, carried a knee injury and had trouble keeping up on the morning runs. Fekler was a slim, highly strung Frenchman much given to theatrical hand gestures.

Contein was a French farmboy with the longest vowels I had ever heard. Lebeck, also French, was reserved, thickset, and in his early thirties; he was starting life over again in the Legion and never did tell me why. And I never asked.

Frenchman Millard had a round, open, garrulous face that seemed to find enjoyment in all things, particularly in cooking. Locolo was swarthy-skinned with long-lashed, stormy eyes. The Spaniard had joined Millard as a *3ème Section popottier*. This job had its advantages and disadvantages.

Some saw a benefit in not having to run every morning, for instance. At least one of the *popottiers* had to stay behind to prepare the *casse-croûte* of omelette, fried or scrambled eggs for the staff. Plus, by being *popottier* you got to eat any leftovers. Not just eggs, but also fruit and fresh vegetables.

The significant disadvantages of being a *popottier* included being abused, humiliated, and slapped, as well as having to be up well before everyone else to make coffee for the *lieutenant* and his *sous-officiers*. One morning I heard Malvina, the Argentinian *caporal*, giving Millard an earful. '*Dépêche-toi*,' he shouted, '*ou je vais t'enculer à sec!*' (Hurry up, or I'll arse-fuck you without lubrication!)

During our time at Bel Air, morale was very low. More than ten recruits – almost one third of the *section* – asked the *lieutenant* for permission to leave the Legion. Their reasons included the lack of contact with home. I wondered what they had expected. Contact with the outside world was strictly controlled, that much was obvious from everything they must have read or heard before joining, surely.

But the other point was that the Legion instruction was hardly onerous, judging by what we'd seen so far, and compared, say, with the experience I'd had as a recruit in the Australian Army Reserve. The three weeks of training I had in Australia, around Ingleburn and Holsworthy in the west of Sydney, with Regular Army officers and non-commissioned officers, taught me more about the military, my rifle and the value of time than anything I had yet seen in the Legion. It seemed to me that maybe the Legion's recruit course wasn't about instruction at all, at least not as I understood the term.

While the Frenchmen were complaining about the lack of contact with home, the Brits and the Germans complained that the Legion was like the Boy Scouts. I agreed with them on that score – although that's probably being hard on the Scouts. While the Legion's reputation promised plenty, the reality of the farm fell way short of that promise. The instruction was poor and the discipline not controlled to a specific end. Instead it seemed designed to fuck you around for no apparent reason, with a slap and a kick to round things off. There was simply no consistency to the Legion's idea of discipline.

Anyway, given the number of people who had asked to leave *3ème Section*, *Sergent-Chef* Mahmood was now decidedly nervous. He formed us up in three ranks and said that, given the threat of desertion, we would not be able to go for a piss except as a group.

While I couldn't be certain it was connected with the *sergent-chef's* comments, next morning LeCoq went completely mad. His anger was apparently not focused on anything. It was as if he were possessed; his face and ears burning red, his lips drawn back from his teeth.

I put my finger to my lips, and when he saw that being mad near me would get him nowhere, he stormed off. He beat the shit out of another recruit, Godber, punching the harmless Frenchman till he was unconscious. No one really looked after Godber; they simply put him into his bunk and revived him for the morning run an hour or so later. How Godber made it through the day I was not sure. One thing though – he was never quite the same again.

7

GARDENING AND *KÉPIS BLANCS*

Fais gaffe, Mason, *fais gaffe* . . .
(Look out, Mason, look out . . .)

Behind Bel Air, beyond the grassy football field, there was a wood. The ground there was carpeted in vines and the crowns of the trees met to make the place shadowed and dark. Through the wood were paths worn by thousands of Legion feet. One afternoon in late June, we went patrolling – or more accurately, for a lesson in French Foreign Legion movement in close country.

The French idea was to follow a track, with the patrol moving along it in single file. The numbers one and two in front kept an eye out while the rest simply followed on, rifle over shoulder, probably day-dreaming of sex. There was no sweeping of the rifle through a designated arc, eyes following where the barrel of the weapon pointed.

Sergent Bronski asked me to demonstrate some of the techniques I had learned back home. I indicated that in Australia we never walked on tracks and that everyone participated in patrolling. I then demonstrated how we looked through vegetation, not at it.

All this was greeted with a 'Très bien' from the sergent, but according to him, the methods I described were far too slow. Anyway, as he put it, when patrolling the Legion way, if you did get ambushed, there were always people to back you up. Essentially then, individual patrol skills were not a priority.

I looked at Bronski, then at my fellow Legionnaires, and thought how many Australian Army warrant officers simply wouldn't believe it.

On Sunday, 26 June, Layman, the tallest member of our *section*, was sent to the *infirmerie* back at Quartier Danjou. He had what looked like ulcers on his legs; red, raw, angry pustulant things. Layman was tired and run down, with dark smudges under his eyes. I thought he could've done with more vitamins and better sleep. Then again, I was sure we all could've done with much better food.

As the Belgian was driven off, we squatted down and spent another Sunday weeding, with *Caporal* Dober again standing over us. As on previous occasions, our only tools were our hands. So, thirty-six young men, volunteers for what we had believed was one of the best fighting forces in the world, spent another day squatting on haunches, pulling out weeds.

Dober came to this regiment from *6ème Régiment Étranger de Génie* (6 REG), the Legion's Engineer Regiment. Like Kronk, he had been sent to 'instruct' one or two recruit courses before being allowed to do his *sergent* course. These hopefuls hated it at Castelnaudary. They were paid less than in other regiments in France yet never enjoyed any trips overseas, just the soul-destroying processing of men, many of whom preferred to desert than remain. It was a reason why our *caporals* treated us as a step to their own ends, rather than as men needing training.

It appeared that for the most part, the *sous-officiers* who instructed had returned from a two-year posting overseas and found themselves sent to Castelnaudary. The carrots offered them were certain promotion and a position overseas at the conclusion of three or more years with the Training Regiment. From their point of view, the rewards were hardly commensurate with a posting generally viewed as the least desirable in France.

But to return to Dober; he began to look more and more like a dog. Coincidentally, although perhaps this informed my view of him, he wore a badge on his chest that proclaimed him a dog handler. During our weed-pulling sessions, Dober would prod some hapless fellow with a switch and demand he sing. When inevitably my turn came, I gave what I thought to be a stirring rendition of 'Waltzing Matilda'. It provoked a round of applause from my fellow gardeners, but I noticed Dober's upper lip raised in a sneer, revealing tobacco-stained teeth.

Next day more weeding, and again the day after. We spent days weeding with our hands yet received just two pathetic lessons on the FAMAS. A run after breakfast, a bit of drill before lunch and weeding in the afternoon – what sort of instruction was this? While it degraded us as things not worth teaching, it also diminished those who had responsibility over us. Like my fellow recruits, I was looking for leadership and direction. There was none.

On Saturday, 2 July, during morning *rassemblement*, with us in sports kit and before the *tricolore*, *Sergent-Chef* Mahmood had an important announcement. On Tuesday, we recruits were to undergo the Legion's rite of passage, known as the *Marche Képi*

Blanc. Carrying 20-kilogram *sacs* and rifles, we would march up to 40 kilometres in a single day. If we succeeded in finishing the march, Mahmood went on, we would win our kepi and during a ceremony on Wednesday, the *Remise Képi Blanc*, be granted permission to wear it. Although our period of instruction was far from over, this at least would finally mark us as Legionnaires. Listening to his speech, I hoped this would sort those prepared to work hard from those who were not. I looked forward to it.

The following day, a Sunday, I rose at 0730. It was marvellous to get something of a sleep in and startling to wake up to so much natural light. Unfortunately, a voraciously successful mosquito had attacked me and my left eye was very swollen. Kronk assumed that LeCoq and I had been fighting and laughed.

We spent much of the day preparing our combat parade uniforms. There was not much to them. French Army combat clothing was not at all like those of other armies. Americans, British, Australians and New Zealanders all have baggy combats with lots of pockets. The French, on the other hand, go in for *le look*: the uniform looks very attractive, very smooth, and everything is tight. We were never to put things into the trouser pockets, the only exception being some tightly folded paper to add to the percussive post-salute effect; in the vest pockets, cigarettes and a notebook and pen were permitted. Anything bulky would upset the line.

The parade epaulettes were fixed to the vests by threading them through the standard epaulette and attaching each one with a Legion button, liberated from an issue greatcoat. On the right-hand side of the vest was pinned the badge of our regiment, *4ème Régiment Étranger*. On the upper part of the left sleeve was the *flamme Légion* and on the right, two finger-widths from the shoulder seam, the divisional badge.

The bottoms of the trousers were elasticised and fitted over the first buckle of our boots. The French had a system whereby the boot was laced and a leather flap was then taken around the top of the boot and buckled up at the outside. It wasn't a bad system, in that sticks and stones couldn't find their way into the boot, but it meant you needed more time to get the boot on and off. Another disadvantage was that when you marched, the buckles rattled and sung like a Morris dancer's shoes.

Less focused on *le look* – and distinctly lacking in any form of style or elegance, in fact – was our soccer match that afternoon. For the first time at the farm, it was francophones against non-francophones. The game turned out pretty much as I'd anticipated.

More or less adhering to the rules, the match was hard and firm, but definitely not fair. I felt my blood pressure rise at *Sergent-Chef* Mahmood's playing technique – hacking – and decided to apply the same technique against him. As I got up from a particularly successful swipe at his leg, the Algerian grabbed me from behind, his forearm across my throat, crushing. With his dark, monobrowed face right up against me, he breathed into my ear: '*Fais gaffe, Mason, fais gaffe . . .*' (Look out, Mason, look out . . .) Then he released me.

We continued to play for a short time longer, the game deteriorating into isolated brawls as guys took the opportunity to let off steam and settle up accounts. The match ended in a two-all draw, with bloodied noses, thick lips and swollen eyes. We never played soccer, or any team sport, ever again.

During a quiet moment that same Sunday, I tried on my kepi for the first time, just for size. I held it in my hand, fingers on the black plastic peak brim, taking care not to touch the virgin-white cotton of the cover, and considered it for a moment. In my hand was the thing that more than anything else told the world I was a Legionnaire.

Having read up about the kepi before I joined, I knew something of its origins. It was *Général* Paul Frédéric Rollet, the so-called 'Father of the Legion', who made the white kepi the iconic symbol it had become. I'd seen his portrait on the utilitarian wall back at Aubagne. Rollet was the Legion's greatest advocate and, between the world wars of the twentieth century, fought against the risk of disbandment. He worked to create cohesive ritual and traditions among Legionnaires, and so pushed for the revival of the kepi, the red-and-green epaulettes and the long woollen waistband known as the *ceinturon bleu*. After almost fifteen years, Rollet's work was rewarded when, on Bastille Day 1939, the Legion paraded in white kepis down the Champs-Élysées in Paris. As I tried on my new kepi now, I wondered if there was anything significant in it not fitting me properly.

The day of the *Marche Képi Blanc*, Tuesday, 5 July, dawned clear with soft light so typical of Europe and so different from Australia. In preparing themselves for the march, some men wrapped their feet in surgical tape; others begged band-aids from a *caporal* and taped up vulnerable spots like toes and heels. Knowing that marching a fair distance caused the feet to swell, I simply made sure my socks fitted snug and smooth and that my boots were laced firmly but not too tight.

On that beautiful day of golden glows and soft light, we marched around 35 kilometres in nine hours into the countryside north of the farm. In our group we lost Contein, who just didn't have the stamina. Then Locolo, the Spanish Legionnaire, collapsed. We took turns to carry his pack and rifle so he was able to manage the last few kilometres. *Caporal* Kronk was completely exhausted. Unlike us, who had to carry a range of useless items amounting to 20 kilograms, the tiny Frenchman carried very little in his *sac*, except water and some food.

The countryside through which we moved was France as I had always imagined. There were old villages with friendly faces and warm cries of '*Vive la Légion!*', rolling hills, green valleys and ancient watercourses. We marched by farmhouses and through medieval hamlets of cool, almost-brown terracotta brick, and alongside moss-covered rocks that formed wells, or old walls between houses and fields. We marched from dark into light, from the cool of an old elm's shade and out into the harsh scrutiny of the sun.

Disturbing my mental equanimity somewhat was *Sergent* Bronski's sense of direction, our steel-toothed *chef de groupe* leading us in circles on one occasion. While he flourished a map and compass, apparently taking bearings, we ended up at the same point twice. I asked myself if he'd ever considered planning the route upfront and marking it on his map, and thought probably not. All in all, it compounded our sense of alienation. We dumb recruits were not shown where we were going or told anything about the country in which we marched. Not one thing.

For the actual presentation of the kepi, the *Remise*, our *section* was formed up into ranks at Bel Air, each man holding the brim of the hat in his right hand. Not for the first or last time, it seemed that the information *Sergent-Chef* Mahmood had given us was not entirely correct. As it turned out, everyone would receive their kepi, whether they'd made the march or not.

Standing rigidly to attention, we awaited the order from the *lieutenant* before donning our *képis blanc*. The bemedalled commanding officer of *1ère Compagnie*, *Capitaine* Rayoume, then addressed us.

He told us we were now members of the *grande famille* that was the French Foreign Legion. After the weeks I had been through with these fellows, I didn't feel part of any grand family or brotherhood, and nor did anyone else. Even the French among us, including Becker with whom I'd had the altercation on the train, were not at all impressed with what we'd experienced. According to LeCoq, it was all *cinéma* – nothing more than a charade, a fantasy. As for us anglophones, we agreed that as far as significant rites of passage went, it was a very poor performance.

After officially receiving our kepis, we drank beer around a fire, singing songs; reminiscent again of Hitler Youth documentaries. We were limited to two small bottles each, and though I looked for them, not one of our *caporals* appeared to congratulate us. This was probably because, even with only a couple of beers in us, we'd be inclined to thump them. Instead, Dober, Kronk and Malvina skulked away to where they could be on their own.

The award of the *képi blanc* was the one significant ritual of my Legion career up to that point. But the fact that it was awarded to recruits who hadn't been able to complete the *Marche Képi Blanc*, to those who could not run or march or use a rifle, was a clear sign that this Legion ritual was not about recognition of accomplishment. Instead, it was about integration into a group; a reward of sorts and the price paid by us was silent endurance and humiliation.

8

BACK TO DANJOU

Je m'en fou.
(I don't care.)

Having already packed up at the farm before the presentation, we were trucked back to Quartier Danjou very late that same night. Allocated to the cookhouse first thing the following morning, I met Chator, a South African, from one of the other *compagnies d'instruction*. We shouted across to each other over the noise of pots and pans being dumped, scraped and hosed, and I was dismayed (though hardly surprised) to find that he had nothing positive to say about the Legion. He intended to leave and go back to civilian life after completing instruction at Castelnaudary.

I asked him how he knew he could do this. He looked at me, his shoulders drooped a little, and he said, 'My God, I have to try – this is bullshit.'

Chator told me about his company's equivalent of the Bel Air experience. Two *caporals* from the Legion's Parachute Regiment were attached to his *section* to do their time before being sent off on their *sergent* course. One recruit had his nose broken and another his left front tooth knocked out. These *caporals* would rip everything out of the lockers, dump it all in the middle of the floor, jump on it, mix it up, piss on it, and leave it to the recruits to sort out.

If the *caporals* were not enjoying their time at Castelnaudary, the Legionnaires certainly weren't. The following day I put my thoughts down in writing, albeit a highly sanitised version, for my mother back home in Canberra. In some ways, the letter was long overdue.

Friday, 8 July 1988

Dear Mother,

I am sorry I haven't been able to write to you much sooner to tell you of my decision to join the Foreign Legion.

I have entertained the idea of joining for some time. It must be one of the last great adventures. Just what I need. Places like Djibouti and French Guyane beckon like whispered promise. I must look and find out.

It is now the afternoon and we've just had another series of injections. We go to the *infirmerie*, take off all our clothes except underwear, and in alphabetical order, form a rank facing the wall in the off-white painted corridor. A trainee medic swabs our backs with wet cotton preparatory to the injections. I am troubled that despite asking, we are ignorant to the contents of these injections.

We file into a room, two by two, where four *stagières* (trainee medics) wait with syringes held high. Standing with my back to these medics, the first grasps the skin over the shoulder blade, near the spine and slips the needle into the flesh. He withdraws and I take a pace to my right, where the same process follows with a swabbing down with cotton.

During the injections, *Caporal* Dober (one of my instructors) waited at the doorway and looked me in the eyes. I tried not to flinch. According to some we've been injected with steroids. I do not believe a word of this; just disappointed we are not told.

Have just done a count – I think that I have already had nine injections or takings of blood. Don't know why but the French seem to have a particular interest in taking samples. I guess I will have to get used to it.

It is 1830 and just back from dinner, which is a very loose use of the term. It was just a bowl of soup, bread and yoghurt; usual for those who have had injections.

At last I am able to send this letter. It has taken some time because some low-life stole the *section's* stamp money. So, for a couple of weeks, we've been awaiting stamps while the *lieutenant* and the *caporal* knew very well that the money had, as they put it, disappeared. We've have to put more money into the kitty. Most have no money at all.

You can understand that I hope things don't continue like this, though I'm not very optimistic. But in any event, I can look after myself in this environment so there is no need for you to worry about me.

Love to all,

David

PS. If you can think of any girls who would like to write to a lonely Legionnaire, please give them my address.

I never did receive any letters from women who might have wanted to correspond with me. Perhaps my mother forgot or thought that this flirtation with the Legion would be short-lived like my other solitary unannounced journeys away from home. Or perhaps she underestimated what such correspondence would have meant to me. In any event, I missed women very much. It was not just sex – which I missed and ached for when I thought about it – I missed speaking with them as well. And I knew I would not laugh with or hold one for months to come, perhaps years. The cost of being a Legionnaire seemed to be going up.

I didn't receive letters from my father either. We did not talk much. In fact, for years we had rarely spoken and never about anything meaningful or substantial. His legacies to me were an education and an intolerance of men who were less than themselves. These were men who let their decisions crush them, and who let little things become important, like a new car, a new house or a new job. I used to wonder whether there was something in my father, a passion or a fire that had been crushed, spent or extinguished.

He'd never spoken of it, and in fact he never would in his lifetime. I broached it with him twice, years apart. I wanted to understand from him a little of what he was and why. It was too much for him to answer, and on both occasions he shuddered, gasped and shook his head.

LeCoq found out we were due to finish our recruit course on Sunday, 18 September, the day before my twenty-eighth birthday. We had around seventy days to go . . . and then, where to? Part of an answer came in a talk given to us by *Lieutenant* Hildebrandt. After telling us more about the Legion's various regiments, he mentioned that one recruit in our *section* could go straight to *caporal* training at the completion of our current instruction.

Following this presentation, the *lieutenant* called me to his office. I could be that rapidly promoted *caporal*, he said, but selection was dependent upon my greater mastery of the French language. Then he waved me away.

I wondered how my language skills could improve given the few French lessons we'd received so far – presumably by osmosis. This was supposed to be the purpose of the *binome* system, although much depended on the relationship with one's binome. In my case, given that LeCoq was bilingual and generally happy to converse in English and French, it worked well. Even so, other than basic vocabulary, the only French phrases I had mastered thus far were '*Ne me casse pas les couilles*' (Don't break my balls), followed closely by '*Va te faire foutre*' (Go fuck yourself); both were useful in my current situation, but hardly sufficient. Through LeCoq and others, I'd picked up a few more phrases, but most of the French I'd learned in the last two months was simply parroting the obligatory replies to the constant orders being yelled at us.

It was not a requirement that you knew the language before you joined – the Legion claimed it would teach new recruits everything they needed to know, after all. But this official position was somewhat different from the reality. With so few French lessons available to non-francophones, you had to pick the language up very quickly by yourself or suffer the wrath of unsympathetic *caporals*. I tried hard to learn, and it was certainly another challenge.

But this rapid-promotion-to-*caporal* route was not all it seemed either, and I already had some doubts about its advantages. I realised that from Hildebrandt's point of view, as *section* leader, he had to find someone credible who could perform and succeed on the *caporal* course. The difficulty for a person taking up this rapid-route challenge, however – as opposed to the likes of Dober and Kronk, who'd put in the years with the combat regiments – was that it subverted the most important thing underpinning respect in the Legion: time in service. Every time you presented to someone superior, they and everyone around them knew instantly how long you had been in the Legion. For a rapidly promoted *caporal*, this was not an advantage. We lived in such a small world that every change and nuance was tasted, discussed and measured.

The joy of a Sunday siesta gave me time to reflect on this and other things. At 1400 the sun was as warm as a languid lover's thigh and birds lazily choraled the pleasure of a perfect summer's day. Almost everyone in the *section* was in bed for a couple of hours.

I sat on the balcony of *1ère Compagnie,* overlooking Quartier Danjou's red-tarmac *place d'armes.* From where I sat, facing roughly south-west, I could see the boom gate, some 200 metres away and almost directly front of me. The boom was down and a guard in parade uniform stood by it, rifle across his chest. Now and again, a Legionnaire was delivered by taxi from town along the Route de Pexiora and entered the camp in an apparently drunken state – telegraphed by a wobble, a stagger or even a fall from the cab. Even so, each one that arrived paused, set his kepi straight on his head, and managed a salute to the guard commander.

To the left of the gate, inside the camp, was a statue of a Legionnaire. Half of his body emerged successfully from the block from which it was carved. Titled *Légionnaire Batisseur* (Legionnaire Builder), did it represent the Legionnaire's struggle with himself and the elements, I wondered, or was it a comment on the difficulty of finding an identity beyond the monolith that is the Legion?

Beyond the Route de Pexiora, and running parallel to it, was the railway line. Railway traffic we saw and heard at all hours. There was one train that woke me every morning at 0245. I didn't mind this at all, and sometimes I even left my bunk to go to the window and watch the train pass by the camp. It spoke to me of another world, a place of human warmth and friendship, a long way from where I was now.

A few days later, *1ère Compagnie* practised drill for the upcoming Bastille Day parade. We wore our best combat greens, with *épaulettes de tradition*, kepis and rifles across our chests. Practice began with us in *section* formation. We were then ordered to form up in one long column, called out by height, from the tallest to the shortest. The *sergents* acted as sheepdogs, urging us to move forward to the man in front – '*Bite au cul!*' (Cock to arse!) – so they could see the heights were true.

Once the *sous-officiers* were satisfied, we numbered from one to six, and at the seventh man, recommenced the numbering. This was the basis for forming the *peloton*s – Legionnaires six by six, with *sergents* in the front rank of each 36-man squad, and in front of them, the *section* leaders, either *adjudant* or *lieutenant*. Leading the first *peloton* was the company commander, *Capitaine* Rayoume, and before the next one, his second-in-command. The oldest *sous-officier* in rank would carry the company flag, just ahead of *Capitaine* Rayoume.

Thursday was the big day: 14 July, Bastille Day, when the nation celebrates the storming of the Parisian fortress-prison and the birth of modern France. Along with other taller recruits, I was selected to march. It was worth tolerating the yelling and abuse from the NCOs for this. Parading in town that morning was a very stirring affair; bands playing, crowds clapping, speeches, medals on chests, and the trees full of the green of summer.

Naturally, we recruits didn't get to mix with the locals. Instead, we were herded onto a bus and ferried back to Quartier Danjou, where we were confined to the *compagnie* building and forbidden, against pain of being locked up in jail, to drink alcohol. By the end of the day, however, even the *sergent de semaine* was drunk and there were Jackson Pollock splatterings of vomit across the parade ground.

The following afternoon we marched to the new indoor rifle range within the camp boundary, in the west of the *quartier*. I was anticipating some instruction on how to hold the weapon correctly, perhaps breathing techniques and how to squeeze off a round. But at least I'd had some experience with firing a rifle. Most of my fellow recruits needed help, but received no guidance at all, so they continued to shoot badly. Predictably, this led to further kicks from our *caporals*.

Along with the lack of instruction, there was a shortage of rounds, just like at Burnell. We fired nine this time. Was it because our leadership wished to instil in us an appreciation of the round and its worth? On the other hand, having spent the best part of an hour firing the weapons, we did spend another six hours cleaning the damned things . . . Anything, I supposed, to use up the time of us worthless things.

Soon there was something new to break the routine. *Première Compagnie* had been allocated *garde 24*, camp guard duty for twenty-four hours, and our *section* was to do it. We spent until 0100 getting our uniforms to the standard *Caporal* Kronk expected. I had already paid one of the Frenchmen to iron my parade and walking-out uniforms. There were parallel vertical creases to be ironed above pockets, others along the back and sleeves, and it was a job that was required to be done once – perfectly. I kept those uniforms my entire Legion career, in fact, and only ever had to follow the lines when ironing. In return, I bulled his parade boots for him. That is, I spit-polished them over a number of hours so he could see his face in the caps.

Next morning, Tuesday, 19 July, we were up before dawn, at around 0445. Forbidden from drinking coffee (in case it got spilt onto our parade uniforms) until after 0800, LeCoq and I shared a chocolate bar and drank a large mug of water. Morning blood sugar levels were very important, especially for him.

Then, forming up in one column, nine of us, including the *sergent* and a *caporal*, were led to the guardhouse – to the immediate left of the entrance – by the bugler, who announced our impending arrival. After the formal handover, we slipped into the guardhouse routine of two hours on and four hours off. For two hours I was at the front gate, with the FAMAS held in place across my chest by the *bretelle* (sling), and twenty rounds in the magazine. I was in turns at ease, at attention or at present arms as the various *officiers* of the regiment came through the gate. If I didn't look like a marionette I certainly felt like one.

It was during the first period of four hours off that things came to a head between me and LeCoq. Over the previous day or so he had become terse and dismissive. In my state of awareness, alert to every little harm or slight done to me, I realised I would have to assert myself or risk being seen as being dominated by him. In the guardhouse, that chance came after he refused, for reasons known only to him, to pass me a tube of toothpaste. The discussion became heated and led to him pushing me off my chair. Just as I got to my feet, but before I could respond, Kronk intervened – putting his forearm across my throat and yelling into my ear to calm down.

As I sat there, smouldering with frustrated anger, I knew I couldn't let LeCoq get away with attacking me. It was almost suicide to appear weak in this environment. For others to think so would only invite many more problems; so, to prevent having to pull myself from a deeper hole in the future, a stand had to be taken.

In the evening we went back to the barracks to shower and change from our parade uniforms into army combat greens. Just as I was about to get into the shower next to our room, LeCoq pushed by me and went in. I knew it was time, so I gritted my teeth and took my opportunity.

I reached into the shower, grabbed his wrist, yanked and dragged him from the cubicle. Wet, naked, and slippery, he escaped my grasp. When he turned and looked at me, it was with a mixture of bewilderment and anger. I told him that the next time he laid so much as a finger on me, I would be delighted to *bombe sa fucking gueule* (bash his fucking face). My French was getting better. Our voices became raised and I called him some of the more colourful terms I'd recently learned: *tête de pine*, *suce bite* and *connard*.

We exchanged punches and the fight moved out of the *salle de bain* and into our room. We slipped and slid on the white tiles, two naked writhing bodies punching out our frustrations. A crowd from our *section* gathered.

For a moment we stopped, breathing deep, and I asked him if he wanted to go on. We could stop now, I said, or fight every day – it was up to him. LeCoq shook his head, but after a couple more blows to his skull, the fight went out of him. I even offered to shake hands, but he refused.

Looking around at the growing number of spectators, I decided to settle things once and for all. This wasn't just about me and LeCoq. So I offered to fight any Frenchman who thought they had a problem with me. With my hands on my bare bony hips, I looked into the eyes of everyone in that room. Not a soul moved to take up my offer.

I took a deep breath and said in the best *français* I could muster: '*Vas-y, les mecs. Vous avez peur. Normale vous êtes Français!*' Which wasn't too far off meaning: Come on, lads. You're afraid. That's normal – you're French!

In response to this outburst, there appeared to be a lot of gazing at the floor. What a pathetic bunch they were.

But what a mad fool I was. After all, it wasn't really them I wanted to fight. I wanted to vent the frustration I felt at this woeful instruction we'd all had to endure. I kept looking, waiting and hoping that things would improve. I was an optimist, but there was only so much optimism to temper my impatience, so I took it out on the hapless Frenchmen who no doubt shared my misery. It was unfair of me and I should have known better. Even so, the practical effect of this episode was that my fellow recruits left me alone; they were conciliatory, even deferential. In the Legion, displays of bad temper clearly had their uses.

Back in the guardroom, Bronski asked why we had been fighting. Of course some sneak must have told him. He didn't seem angry, just curious. Kronk smiled. I said nothing, nor did LeCoq, so the *sergent* let it go.

Finishing the *garde 24* next morning, and after having handed back weapons to the armoury, we went without breakfast because Dober, the *caporal du jour*, forgot to collect some for us. Instead, we went straight on to a couple of lessons. The first was French: *le sac*, the bag . . . *le fusil*, the rifle . . . *je suis*, I am . . .

The lesson was given by *Sergent-Chef* Mahmood. It was delivered in a large room on the ground floor of the *1ère Compagnie* building, with industrial grey-white tiles on the floor and white painted walls. We sat on hard wooden seats behind children's school desks. Despite the odd slap to the back of the head from the patrolling *caporals*, most of the class was dozing after just fifteen minutes of a lesson that droned on for over an hour without a break. It was a waste of time.

The second lesson was on *secourisme* (first aid) – or rather, the use of bandages. It dragged on for two hours and deteriorated into a torrent of verbal abuse in franglais, courtesy of our instructor, *Sergent* Romett. The Englishman's thin face turned crimson, spittle flying from his mouth and out across the room, towards a couple of our number who'd been unable to tie some knots correctly. It was a sight to behold but, alas, another waste of time.

These lessons and the other mindless activities we did highlighted one certainty for us. There was no predicting what might be of significance to a person in authority, a *caporal* or above, at any given time, and therefore what sanction might follow some failure. We had no power over what was important, what was not important, or what might be. So we felt extremely vulnerable; exposed to the capricious whims of others. We existed in a constant state of stomach-tensed hypervigilance, all the while trying to make some sense out of a world in which we were shuttled from place to place, from activity to activity, in a muddling fog of uncertainty as to what fate had in store. Probably because the world was not ours, most of the time it just didn't seem to make any sense at all.

9

MARCHING, WARGAMES AND MOUNTAINS

*Chaque Légionnaire est ton frère d'armes, quelle que soit
sa nationalité, sa race ou sa religion.*
(Every Legionnaire is your brother in arms, irrespective
of his nationality, race or religion.)

I always enjoyed marching and getting out of the *quartier* and
into the countryside. This was fortunate because if the Legion
was good at anything at all, it was forcing men into marching
long distances with heavy loads on their backs. Along with the
telltale short haircut, a Legionnaire is distinguished by his lean
form, a product of poor food, plenty of *footing* (running) and
endless marching.

Driven out to Bel Air in trucks we did what the Legion
called *combat*. This included the entirely expected: everyone
marching along a road and someone sniping at us. As I had
learned, there was no patrolling, no formations, no field craft;
just a single column walking up a track, waiting to be ambushed.
It felt like the tactics of the nineteenth century.

I made a fool of myself that day. On the first occasion Kronk opened fire on the column, I saw his position and yelled out 'Ambush right!' and charged, firing blanks at where he lay. This was the drill in the Australian, British, New Zealand and US armies, at least. By the time I'd run the 15 metres to Kronk's position, I realised no one had followed me. I turned to see a very bemused *Sergent* Bronski, rifle slung, hands on his hips, indicating with a tilt of his head that I should return to the track. Kronk simply said, '*Idiot.*'

'In Legion, wait for orders,' Bronski said in his broken English. '*Nix* "Ambush right", do again and boom-boom' – and he punched the air in front of him, indicating the penalty for any repeat offence. He let out a belittling laugh as the other recruits looked at me and smirked.

I couldn't believe what I was hearing, and asked for some clarification. '*Je tire quand?*' (I shoot when?) At this the *sergent's* brow furrowed and I wondered if I'd gone too far.

'*Tire seulement quand je te donne l'ordre.*' In other words, only fire when ordered to; show no initiative or thought, just be a target.

At the conclusion of this brief exchange, I blushed so hard my ears felt hot. To his great credit, a few minutes later Northam sidled up to me and, with a shrug of his shoulders and a sigh, said, 'Mate, I don't have any idea what's going on.' For what he did that day, I liked the Englishman more than I could tell him. He didn't have to say anything at all, and most recruits did just that. When we observed another *section* member being undeservedly humiliated, some among us would try to say a few kind words to the victim, give him a nod, a squeeze on the arm or a pat on the back. We were all in the same position, powerless and weak. Of all the things I took from instruction, it was the recollection of those unsolicited, thoughtful actions that gave the period any redeeming memory at all.

We left Bel Air and commenced the march around 2300, arriving back at Quartier Danjou over three hours later. Like the other Legion marches I'd done so far, it was not too taxing, but during the later stages we had to walk along a disused railway line. As long as you were very short, the distance between sleepers was just right for your stride. For 90 per cent of us, however, it was tedious, having to be constantly alert to tripping over the wooden sleepers laid between the tracks.

We arrived just outside the front gate at around 0230, having run the last few kilometres with our *sacs* and rifles. For some reason, Locolo and Fekler took this as an opportunity to start a fight, going for each other with fist and rifle. They soon tripped and fell to the ground amid grunts and the clatter of plastic and metal. As they writhed about with the dust of the road wrapping around them, *Sergent* Bronski stepped up to the pair and, using the butt of his rifle, struck each man on the head, the sound of hard rubber on bone preceding even loader groans. Moments later, as they lay there stunned and limp, the *sergent* ordered us to carry them into camp and up into our room. We were tired, dripping with perspiration, and carrying these two and their gear was not something we welcomed.

A few hours later, when we were woken for breakfast, Locolo and Fekler complained of headache and blurred vision. There were no kind words or reassuring nods for these two, they had brought their problems on themselves.

For some members of *3ème Section*, Friday, 22 July was PI duty – *piquet d'intervention*, the regiment's internal rapid-reaction force. That is, nine of us sat in our combats inside a humid room, on the ground floor of the 3rd Company, for twenty-four hours. This room had a toilet, washbasins, a bed for each recruit and a television that was never turned off.

The tedium of the early part of the day was relieved by unloading a large truck supplying goods to the foyer. This articulated vehicle had *Légion Étrangère* emblazoned on its side and was driven by a *caporal-chef* whose sole job was to travel between regiments delivering beer, T-shirts and running shoes. I was coming to understand that the Legion was almost entirely self-sufficient and self-managing. There were no cleaners, plumbers, electricians or civilians of any kind in the camp; Legionnaires did everything.

Not only that, but the Legion also managed itself legally and financially. On the legal front, the Legion awarded punishment according to its own guidelines, without review or appeal to a wider forum within the French Army. And all financial affairs were likewise handled internally, rather than through the Defence Ministry, including property management on the chateau next to Quartier Danjou, used as an officers' mess. The Legion was a law unto itself, and remains so today. Whether this, in a world of professional militaries, integrated interoperability, transparency and accountability, is efficient or appropriate is an entirely different question.

More relief from the confines of the PI room came at 2100, when we commenced cleaning the foyer after the Friday-night drinkers had left. There were broken beer bottles, junk-food wrappers and cigarette butts on the tables and across the tiled floor. Someone had smeared shit on the latrine wall and there was vomit on the floor. We spent the hours until midnight scraping, scrubbing and cleaning. It was what we were good at.

Cleaning certainly seemed to take priority over training – unless, of course, the cleaning of things was our training. Too often I'd seen lessons cancelled because the *lieutenant* had found a mark on a bathroom floor. Were lessons on the rifle or the French language really a privilege that could be lost? I wondered what commanders in the combat regiments had to say when they received such poorly trained men.

The emphasis appeared to be not on training but on 'forming' a Legionnaire. That is, the organisation wanted us to bend and become compliant. On the outside, we were compliant. But inside, many of us were forming a cold hard stone of anger. We were learning that the reward for compliance was a kind of servitude. This was too much for some recruits, and though they were good men, they planned to leave in the weeks to come, at the end of the course.

Back at the *compagnie*, Blacker and Blackest had deserted. No one minded that they'd gone; but we were all severely pissed off that the two brothers had stolen 600 francs from a Frenchman in the *section*. They'd broken a fundamental rule: do not steal from those in the same pitiful position as you.

In another welcome change of scene from Quartier Danjou, our *section* was off to Camurac, some 60 kilometres due south of Castelnaudary, not far from the Andorran and Spanish borders. As usual, I learned this much via the Frenchmen in the *section*. There was no information given to us by an NCO, of course, nothing posted on a noticeboard – just orders shouted at us to do things. As typical as this was, it didn't make the situation any less frustrating.

We arrived at Camurac, high in the Pyrenees, in the early afternoon of Monday, 25 July, as the sun cast solid dark shadows across cobblestones and the stone walls of the little town. After disembarking from the trucks, we stood in ranks in front of the

Legion's three-storey farmhouse, on green grass, waiting to be told to go on into the building.

The ground floor had accommodation for *Lieutenant* Hildebrandt, his *sous-officiers* and *caporals*. Here, too, was the cookhouse. The first floor consisted of a refectory, which doubled as a lecture room; a sole squat toilet for the thirty-plus recruits and an armoury. The top floor, or attic, was where we slept. Access to the upper floors was limited to an extremely narrow staircase, so a fireman's pole had been connected to the building's outer wall for our use whenever we were to go outside.

At night though, the shutters were closed and locked, while a *caporal* slept in the attic with us – both precautionary measures against more desertions. Smoking in this room was strictly forbidden, and I just had to hope that a fire never broke out; with the locked shutters preventing escape down the fireman's pole, and the stairs wide enough for only one man to descend at a time, the place was a death trap.

If we ran at Castelnaudary and Bel Air, at Camurac we did it further, faster and higher. We ran along paths through forests and on dirt roads, up hills and down again. The first morning was the hardest run in all our months of recruit training. After sweet coffee and bread for breakfast, we ran for almost two hours. Up narrow trails bordered by conifers, we went, and as we rose into the mountainsides, the views across the valleys were storybook magnificent. The air was champagne sweet, the sky china blue and in the distance, the farmhouses were dark wooden matchboxes set among the greens of the forest. As exhilarating as the *footing* was, it was exhausting too. Towards the end of those two hours, even *Sergent-Chef* Mahmood was bent over and panting. Malvina broke into a walk so we left him behind to make his own way back along the narrow paths.

Running as we did, we needed to be properly fed, and food was a subject close to the hearts of all. We questioned why we had to be fed such rubbish. Everything we ate came from a can and, personally, I wasn't keen on the *cassoulet*. According to LeCoq, a *cassoulet* can be a delight, particularly in winter. Maybe so, I'd reply, but when served during summer on our metal trays, it was just beans swimming in fat with a lonely, submerged sausage. I would have given a lot for an orange or a crisp apple. With the combination of mountain running, frequent marching and insufficient food, we all lost weight even more rapidly than we had at Bel Air. In addition, a few of us started to develop disgusting green-scabbed, weeping sores that would not heal, especially around the corners of mouths.

Early next day we set off on a long march, after which we would be camping out at a prearranged bivouac for the night. As with the previous day's footing, it was a hard slog. Late in the afternoon, at the conclusion of two very steep rises, I was the only person left with *Sergent* Bronski, the rest of our *groupe* having fallen back as the pain in legs, shoulders and chest became too much. My thighs were tearing fire and my lungs great bellows heaving against the straps of my pack.

At last the two of us stopped. A veteran of 2 REP, Bronski turned to me then, sweat dripping from his face, and waved his hand in the direction of the others. '*Ici*, REP . . .' he gasped. '*Pour le reste, même pas Légionnaires.*'

The meaning was clear enough: what we'd just achieved was worthy of a member of the fabled Parachute Regiment; as for the stragglers far behind us, they weren't fit to be in the Legion at all. As flattered as I was to be included in such exalted company, Bronski was selling short the others' efforts. I knew his *sac* carried no more than a sleeping bag and some water, whereas we recruits were hauling over 20 kilos in ours.

The conclusion of that day's march was for me the proudest moment of my entire recruit course.

Later, once the *section* had regrouped at the bivouac, a few of us were detached to prepare *la bouffe* (food) and the rest sent off to gather firewood. I had yet to see anything resembling a tactical day or night formation. Instead, after first surrendering our weapons, we made a bonfire and lay out our sleeping gear in ranks. Better, I supposed, for the NCOs to be able to count us during the night.

Preparation for the night highlighted the inadequacy of our equipment also. The poncho, for instance, had no eyelets in the corners to allow it to be strung up in case of rain. Nor was it long enough, whether suspended above us or cloaked around us on the ground, to ensure the sleeping bag didn't get wet.

The triangular piece of camouflaged canvas that we each had should've been useful as one part of a four-man tent, but with no logic to the issue of these pieces, each on its own was useless. Then there were the four 30-centimetre-long wooden pegs intended to serve as interior poles to the canvas shelters we never set up. Instead, we used them to square up the *sacs*, to act as an inner frame.

The *sac* itself wasn't much good either. Aside from it having no frame to keep the pack rigid, its design made access to the inside pocket far from easy. Making life harder was the ludicrous order that the one other pocket, a zippered *pochette* on top of the pack, was only to be used at the direction of *Sergent* Bronski, our *chef de groupe*. The upshot was that we had to pull everything out to get to the sleeping bag, resulting in gear being spread all over the ground.

To ensure one of us didn't run away with a weapon, no doubt, our rifles were grouped together near the fire, with a cable passed through the upper hand grip and the ends joined at a padlock. One of the two men on guard listened to the radio and watched over the weapons. The other moved about carrying a chunk of wood, with strict orders to bash any Legionnaire who got out of hand or tried to wander off.

Marching back to Camurac next morning, Bronski took us on another one of his shortcuts. Rather than follow the ridgeline on its lee side, 20 metres below the crest, he insisted on following the windswept ridge. He got a couple of turns completely wrong and we found ourselves having to turn back on three occasions, all the while accompanied by the *sergent*'s frequent curses of '*Putain de carte*' (Bitch of a map).

As soon as we arrived back at the farmhouse, we had an orienteering course. This I won, with Northam coming in a close second. In fact, the only people who were capable of navigating at all were those who'd had training in other armies. The half an hour of so-called instruction on map and compass reading was never going to be sufficient for the beginners among us, especially when the instructors were themselves less than competent.

As a break from the exhausting trio of marching, running and non-instruction, that evening we were escorted to the Edelweiss bar in Camurac. But not before a talk from *Sergent-Chef* Mahmood. The monobrowed Algerian introduced us to the notion of *détente* – a period of relaxation. If anyone took too much advantage of the *détente* and his good intentions, Mahmood warned, we would be up all night running off our enthusiasm on the roads around the town. So, in the Legion's fetching *tenues de sport*, we had a few beers, played some pool, made too much noise, and in so doing frightened away any likely females who might otherwise have been courageous enough to enter the bar.

We often talked about women, not solely as objects of pleasure, but as civilising creatures who made a man reflect and reminded him that there was more to life. In time, after a few years in the Legion, many of these same men, or men like them, became dislocated from women, in the sense of being able to connect with them on any emotional level. If women were not objects before they joined the Legion, for many they became so, in the brothels of Djibouti, French Guyane or Marseilles. If this was not a conscious choice, it was something that few Legionnaires recognised. For those who did, it was a lot to pay, since the tariff of reconnecting with women was fear, tears and, too often, failure.

There was no breach of *détente* etiquette and no all-night run. But we ran next morning – of course – for some 10 kilometres. The mountain air was particularly cold, damp and clammy that day, the fog thick around us. For many in the *section*, this run proved very difficult and some were genuinely ill, including LeCoq and Becker, as well as a Yugoslav named Dazinovic.

LeCoq looked positively cadaverous, skin stretched taut over his cheekbones. As we pounded up yet another hill, he groaned and gasped as a stinking mess slid down a leg to stain his Legion sock. When we got back to the farmhouse, I helped him out of his clothes and put my arm around him to support him to the shower. Under his breath he thanked me, before announcing loudly that he didn't need my help. I smiled at the irony; none of us wanted to appear weak, as I well knew; that had been the same motivation for our violent altercation outside another bathroom a week or two before.

It was shameful that many of us had bad diarrhoea, caused no doubt by the dreadful food we received. Or maybe it was something they caught in the pitiful excuse for a latrine that we all had to line up to use: that one squat toilet, stained a greenish brown and stinking like rotten flesh.

Despite the shortcomings and hardship up at Camurac, I still counted myself lucky to be outside four walls and barbed wire, and in fresh air and sunshine most of the time. Anything was preferable to the initiative-sapping guard duties and mindless *corvées* that defined life at Quartier Danjou.

Something I had noticed back at Aubagne was still troubling me, as it was very much a part of our everyday life in Castelnaudary. No one took the time to banter or offered anything freely in conversation; there was no place for light-heartedness at all. Instead, when people laughed, their laughs sounded false and hard. There was no fun in this laughter, and you could always be sure that any merriment was at the expense of someone else. I couldn't help thinking that it must've been the same for inmates in a prison. After all, if you showed you genuinely enjoyed something, then other people could see a part of the real you, and you became vulnerable. If people could see a part of you, they could hurt you. So no one really laughed.

Too soon for me, then, on Saturday, 30 July we loaded up the trucks, climbed in and descended the Pyrenees on our way north to Castelnaudary. Once back at Danjou, we discovered that the idiot brothers Blacker and Blackest were in jail. They never did rejoin the *section*.

The day after we arrived, I was back in the *ordinaire* and doing the very things that I'd relished being free of while out in the mountains: assigned to tedious *la plonge* duties, scraping and scrubbing at the huge stainless-steel basins with little or no detergent, and having to put up with the appalling behaviour of some Frenchmen. I almost had a fight with one.

This narrow-eyed fellow with thick, aggressive lips seemed to think work was somehow beneath him because he had finished instruction and was on his way to French Guyane. It didn't bother him one bit that by refusing to work, he was making the rest of us labour that much harder. With support from my old friends Tom and Teabag, *2ème Compagnie's* contributions to the *ordinaire* that day, I soon sorted out the Frenchman's attitude, with a kick that sent him scuttling away and the voiced conclusion that French Guyane, with its tropical rot, mosquitoes and disease, was just the place for him.

It was more evidence that while the Brits stuck together, the French were often self-centred bullies. I had never heard of, and could never imagine, a Brit trying on this sort of rubbish. The fact was, his mates would've sorted him out before anyone else had to.

The following day, I got to see how things were done next door when, at 0700, I was sent to the *sous-officiers'* mess. Here, *sergents, sergent-chefs, adjudants, adjudant-chefs* and *majors* ate and drank, away from the rest of us. Their mess was in the same large building as ours, between the running track and the parade ground, and I'd always wondered whether we shared the same food.

It wasn't long before I knew, and in knowing this I also learned why it was that so many of the senior NCOs were overweight. Their food contained a great deal of cream and fat, and this together with the quaffing of wine at lunchtime probably explained why our *sergents* were often sullen and moody in the afternoons.

I watched their red faces, their chewing, and their swallowing. They comported themselves like pigs – snorting, shovelling and squealing with glee whenever a senior among them made a joke. I was disappointed and disgusted.

Sergent-Chef Mahmood saw the look on my face and took me aside. 'This is a training regiment, Mason,' he said, in English. 'What happens here is not what happens in a combat regiment. Things are better and more disciplined there.'

I doubted this somehow, and felt brave enough to ask, 'Why should there be any difference?'

He shrugged his shoulders and concluded, *'Je m'en fou.'*

Perhaps he really didn't care, but I found myself still caring; still driven and searching for some meaning to all this. As always, being free of the negativity within the camp's four walls was more conducive to helping me stay motivated and passionate.

Assembling the next morning on the towpath parallel to the Canal du Midi, in the golden light under the long lines of plane trees so typical of southern France, was a perfect antidote to my disappointing few days back at Danjou. We were there to run, of course; first 1500 metres, as a 'warm-up' preliminary, then 8000 metres. For both these runs, we wore our combat greens and boots, and carried a rifle, along with a *sac* weighing 11 kilograms. I came first in the 1500 metres and third in the 8000, after *Sergent* Bronski, who again carried next to nothing in his backpack, and the snivelling Asnol, who felt the need to gloat about his victory later in the day.

The *footing* was not easy, the variously gravel or sandy towpath being difficult surfaces compared to the smooth track at Quartier Danjou. Running in a north-westerly direction into town, the canal formed an outer border to the camp, just beyond a 3-metre-high chainlink fence. And what a world away it was out here: the gentle waterway filled with the lazy progress of pleasure craft, converted barges and spluttery old penichettes taking their holidaymaking crews north to Toulouse, and beyond as far as Bordeaux and the Atlantic, and south down to the Mediterranean at Sète. It was an artery, like the railway on the other side of the camp, and it also carried memories and a life very different from within the camp. I smiled inside at the startled faces that appeared from the shaded cabins of barges; faces that watched open-mouthed the grunting sweating men running by their moored vessels in the early morning.

That early Tuesday morning, I felt joy at the physical pain that came to me only when challenged. In that place of green moisture beside the canal, sweating and suffering, I experienced some of the magic of life. It felt good, and I looked forward to more runs that made me hurt and sweat and want to win.

Later that day, after the midday *soupe*, *Lieutenant* Hildebrandt indicated that the decision regarding my staying in Castelnaudary as a rapid-promotion *caporal* or leaving for one of the regiments wouldn't necessarily be mine to make. This was hardly what I wanted to hear, given my original doubts about the merits of that particular route.

It happened during a brief talk he gave on the Legion's Parachute Regiment in Calvi, on Corsica, when he asked who among us would want to be posted there. Along with some others, I put up my hand. Of course it would be my first choice; it was the Legion's elite unit and I loved parachuting. But the *lieutenant* just looked at me and shook his head. With his right index finger, he pointed to me, then down towards the ground.

Hildebrandt must have sensed my disquiet, because he called me into his office afterwards. He made promises and told me what would be required: I would do the nine-week *caporal* course starting in early November; once that was completed, in January, I would do two *sections d'instruction* – that is, two fourteen-week training periods as *caporal* here with the *4ème Régiment Étranger* – before going to the regiment of my choice.

In the time between the current instruction finishing and the start of the *caporal* course, about seven weeks, I would receive specialised lessons in French and in weapons. I wondered if I should believe him.

Soon enough, I'd learn that the scheme behind a rapid-promotion *caporal*, better known as a *fut fut* (short for *faisant fonction*), was designed to promote a recruit with previous experience and have him provide a basic level of command and control over the next batch of recruits. This 'command and control' was not instruction per se; it was about showing the new recruits basic things and having them at the right place at the right time. In basic training, the *sergents* and the *caporals* going on to the *sergent* course were the instructors. Or at least, they were supposed to be – that was the idea.

The following day, supposition and grand ideas were very much to the fore again. LeCoq and I found out in the morning that we would be part of a demonstration of Legion training for a visiting Mayor and his entourage from the United States. In fact, rather than a demonstration, it was a public relations exercise, pure and simple.

Some *capitaine* I had never seen before told the guests that a Legionnaire had to march at least 100 kilometres to win his kepi. A complete lie – no one ever did. The Americans lapped it up though, as LeCoq and I stood on a stage brandishing our weapons, our uniforms and faces made up with camouflage, complicit in the lie.

To distract myself I looked among the Mayor's team and imagined myself having sex with the woman who sat to his right. I must have looked at her for too long, because she blushed and began shifting in her seat. Inwardly I sighed; I knew it was fruitless. So I lifted my gaze to the back of the hall and imagined myself a long way away.

We'd been selected because this *capitaine* wanted what he called '*l'équipe choc*', the best *binome* pairing in *3ème Section,* which was LeCoq and me. By performing this task we missed out on a trip to Bel Air to do combat training and, even better, the night march back to camp over the railway sleepers. All in all, it was a holiday for the two of us. And it gave me a chance to write up my diary that evening.

The others got back at 0215. LeCoq and I simply rolled over and went back to sleep because, after the ludicrous little show for the Americans, and despite the most imaginative threats from the *sergent de semaine,* we'd enjoyed a few beers in the foyer.

Days later, during the *garde,* a report came through that Layman had deserted from hospital. Apparently, his father had driven down from Belgium to pick him up, and then the two of them had gone straight home. Layman had been in hospital undergoing treatment for various sores and eruptions he'd picked up while at Bel Air. The last time I saw him he was pale and sickly, the sores on his body were suppurating, leaving wet blotches soaking through his clothes. He would be better off in a Belgian hospital.

As usual, *Caporal* Kronk woke me in the middle of the night, thinking I was someone else due to go on guard. The simple expedient of allocating bunks, depending on which *binome* was on which relief, was beyond him. I suggested the idea to him while lacing up my boots before my stint, and he nodded in mulish agreement. He never thought to implement it though, so I did. The others agreed it made sense and we all benefitted from that precious thing: uninterrupted sleep.

Later the next day, we had to learn and sing another Legion song. It was difficult to feel motivated when we were being abused and harangued. Malvina was in particularly bad humour, furious at having missed out on a rare weekend *permission* (leave pass). After the lesson, he went to the foyer, bought himself a case of beer, and drank himself stupid. Lying on my bunk that night, I listened to him singing sad Spanish songs and wondered what had brought him to the Legion.

More duties the following day, and another dreaded *piquet d'intervention*. While we were engaged in one of the perpetual sweeping and mopping jobs in the building housing the *ordinaire* and the foyer, LeCoq came out with another of his priggish remarks. 'You'd better hurry up and finish your job,' he called across to me, 'because I've almost done mine and so have the others.'

I leaned on my broom, contemplated LeCoq and reflected for a moment. He began to look nervous. Even though our episode had done much to calm relations between me and his compatriots, such comments were all too common from the Frenchmen I dealt with in the *section*. Their work ethic appeared to be a simple one: Get yourself the smallest job possible, finish first but not too quickly, and then harp noisily about how one's *binome* had not finished – and definitely do not offer to help. Rather, stand around, bleat and watch.

I looked up at LeCoq again. If he were an Australian, I told him, he would've lent a hand without comment until the job was done. He asked me why, and I told him he could shove his broom handle up his arse.

Another *garde 24* on Tuesday, 9 August. LeCoq and I did the last full shift, from 0300 to 0500, and a couple of hours later ran the 1500 and 8000 metres, again with boots, rifle and 11-kilogram *sac à dos*. This time I came first in both, and broke the forty-minute barrier for the 8000. After the run, our new *caporal*, El Wahad, destined for *sergent* stripes, asked me to arrange his pack, to put it in line with the others. Moving the *sac,* I found that there was next to nothing in it. In the Legion, rank exempted you from leadership.

Then I was in the kitchen again. The thug who supervised us was a Spanish *caporal-chef*; exploded blood vessels on blue and florid cheeks marked him as a drunk. From 0700 he stood at the beer-dispensing machine pouring himself drinks, reassuring himself that there was a good regular flow, and that no one else indulged of the precious amber fluid. Recruits were forbidden alcohol.

And when he didn't have a glass in his hand, he was on the warpath. His fists clenched tight, thumbs to the fore, shoulders hunched, he'd lurk about, always approaching any presumed transgressors from the rear. Anyone speaking a language other than French, indulging in a brief unauthorised rest or having a smoke met with either a punch to the kidneys or a slap to the right ear. The latter risked perforating an eardrum. The two men I saw hit both dropped to the white-tiled floor like cattle shot in an abattoir.

From a Spanish bully in the kitchen, it was an Austrian and a Frenchman trading blows shortly after my return to the *1ère Compagnie* block. Stein and Fekler had a splendid fight out on the balcony that evening. Not surprisingly, given the location, the ruckus attracted the camp authorities. The *sergent de semaine* was alerted and quickly made his presence felt. A couple of rapid *baffes*, bloodied noses and cauliflowered ears to each, and the affair was over. For the time being, at least.

As I could testify, ongoing problems with one's *binome* were entirely normal. From the nonfrancophone's point of view, we had high expectations of our French partners – in the absence of any information from the NCOs, surely they could tell us what was happening; we pressured them to provide information. As it turned out, this was quite unrealistic, and perhaps even unfair to our *binomes*. How could they tell us what they didn't know?

Sometimes the Legion offered dental care, and around this time LeCoq went off to hospital to have a tooth out. If what we'd heard was any indication, he needed to be sure they took out the right one. Experience taught us that the French Army did not fill teeth, it extracted. One recruit woke up in the chair to find all his teeth gone, having expected a filling or one extraction at most. That recruit went back a few days later to receive a splendid set of new false teeth. Maybe he was grateful.

On his return from the military hospital in Toulouse, late the same evening, LeCoq was appalled. He shook his head and said, 'For the people who can't speak French, the people in the hospital just don't care.' Maybe they were too busy or distracted.

For members of *3eme section* now in the final month of training, distraction was something we welcomed in one sense but dreaded in another, because of where it could take us. I found that during the day, at what might have been the oddest moments – when scrubbing a toilet bowl, for instance, or refolding uniforms – I'd have flashbacks to events in Australia. A march with the Army Reserve . . . Me as a child in a swimming pool . . . A woman's face across a dinner table thrown into shadow by candlelight . . . It was my mind finding distraction in the past, for here there were no distractions, simply enforced tedium.

Parts of my mind appeared to be becoming disconnected as they were not being used. Those parts included love, poetry, passion, happiness and intellectual reflection. All these things were irrelevant now and of no use; even worse, they could compromise the ability to endure. They could compromise my endurance, because in thinking about these things, it made me realise what I had given up.

The Army Reserve was about camaraderie, but there was little of that here. In fact, it appeared to be implicitly discouraged – which surprised and disappointed me. Swimming reminded me of warm summer days, warm water wrapped around me as I spun and held my breath underwater, experimenting with my body. Here my body felt abused and uncared for, except as a tool for carrying a pack. And as for women, poetry and love, there was none of that here either. The fact was, I did not expect it. Nor did I really expect to be well treated. But I wondered whether the trade was worthwhile; and every part of me wished and hoped it was.

At least one young man in our *section* did not consider the trade worthwhile. A Frenchman named Ramon cut his wrists in one of the toilet cubicles. Because we used only plastic razors, cutting one's wrist was a rather tricky activity, so he broke open the head and extracted the blade. He should've used the wooden-handled knife we were all issued, to make sure of the job. Coupled with the fact that he cut himself across the wrist rather than lengthways, I thought it quite likely he didn't really want to kill himself. He just wanted to tell the world he needed help.

There was a long swathe of Ramon's blood on the tiles and, just my luck, it was me on *les chiottes* that night. I supposed mopping up the blood was a change from slopping down the backs of toilet doors to swill off the semi-dried semen. There was no sympathy for Ramon for he tried to take the easy way out. We dragged and carried him down the stairs and across the ring road to the *infirmerie*. We were wrong to assume it would be the last we'd see of him.

•

By the end of August, just weeks away from completing instruction, we were all truly fed up with the cleaning and the guard duties, particularly *piquet d'intervention*. Next time it came around, we did PI under the supervision of *Sergent* Romett and *Caporal* Malvina, but it really didn't matter who the NCOs were. PI was always the same – the same equipment, timings and location.

The preceding evening at 2030, we would be ordered to get our *sacs* and meet in the corridor. We'd then be ordered to empty them onto the tiled floor. What fell out were a sleeping bag, poncho, canvas and four wooden pegs.

Having emptied our *sacs*, Malvina would hold up an item to general view, commencing with the sleeping bag, and then give the order, 'Dans sac.' Everyone duly put the sleeping bag into the pack, followed in turn by the poncho and canvas, one *tenue de combat*, one *tenue de sport*, a full water bottle and boot polish; finally, the four pegs would go in to provide some structural rigidity.

The *sac*s were then closed, inspected by Malvina, and placed at the foot of the bunks. Our washing and shaving kits we'd place on top of the packs, ready to go in the morning.

Réveil at 0500, followed by *appel*, then assistance to the driver of our truck, loading up everything from picks and shovels to screwdrivers. In combat greens and berets, we would place our *sacs* onto the back of the truck, a 1950s Marmon or Simca troop-carrier, with bench seating set up at 90 degrees to the cabin. We then marched off to the armoury to draw our weapons, our visit always prolonged by having to wake up the armourer on the ground floor of the *compagnie commandement et de service*.

Having been issued the weapons, we marched to the *salle d'alerte,* where we'd unload the truck, say hello to the lads from the other company stepping down from service, and make our way into the *salle*. Once inside, the television came on and, if there was little to be done during the day (except the usual sweeping and mopping), we would try to sleep, read or write letters.

From 1800 till 0530 there was a guard placed at the perimeter of the camp, near the *officiers'* mess, and one behind the foyer, near the athletics field. Two hours on and four hours off. The *caporal* had to effect the change every two hours, while the *sergent* slept all night. Some rank had many privileges in the Legion.

Next morning there was an orientation session to discuss where we would all be going once the course had finished and we left Quartier Danjou. When my turn came, the *lieutenant* again told me I was to remain at Castelnaudary and be rapidly promoted. According to him, I had a '*belle carrière*' (a wonderful career) ahead of me, and no choice in the matter anyway. If I refused, he said, he would '*baise ta gueule*' – fuck my face.

And that was career counselling, Legion-style, I supposed. In the more immediate future, I knew we had tests over the next few days, then the *Marche Raide* starting on 5 September, and finally, the week after, packing up – the end. Sunday, 18 September couldn't come soon enough for me. Among other things, I needed a rest from LeCoq's episodic madness and the pressure of trying to be the best all the time.

If I was passionate and driven to succeed I would always do my best. But here in the Legion, it was something more than that. I was a representative of my country and the only Australian most here had ever met. I had to be the best, or at least give it all I could. I never wanted anyone in the Legion to think that

Australians were anything other than honest, straightforward and willing to try until they fell over and could do no more.

I sat in our room at the desk we all shared, revising some of the material on mines that had been presented to us over the last week. In addition to this, there was a second piece of homework I had to do, namely trying to memorise the official *Code d'Honneur du Légionnnaire*:

1. Legionnaire, you are a volunteer serving France with honour and fidelity.

2. Every Legionnaire is your brother in arms, irrespective of his nationality, race or creed. You demonstrate this by an unwavering and straight forward solidarity which must always bind together members of the same family.

3. Respectful of the Legion's traditions, honouring your superiors, discipline and camaraderie are your strength, courage and loyalty your virtues.

4. Proud of your status as Legionnaire, you will display this pride, by your turnout, always impeccable, your behaviour, ever worthy though modest, your living quarters always tidy.

5. An elite soldier, you will train vigorously, you will maintain your weapon as if it were your most precious possession, you will keep your body in the peak of condition always.

6. A mission once given to you becomes sacred, you will accomplish it to the peril of your life.

7. In combat, you will act without passion or hatred; you will respect the defeated enemy and will never abandon your wounded or your dead, or your arms.

There certainly was a lot of talk about being *élite*, about *honneur* and *fidélité*. I hadn't seen any of it personally, but then I had four and a half more years to find it. The problem was, after four months, I was now beginning to doubt I would find it at all. This scepticism was beginning to colour all I did in the Legion, compromising my enthusiasm and hope for the future. I fought its pernicious effect – I knew I had to, to survive.

10

THE FINAL TEST

Vous êtes tous crétins et idiots.
(You're all cretins and idiots.)

In just one week we had more lessons than the thirteen previous weeks combined. It just showed what could be achieved when there was a deadline looming, I guess. Our classwork done, we were then trucked out to Bel Air and given weapons exams.

One thing I always did whenever we were issued with rifles was to put the safety catch to safe, take the magazine off, cock the weapon and look inside the chamber. It was just a standard safety procedure, although also, admittedly, a legacy of my training in Australia. Eleven of the just over thirty men remaining in the *section* failed to do this basic check, however, and ended up firing off the exercise round that had been put into the chamber. With Mahmood nodding his assent, they got a good kicking from the *caporals*.

So, after close to three months of instruction, a third of our number were still ignorant of basic weapons-handling drills. This was a sign that something was not quite right, surely – this was serious. But no one seemed to care, of course. The *sergents* just shrugged while the *caporals* laughed and said, 'Vous êtes tous crétins et idiots.'

We had further exams for the *Certificate Technique Éléméntaire* (CTE), the basic test for recruits. It included French language, mines and first aid, and we also ran the usual 1500-metre and 8000-metre distances as part of the physical element of the certificate. I came first on both runs, with *Caporal* El Wahad and his near-empty *sac* running beside me. He kept screaming in my ear that if I was a real Australian, I had to win. I couldn't argue with that, but it wasn't as if the *caporal* was genuinely trying to motivate me. He was simply performing for *Capitaine* Rayoume, who had come to see how his charges were getting along.

But there was no performance, no play acting, come Monday, 5 September. That was when we were trucked to the countryside and set up camp next to a small vineyard from which we would begin the *Marche Raide*. At last we were off on the march that would be our rite of passage as Legionnaires and the endpoint of our recruit course.

It was late summer in Europe, and despite threats from the *section* staff, those ripe, plump red grapes on the vines were just too good to ignore. At a guess, the owner of that vineyard must've lost around 25 per cent of his crop as our *section* of Legionnaires ate through kilos of the delightful fruit, the like of which we hadn't tasted in months.

We set off on the first of four days' marching early the following morning, in our groups. I had the usual suspects around me: *Sergent* Bronski, *Caporal* Kronk, LeCoq, Stein, Fekler, Contein, Lebeck, Locolo and Millard. It was Lebeck's *binome*, slow-talking country boy Contein, who was the first to fall.

The young Frenchman went down – literally, falling to the ground, with his *sac* on his back – late that first afternoon. We gathered around to see that his lips were flecked with dried spittle and dried sweat had drawn lines of salt on his cheeks. With imploring eyes, Contein begged me for some water, as I was the only one who had any left in his canteen. I poured a measure of the precious liquid into the cap of his empty bottle. He slobbered at it just enough to moisten his mouth.

Having had no instruction on the subject in the last few months, not one of the men I marched with had any idea of water discipline. Me, I was fortunate in that I'd had experience in an army that valued water, because the Foreign Legion was obviously never going to enlighten us. Then again, there's lack of education and there's plain stupidity.

And so it was that on day two Malvina collapsed, having set out on a day of blue sky and blinding sun, carrying eleven bottles of Kronenbourg beer in his *sac*. Like many things I witnessed in the Legion, had I not seen it myself I would never have believed it.

At the end of that Wednesday, having climbed escarpments and marched along country lanes since 0700, the *groupes* assembled around a natural spring fringed with green vegetation, and there we found the Argentinian, writhing in the dust. He was just a dirty-green form of spasming muscles and dried salt sweat. Malvina had dehydrated himself so badly he could barely speak and was incapable of walking without help. He probably should have been evacuated to hospital, but instead he was put in his sleeping bag with bottles of water to hand. For the rest of the march, he rode in the liaison truck that carried the injured and jerry cans of water.

In the course of the *Marche Raide*, we marched up to the base of some Cathar stone ruins, called Peyrepertuse, meaning 'pierced rock'. The Cathars were a religious sect in the south of France from about the middle of the twelfth century. The last of them were burned as heretics in 1320. The ruins included a large stone castle perched on the crest of an 800-metre-high rocky outcrop at what used to be the old frontier between France and Spain. From its elevated position, and with weather permitting, the Mediterranean was visible to the south-east. I only got to know all this after talking to a beautiful young woman with blonde hair, round melon breasts and a smattering of English, who was selling ice cream in the castle's car park.

My subsequent reflections on breasts and battles were crowded out and displaced by a difficult descent, down steps carved from rock and along a path made almost impassable by vines and overhanging trees. Later, while climbing the other side of the valley, Locolo dropped to his knees and cried out that he couldn't carry on. *Sergent* Bronski turned back from his position in the lead and gave him a kick to the ribs that had Locolo sprawled beside the track. With tears dripping from his cheeks, the Spaniard finally lurched to his feet and marched on.

That evening we camped by a stream, the surface calm and placid, its waters cool and soothing. Where this picturesque spot was exactly, though, we had no idea. Because we were given no maps, nor told of our route or destination, we were ignorant tourists. We knew we were heading in a roughly northern direction, and we knew we were following GR36, a path through the west of Languedoc-Roussillon and part of the *Grande Randonnée* network of walks crisscrossing France. That much was clear from the sun's position at any given time of day and the red painted arrows on boulders and trees along the route – the Legion couldn't hide those basic facts from us. Even now, did the *section* staff fear desertion, or was it because they simply couldn't be bothered to tell us where we were going? Whatever it was, it meant that most of us walked with head down, the weight of packs and thoughts ensuring that eyes were on feet, one foot in front of the other.

Five days after we left the camp, our *groupe* finished the *Marche Raide* by a copse of conifers atop a windy plateau. The ten of us sat there on our packs, waiting for the rest of *3ème Section* to arrive, and ate sardines and bread slippery with oil. Soon we were all trucked back to Quartier Danjou on a road passing just to the south of the old fortified town of Carcassone. There, early on this Sunday evening, the magnificent castle was lit up, inviting me to think again of warriors and battles past.

Sergent Romett interrupted my pleasant reverie with that most unexpected of things: some volunteered information. By his reckoning, we had marched about 150 kilometres. Looking at his pinched face, I couldn't even be sure he was right about that.

Mid morning the next day, LeCoq rushed into our room, excited, obviously keen to share some major news. 'Mason, you are the best!' he said, for once a big smile set between those giant ears of his.

Sure enough, on a wall out in the hallway, was posted a list of our names with a number next to each one corresponding with where we'd finished at the end of instruction. Beside my name was the typed 1. It was worth trying so hard all these months, if just for that single digit after my name. For the rest of my life I could carry with me the satisfaction of having topped my French Foreign Legion recruit course. If it sounded good, it felt even better.

Just so we didn't get soft or start taking our achievements too much to heart, we still had five days of intense cleaning and packing up to look forward to. Then, on the Sunday, we all participated in the *4ème Régiment Étranger* half marathon. Legionnaires from all of the Legion's continental regiments and French civilians participated in what was a truly colourful event around Castelnaudary. From the air, the different colours of the various *compagnie* and regimental T-shirts must have looked a pointillist painter's delight.

It was quite a day. I finished in just over 78 minutes, even though we had done little footing over the last few weeks. I was sure I could easily have run a full marathon if we'd had to. It felt that good. Not so good was the prospect of days of parading, cleaning and getting ready to leave; for everyone but me that is.

Next day, Monday, 12 September, we had to wear our combat greens and kepis, for this was it; we were being posted to our respective regiments. Every week a *commandant* (equivalent to a major in the Australian or British army) travelled to the *4ème Régiment* from Aubagne, the Legion's headquarters, to meet with those who had just completed their recruit course. This senior officer, along with the relevant *section* leader and another *lieutenant* from the regiment, sat on a panel that decided the regimental destination of each new Legionnaire. Why there was a panel, who knew, as it wasn't as if any discussion ever took place, just allocation. Others had already planned each recruit's Legion destiny.

Having topped the course, I was the first to enter the room, which was next to the *bureau de semaine* on the ground floor of the *1ère Compagnie* building. As was customary, I presented myself, held my kepi by my left side, and remained at attention. When the *commandant* put it to me that I had a '*belle carrière*' in the Legion if I so wished, *Lieutenant* Hildebrandt and the other junior officer nodded their heads. He told me that I was valuable to the Legion, and in return for all my hard work, I would be rewarded.

I'd known for some time what my prize was to be, of course, and all the commandant did was reiterate Hildebrandt's offer (without the 'fuck your face' threat, thankfully). I would be in Castelnaudary until the end of the following summer on the fast-track route to *caporal*, and then on to the regiment of my choice. At present, my thinking was either the Parachute Regiment, or more likely, the Legion's unit based in the Republic of Djibouti, in the Horn of Africa, but that was all a long way off right now. My choice would depend on what I heard in the meantime.

After I left the room, Dober and Kronk took me aside. No words of congratulation from these two, no begrudging respect even; far from it, in fact.

Dober sneered, revealing his yellow, stained teeth, before hissing, '*Tu vas deserter, toi. C'est sure.*' (You'll desert. It's certain.) Little Kronk, the quasimodo–pixie cross, nodded in agreement.

'*Jamais!*' I spat back – and it was true, never would I have even considered deserting.

And then I let the pair of them have it, in English, some of which they understood. I said that slimy, lying, ignorant bastards like them would never make me quit. Not only was I fitter, more intelligent and better trained than them, but most importantly, I was here of my own free will; I wasn't some political or economic refugee concerned only with the acquisition of a French passport. I could desert the next day if I wished, but no bastard would make me, and certainly not the likes of them.

At this outburst, my first after close to four frustrating months in the Legion, the two loathsome *caporals* appeared taken aback. I thought they might hit me, and I wished they would – for I would fight these bastards and fight until I dropped. Instead, they just looked at one another, and then Dober, with a shrug of his shoulders, simply bleated, '*Je m'en fou.*'

I had no respect for these two. Had they taught us anything? Had they even attempted to encourage teamwork? No, not at all. They'd been amusing themselves with us on their way to *sergent* course. They were the embodiment of everything that had driven me mad about Legion life since arriving at Aubagne. Where in these characters was the *honneur*, *fidélité* and *fraternité* we'd read so much about, this esprit de corps for which the Legion was famed around the world?

But maybe I had a question of my own to answer. Was I a masochist to stay on here after all the problems I knew to be real, and all the negativity that had been passed my way from the *anciens*? Perhaps I was, a little. Even then, though, I knew that in life, nothing that is strong, valuable and enduring comes from doing things the easy way. I wanted to demonstrate to myself that I could complete the full five years.

Besides, why did I have to desert to express my contempt for the training I had received? Why not stay and see what else was on offer? After all, this was meant to be an adventure.

Years later, when I look back on that decision to remain in the Legion after instruction, I shake my head at a young man's ability to be so analytical and sure. Generally, people understand and empathise with those who give up or fail far more readily than with those prepared to fight and endure. Failure invites pity and compassion. On the other hand, fighting and enduring, as I was to find, too often involves compromises that are difficult to explain. In retrospect though, I was right to remain. I had committed to five years. Moreover, only a few months into the five years, as I was at this point, I'd seen very little and I longed to see much more. If a hellion drove me to join, it also taunted me into leaving. Although I ignored it, its whisper lingered like a promised kiss.

What I did know back then in mid September 1988 was that the Foreign Legion recruit course at Castelnaudary was rubbish. Instead of making recruits proud, it made us angry and resentful. Knowing that, it was little surprise that so many chose to desert or leave, and of those who stayed, that so few wished to return as instructors to continue the lie.

At the conclusion of that morning, once free of the odious Dober and Kronk, I had a chance to see what sort of a bearing all this had on my fellow former recruits and what the future held for them. There were fourteen Legionnaires from our *section* allocated to 2 REP in Calvi. They included LeCoq, Fekler, Becker, Dazinovic, Canuk, Schmidt and Gamelin, all of whom would be leaving tomorrow. Of the *section* that had departed from Quartier Danjou the previous week, twenty were also destined for Calvi. If this was anything like the weekly addition to regimental strength, there must have been an enormous turnover of personnel. Where did they all go? According to rumours over at the foyer, the answer was simple: desertions. Coupled with the abysmal recruit training, how was it possible then to maintain an effective regiment, given that so many walked out the front gate?

I sat for a moment and thought through the numbers. There were three *compagnies d'instruction*, each with four recruit *sections*. Instruction was some twelve to fourteen weeks duration. I knew that there was anything from thirty-five to fifty-five Legionnaires in a recruit *section* at Castelnaudary, and that almost every week of the year a *section* completed instruction.

So, if there were some forty Legionnaires like us every week, allowing for desertions and those who went *civil,* that totalled something less than 2000 men a year. The Legion had some 8000 men in total, with *officiers* and *sous-officiers* making up, say, a quarter of that number. Given that the minimum period of engagement was five years, it was obvious that the Legion had a significant retention problem.

If the training was poor at Castelnaudary, I never properly understood how it was to be undertaken in a regiment, as *Sergent-Chef* Mahmood would have had us believe. Any deficiencies at initial training, he'd tell us, would be corrected once we'd arrived at our respective regiments. It seemed to me that he was almost admitting to what a number of us had suspected for some time: Castelnaudary was not training at all; it was a period of indoctrination and desensitisation – an introduction to the new world of the Legion. I would have to wait another year before I could begin to find out the truth for myself.

On Friday, 16 September, we set up one of the *compagnie* rooms in readiness for a *pot,* as the French call a small celebration or mild beer-drinking session. We grouped tables together, then begged, borrowed or stole bedsheets to serve as our tablecloths. Once done, we arranged the various drinks (for which we'd paid through our forced contributions) into the shape of a Legion flame, bordered by peanuts and crisps.

At 1600, the whole of *3ème Section* was assembled for our farewell drinks, including the staff, *Capitaine* Rayoume and the *adjudant compagnie, Adjudant* Jakic. When *Lieutenant-Colonel* Mariotti, second-in-command of the regiment arrived, Hildebrandt presented the *section* and we were treated to a little speech.

Mariotti spoke of us as real Legionnaires. He spoke too of *fraternité*. The *lieutenant-colonel* was slick and too smooth, but at least he was enthusiastic. Looking around the room, I met the gaze of Canuk, the Canadian, and others. Each raised his eyes to the ceiling: that brotherhood, *grande famille* business once again . . . From that moment on, I couldn't believe a word Mariotti was saying.

After months in the Legion, what had we learned? We'd learned the importance of time or service in the Legion over what you had done and whether you were any good at it. How often had I heard '*Quelle matricule de ridicule!*' as NCOs ridiculed the army number each of us had been given. Like them we knew our unique army number told everyone precisely when we had joined.

Sure, it felt pretty special to be the top recruit in our *section*, but in all truth I'd felt far more of a soldier after having completed a three-week Army Reserve recruit course in Australia. In four months here in the Legion, our expertise was handling a *balai* and *serpillière* (broom and dirty rag) rather than anything related to soldiering.

We'd also learned to distrust almost everyone. There was only lip service paid to this *binome* concept. What we did trust in, and what those from *caporal* up to *colonel* officially loathed but indulged in also, was the Legion's 'mafia' system.

Such groups were the strongest social component within the Legion. There was the French mafia, the Brit mafia, the German mafia and generally smaller mafias for other nationalities and language blocs. In the Brit mafia, as for the other ones no doubt, because we all shared a language, common culture and an accepted means of enforcing conformity, we came to rely on one another.

That various mafias existed outraged French officers, because it ran expressly counter to what they wanted to achieve – the integration of all to a common denominator. This common denominator meant that we all became alone, or equally vulnerable, before *sous-officiers* and *officiers* who did not manifest, or even articulate, a concern for their Legionnaires. So we adopted the best means we had and looked after our own. This we did through what was commonly known as *système D* or *démerde*. From replacing a lost or broken part of your kit or obtaining a few extra cans of compressed meat for *casse-croûte*, to getting some wood to set up as targets, you would be told, '*Démerde toi.*' Get it yourself, in other words, through whatever means you can, fair or foul. This was all very well for encouraging initiative, but it also encouraged theft and ultimately added to the atmosphere of uncertainty and mistrust.

And so it was that our drinking partners that Friday evening were decided very much along mafia lines. After the *pot* we were escorted to the foyer by Malvina. He watched us very closely, concerned that we'd start brawling amongst ourselves. We simply concentrated on drinking as much beer as we could in the time allowed.

Ramon the Frenchman cut himself again that night. He was found slumped in a latrine, slashes across his wrists, and a destroyed plastic razor in a pool of blood at his feet. Ramon's latest attempt came after a flurry of others, including another Frenchman in our *section* named Bernhault, to hurt themselves and so be released from their contract with the Legion.

And there was the answer to a question that had been troubling us since June. Despite the clause in the contract that said you could be released if you requested it, this was not quite what it meant. The Legion had to agree that you were not suited to a Legion life. Therefore, there was a presumption that had to be overturned, which is what Ramon, Bernhault and many others set about trying to do.

A medic was summoned and Ramon was transported off again, alive if not well, to the *infirmerie*.

Next day, Saturday 17 September, most of the *section* left Quartier Danjou, to travel to the various regiments in mainland France, or to Aubagne and then on to Calvi. I stayed behind.

11

LEGIONNAIRE ON LEAVE

Dépêchez-vous!
(Everyone hurry up!)

For my own sanity, rather than view the future as one long trial, I tried to break it into stages. Each stage would have its own challenges therefore, and its own highs and lows; some were the people, the training or both.

In the short term, I had to adjust to my new situation and prepare for the *caporal* course. Everyone in our *section* had just departed for their regiments, except for myself, Northam and the others headed to *3ème Régiment Étranger d'Infantrie* in French Guyane, and Bernhault, who would be going *civil* after his wrist-slashing episode.

Bernhault was ecstatic at the prospect of being released from his contract; going home, as early as in the next few days. Perhaps the scars he would forever carry on his wrists matched the ones deep inside. The other slasher, Ramon, was quite mad. I saw him in the *infirmerie*; his eyes appeared to have grown so large, they protruded from his face, and he wore an expression

TOP: *3ème Section* in the field north of Castelnaudary, France, around a newly laid out Legion flame.

BOTTOM: *Remise Képi Blanc – 3ème Section, 1ère Compagnie, 4ème Régiment Étranger*, at Bel Air, near Castelnaudary, in July 1988. The author is in the back row, fifth from the left.

TOP LEFT: An important duty – the author polishing his boots.

TOP RIGHT: Not long a *caporal*! Parade combats with *épaulettes de tradition* and kepi.

BOTTOM: At Castelnaudary during the *caporal* course. The author is in the top row, fourth from left.

TOP LEFT: With a member of the Brit Mafia at Castelnaudary. Another *Remise Képi Blanc*.

TOP RIGHT: Djibouti nightlife.

BOTTOM: At the Forest of Day – revising the *Machine Gun Manual*.

TOP: How many Legionnaires does it take? Bogged near Lake Abbe in the west of Djibouti.

BOTTOM: *Section* on the march in Djibouti, 1991.

TOP: Two *tireurs d'élite* near Ali Sabieh.
BOTTOM: Firing the machine gun in Djibouti.

TOP: Part of the commando course.
BOTTOM: The author sewing hessian strips on combats during the *Stage Tireur d'Élite*.

The memorial at the summit of Mount Garbi, built in memory of the twenty-seven Legionnaires killed there on 3 February 1982 while on a training exercise. In bad weather, their twin-propeller transport hit the side of the mountain killing all on board.

The author in parade dress at Quartier Monclar, Djibouti.

straight out of one of Hogarth's engravings of Bedlam. His was a madness born of determination to get out of Castelnaudary and the Legion. According to an English medic I spoke to, a decision had yet to be reached on Ramon's future.

Stage one of my future began two days after LeCoq and the others moved on – Monday, 19 September. It also happened to be my twenty-eighth birthday and my first day as a *caporal du jour*. I imagined that during the next few years I would be spending a lot of time in the labour-intensive role of *caporal du jour*.

I found myself allocated to *4ème Section* of *1ère Compagnie* and moved to another room on the top floor of the barracks. The men here had arrived as recruits in the first half of July were now entering the final month of their course. They included Rhemes, a Belgian who spoke German, English and French; Hovellet, a black guy from Wolverhampton in the English Midlands; and Dominez, a slim, predatory-nosed Frenchman who spoke English and seemed far too clever to be in the Legion.

Morale in *4ème Section* was particularly low, I gathered. They were awaiting the arrival of their fourth *section* leader and had already farewelled five *caporals*. Six Legionnaires had deserted. From my point of view, whenever the new *lieutenant* did finally arrive, I knew I'd have to ask for some leave; even a weekend would be good. I could feel myself getting tense, my stomach knotting and my jaw clenching; it was a standard reaction to all the usual yelling and screaming that echoed throughout the building and across the *place d'armes*, and the stupidity that was life at Quartier Capitaine Danjou.

I wore a brassard on my right arm and had to present myself as '*Fonction Caporal Mason*'. I was marked out as neither Legionnaire nor *caporal*, just an in-between thing again, caught between two ranks. The *caporal* course was due to start in the first couple of weeks of November, almost two months away.

One of the advantages in having a *fut fut* close to hand for NCOs in the Legion was that the more tiring duties could be passed on to him. After all, what had I done to deserve a break from the tedious, tiring and annoying? So it was that I was the *caporal* who took *piquet d'intervention* that week. I changed the guard at the perimeter and near the foyer at 1900, 2100, 2300, 0100 and 0300. Each changeover took twenty to thirty minutes, the last pair remaining in place until 0520 or so, when I went to collect them and set the men to cleaning the room. In other words there was very little sleep.

And because I was a *fut fut* – or more commonly, the like-sounding and distinctly unflattering *foutre foutre* (fuck-up, or sperm bank) – I found that some NCOs went out of their way to render my every effort a failure. They rarely did this to my face, but they whined among themselves no end. Because the life of a Legionnaire was such an enormous ball breaker, to have arrived at the dizzy heights of *caporal* meant that life could at last be led without the scrubbing of latrines. For many, the rank of *caporal* would not be reached for between three and five years. Little wonder others were jealous. And the rapidly promoted *caporal* had not done it the hard way; he hadn't endured the pain and humiliation of years of systematic abuse.

I discussed this with two other rapid-promotion *caporals*. Coleman was a former captain in the United States Army, and Franko, a Yugoslav who had lived all his life in Germany, and who spoke not only the languages of those nations but also English and French. We three brought differing knowledge and abilities to the Legion, assets one might've thought would be highly prized but, as it turned out, not so. Despite plenty of promises, including those I'd received from Hildebrandt, we got no special instruction to assist us through to *caporal*. We would have to do it all ourselves.

It was little wonder that so many *fut futs* deserted, which was why Dober and Kronk had been so cocksure of themselves that day of our showdown, no doubt. At the conclusion of my five years, I was almost alone as a rapid-promotion *caporal* from 1988 completing my contract in a Regiment's combat *compagnie*, and one of only a handful to complete the five-year contract at all. What a waste it was. If these men were supposedly the best of the best, why did the Legion not work harder at retaining them?

In Quartier Danjou, barbed wire and other people surrounded me. There was no time or place to leave the group, to be alone with my thoughts and not be subject to the capricious whims of others. As always, lives were regulated by whistle blasts, constant counting, orders and threats from early morning to late at night, seven days a week. I felt caged, trapped, with no escape. I knew I had to adapt and let this wash over me. But it was difficult; I didn't want to be blind to or untouched by the world around me. To do so would have been to die a small death of surrender inside.

Instead, simply to help me get up every morning, I put a hot knot of loathing inside myself. It was in a quiet place where I could retrieve it as necessary. Just knowing it was there meant I didn't have to show it to anyone. It was as if I was living a second, interior life. The knot allowed me to still feel, its heat keeping me warm.

Piquet d'intervention came around again on Sunday, 25 September, this time with *Sergent* Fleber of *4ème Section*. At 0530 on the day of duty, he was drunk, barely capable of speaking and certainly unable to direct things. Later that morning he couldn't even lift himself from his cot. So I ran the PI, daytime and night. Craning my head into the small room where Fleber was sleeping, I asked him a question. He mumbled, '*Je m'en fou*', rolled over and continued snoring.

Next day I knew my expectations remained too high. The Legionnaires were set to sweeping and mopping once more, their weapons lessons apparently cancelled because Fleber, the *sergent du jour* responsible for giving the lessons, was too drunk, again. Meanwhile, rather than fill in for their incompetent colleague and ensure that the men got some useful instruction, the other *sergents* sat in the *section* office, feet on desks, drinking coffee. There was never an assessment of their performance, of course, even, it seemed, once we had our new *officier* on board.

Soon after his arrival at *4ème Section*, *Lieutenant* Blithiot collected all the watches, claiming it was better that Legionnaires were disorientated and not a good thing if they thought for themselves. Removing the timepieces meant they couldn't anticipate orders. In this way, our charges were treated like Pavlov's dogs, made to respond only to whistles and bawled commands.

Blithiot was a recent graduate from the military academy at Montpellier and was rarely seen around the *section*. Young and earnest behind his round wire-rimmed Trotsky glasses, he was keen to try out his Legion psychology on the men. Thus he adopted an extraordinarily patronising tone to anyone who wasn't an officer. It wasn't unusual to hear *sergents* and others leave his office with a sneering or despairing '*Quelle con!*' (What a fool!)

Sergent-Chef Solo, on the other hand, was a man not to be underestimated. He was an Italian who spoke English, German and French. Curiously, despite his obvious intelligence, he often seemed preoccupied with the trivial things, such as a missing pillow cover, rather than a Legionnaires's swollen ankle or money missing from the *section's* cashbox.

Autumn progressed and before long the forty men in *4ème Section* had entered the final week of instruction. The *Marche Raide* began on 14 October and was along the same route as mine had been, only without the heat. Indeed, due to the cold we found ourselves sleeping in *gites d'étapes*, the small chalets or huts set at intervals along the Grande Randonnée trails.

During those gruelling days, *Caporal* Jack – like Dober, an *ancien* of the Legion's Engineer Regiment on his way to the *sergent* course – complained of a pain in his knee. According to Jack, the troublesome knee was a legacy of his time in French Guyane. I soon discovered that he'd been there for just a few months, however, and had never in fact gone out on a mission into the jungle. It was no surprise to hear *Sergent-Chef* Solo calling him a '*gross sac de merde*', even in front of the new Legionnaires. All Jack carried on the march was a sleeping bag, to fill things out, and the necessary food for the day. He spent much of his time yelling at the men, jutting out his Punch and Judy chin, and threatening them with beatings and rape, each order accompanied by a screeched '*Dépêchez-vous!*' (Everyone hurry up!)

Within a week the men had been seen off to regiments, after which I had a long discussion with *Sergent-Chef* Mahmood. He reiterated what I already knew: that the life of a *fut fut* was complete shit, something that had to be endured with a soul of iron.

'You are very good, so let nothing touch you,' Mahmood advised, slapping his chest with a closed fist. 'Or you will die small deaths every day. Most people here are shit, you understand? They use this,' he continued, pointing to the coloured rank on his chest, 'to hurt people, because they are nothing.' The Algerian looked at me for a moment through basalt-black eyes before thrusting out his right hand. 'Be strong,' he said, as we shook hands. I knew *Sergent-Chef* Mahmood was right.

The most remarkable thing during this period was that Lieutenant Blithiot had given me eleven days' leave. At last, after five months with no leave at all, I was to have a few days outside the wire.

Sergent-Chef Solo was surprised also. But when I mentioned that I planned to spend my time off in Paris, he assured me there was no way I would have enough money for eleven days there. Why not consider going to England instead? he suggested. Although the Legion held my passport and it was forbidden for us to leave France, we knew that it was possible to cross borders without one, and many people did. Coincidentally, my brother Brett was at Cambridge working on a graduate degree, so why not indeed?

I left Quartier Danjou on Wednesday, 26 October along with Colin Trotter, a cook in the regiment whose leave happened to correspond with mine, and together we set off for Paris on the overnight train. Colin was not actually part of the *compagnies d'instruction*, rather he was attached to the CCS, the *Compagnie de Commandement et de Service*. The CCS provided cooks, plumbers and mechanics to the various Legion regiments and their routine was completely different from those of us working on the recruit courses. Generally, Colin worked from 0700 to 1630, and always had Saturday afternoons and all of Sunday free.

In Paris we drank too much at Irish Tony's, just off the red light district of Rue Saint-Denis, and despite the misgivings of a French customs official on the train to Dieppe, we were able to board a cross-Channel ferry with just our *Cartes d'Identité Militaire*, identifying us as Legionnaires. The true test came in Dover when we had to line up at passport control.

Rather than try my luck in the European Community line, I simply followed Colin and joined the queue under the sign reading UK Nationals. We both then handed our cards to the immigration officer, a very attractive woman in her early twenties.

'Oh dear, what are those?' she asked, as if the problem was too much to deal with. 'Off you go then . . .' And just like that, with a wave of her hand, we were through.

Up at Cambridge, a couple of hours north of London, I stayed with my brother and variously challenged him to a race around Trinity College courtyard, tried to convince the female rowing captain of Magdalene College to have sex with me, and slept. Over the week or so I was there, I slept a lot. And now that I had arrived in a friendly, civilised environment, I thought a great deal too.

I reflected back on the heated discussion with Caporals Dober and Kronk and wrote home to my mother in Australia:

Saturday, 5 November 1988

A letter home from Trinity Hall, Cambridge, England

Dear Mother,
Your letters questioning my decision to join (though not your surprise!) and my short time here in Cambridge with Brett have brought into clearer focus what I have done, and perhaps more importantly, what I have to do to survive. You know I hate giving

up on anything and the fact that I have been fundamentally challenged has galvanised me. That said, I know that I must take care.

One's vigilance must never be lax. Passivity is out. I've given some thought to deserting, but how can I live the next fifty years knowing that I had given up? No, desertion is a last resort, an alternative if my mental wellbeing is under threat.

Love,

David

One of the things about your own emotional wellbeing is that it is very difficult to notice change in yourself. If I knew I was starting to change, to adapt to the Legion, I didn't know what I was losing.

On Friday, 11 November, four days after my return to Castelnaudary, the next batch of recruits for *4ème Section* arrived. The cycle never ended. It was fortunate for me that I'd joined the Legion during the spring, I realised. With winter fast approaching, these new recruits would suffer in the cold.

For myself, I knew that the upcoming *caporal* course would be no picnic, but at least I had a vague idea of what was to come. And I was looking forward to seeing what the Legion had to offer its junior leaders in infantry tactics and training.

Surely the Legion would be offering something in those fields now . . . wouldn't it?

12

CAPORAL COURSE

Tu comprends, tête de noeud?
(Understand, dickhead?)

By 8 December 1988 I was in the third week of the Legion's nine week *caporal* course, or *Certificate Militaire Élémentaire* (CME). I was now '*Élève Caporal Mason*', indicating my status as a student on the course, a considerably more satisfactory situation than being a *fonction caporal*.

Because we were on a course, all students were grouped into *pelotons* instead of *sections* as before. The point was that the eighty or so of us on the course were grouped into two *pelotons* – there being two such groups doing the course of some nine weeks' duration at the same time. My *peloton* was called the 88/10, meaning the tenth *peloton* to do the course that year.

I was due to be going to the course, at nearby Quartier Lapasset, on Monday morning, allowing me Saturday and Sunday to prepare. It sounded perfect. I should have known better, because, mid Saturday morning, I suddenly learned I had just one hour to pack everything together. As it turned out, along with two other Legionnaires from Trotter's CCS, I then waited more than five hours for the bus that would ferry us the necessary few kilometres.

Quartier Lapasset is situated just off the main square in the heart of Castelnaudary and used to be the Legion's main training centre until superseded by the purpose-built facility along the Route de Pexiora. Upon arrival at Lapasset, we were immediately busied with administrative matters. And, naturally, it wasn't long before the subject of time in service raised its head.

I had the shortest service, a trifling six months, and Fiaz from 2 REP the longest, with five years and eight months. There were two other *fut futs* doing the course. Eldron, a too-lean, blond American, formerly of a Ranger battalion in Panama, joined me in 88/10; while Griffo, a dark-eyed Brit with the most wonderful scrofulous sore on his neck, was in the other platoon. Most of the men had two to three years' service, although there were some with little more than a year. Months before, Hildebrandt had told me that people never went on the *caporal* course with less than two years' service (rapid promotions aside), so this last category of *élèves* was something new.

Adjudant Raype, the head of 88/10, formed us up and told us the two things that would see us kicked off his course: stealing and *se branler les couilles dans les chiottes*. Wanking was apparently a common concern across the Legion's training establishments.

Raype was a short, slight, dark-haired and moustachioed native of Portugal. He wore the red and blue ribbon of the *Médaille de la Défense Nationale*, indicating that he had been with the *4ème Régiment* for many years. He had probably been on postings to Djibouti and French Guyane in between three- or four-year stints at Castelnaudary.

Having settled in for a day, we were marched for two days and nights, with just a couple of hours sleep, in the direction of Caylus, over 100 kilometres to the north of Castelnaudary. Picked up en route by trucks and then conveyed the rest of the way, much to our relief, we were deposited at an army camp where some of the buildings dated back to 1853. Inside, it was possible to run your hand over whitewashed mortar into which soldiers had engraved their initials and the years of their artistry.

It was cold, very cold, and it dominated our lives. We slept in stone huts with concrete floors and decaying walls; the icy wind blew through the gaps in the mortar and reached out for us on our canvas stretcher-beds. *Reveille* at 0530 meant a dive for candles and the striking of matches to light cigarettes and mini gas stoves. It was so cold that if you'd left your stove on the floor overnight, under the canvas bed, it refused to work.

As I moved my head from my sleeping bag, the cold seemed to wrap itself around my neck, and even though most of my hair had been shorn from my head, I'd feel the bristles stand up and my skin prickle. Like the other *élèves*, I wore almost everything I had while inside my issue sleeping bag. I wrapped my jumper around the small stove and used it as a pillow. The gas stoves were vital during those winter weeks: without a hot brew in the mornings, there was nothing except cold water to accompany the breakfast of dry bread and a smear of jam.

One evening, for reasons unknown, except perhaps to test our morale, we were made to clean weapons through the night. Then, as the sky went from black to grey with the arrival of dawn, we marched for a number of hours, following the always bulky-looking but almost weightless pack of the *adjudant*. As I looked around me, I could see tired men, men whose ears and noses had been frost-nipped and whose eyes appeared to be dimming. These men were becoming so cold they were losing interest.

Without the help of the Brits on the course, my time would have been infinitely more difficult. One was Malcolm, an Englishman from the Infantry Regiment at Nîmes. He had a dream that sustained him during his five years: to buy a Citroën 2CV, paint it pink and see France. He had three-and-a-half years' service, two of which were spent in French Guyane – an experience that had 'fucked me feet', he told me. Malcolm was a specialist radio man.

Another was Bunt, who came from the Legion's Cavalry Regiment, *1er Régiment Étranger de Cavalerie* (1 REC). Irreverent and pedantic, on occasion he told the *adjudant* to fuck off, though never to his face. Malcolm and Bunt were generous with their advice and patient when I asked what to them must have seemed very stupid questions.

Critically for me, at the rifle range towards the end of our two weeks at Caylus, I injured my Achilles tendon. We had finished firing, had packed up gear into trucks and were ready to embark on an overnight march when Adjudant Raype thought he'd amuse himself by playing a game. At his command, we all had to get into the back of one of the trucks as quickly as possible; then, on his order, immediately dismount from the vehicle. This little game was made more difficult for us as we were each encumbered with equipment totalling some 30 kilograms, plus a single truck was simply too small for forty or so men. In the scramble to descend, I was pushed from behind and landed badly, and painfully. I knew at once that I'd torn the Achilles tendon of my right leg.

I lay on the cold tarmac for a moment, my face in a grimace, and wondered what to do. Should I report the injury? And then what, be thrown off the course? No way. I made up my mind to stay and fight through the pain – marching, *footing*, whatever the Legion wanted to throw at me. I hobbled to my feet while Raype sneered under his black moustache and told me I was slow and weak.

Later that day and all through the night we marched. My ankle swelled up, my entire foot felt leaden, and I was fearful of taking off my right boot. I kept going through the familiar sightings during all night marches of purple elephants at 0330, and hobbled, stumbled and limped to the finish. According to the *adjudant*, we had marched 60 kilometres.

Once back at Quartier Lapasset, on Friday, 9 December, we did two 8000-metre runs with helmet, *sac* and rifle in two days. I could just get the foot into my boot now, but if I touched the inflamed tendon I had to bite my lower lip to stop from crying out. I willed myself to continue.

I was thankful for a quiet Sunday. We were taken to watch a soccer game between the *Compagnie de Commandement et de Service* and the CIC – the *Compagnie d'Instruction des Cadres* – to which I found myself attached for the duration of the *caporal* course. The match was part of a series of events played between various companies in the lead-up to Christmas celebrations. As ever, the Brit mafia were vocal and cheerful.

At the conclusion of the match, our *compagnie* second-in-command, *Capitaine* Schpeck, walked by where Malcolm, Bunt and the rest of us were sitting. Compared to us, he was very plump, and his face carried a smooth sheen that spoke of too much flesh and too much attention to his looks. '*Vous êtes que des hooligans*' (You're just a bunch of hooligans), Schpeck told us. But what got to us was his next remark, which translated as:

'Why don't you shut your arses and give your mouths a chance?' As one-liners go, it was too smooth, too practised. There was a general consensus that this *capitaine* was a sly weasel. Still, it was an easy day for us, and I couldn't complain about that; I just wished the lumps in my tendon would go down.

Come Wednesday, however, we were running another 8000 metres, with boots, rifle, *sac* and helmet. After a shower and some drill before lunch, I found I could no longer walk. It was just impossible to do a couple of turns around the parade ground in *pas de gymnastique*, where the platoon jogged in formation, our boots striking the ground to keep the cadence. My ankle had become leaden again and the pain when placing my boot to the ground each time was excruciating. Tears were soon streaming down my face. But still I wasn't giving up.

Malcolm and Bunt regarded this with a mixture of concern and amazement, shaking their heads at my wanting to carry on. They attracted the attention of *Caporal* Manac, our minder, and I was soon before the *adjudant*. The very first thing Raype did was punch me in the stomach. I bent over double as he stood over me, screaming a series of questions in English: 'Why did you not come to me sooner? Are you acting? Are you really a *pédé*?' As best I could I tried to explain that, being a *fut fut*, I could not give up. I knew that Eldron and Griffo were already in hospital, and it seemed I'd be heading that way too.

At this, Raype said that the doctor would be reporting back to him and if there was nothing wrong with me, he would personally kick my face in. This seemed fair enough to me, and I told him so.

Over at Quartier Danjou, I was examined by the *capitaine médicine*. In reply to his questions, I explained why I hadn't come in earlier and what I had done to perhaps aggravate the problem. After cutting the boot from my foot and seeing the result for himself, he sucked in a breath and called me a fool.

Soon I was sitting on a hard bed in the *infirmerie*, my right foot in plaster for what I was told would be a minimum of fifteen days, and my mind pondering the possibility of being kicked off the course. I realised that if I was to get back squadded, it would mean not finishing till April; in which case, I decided, I would rather abandon the whole rapid-promotion scheme and go straight to a regiment. All this because, by the time I then finished the two full periods of recruit instruction following the *caporal* course, I'd have had over one year and eight months' service to my name yet still no experience whatsoever of the Legion outside of its Training Regiment. I couldn't accept that – there had to be more to the French Foreign Legion and I needed to see it.

A few days later, once I was back in Quartier Lapasset, the *adjudant* punched me again, and yelled accusations that I had hurt myself deliberately and was taking the easy way out. Most importantly, he told me I could continue the course. There were thirty more days to go.

Even with only a month remaining, there was no pleasure to life in 88/10. There was no leave, no opportunity to decompress from the annoyances of others and, the biggest frustration, no respite from the wasteful use of time. There was no real instruction either; no map reading or weapons, just various guard duties, scrubbing pots and cleaning rifles and rooms until late into the night.

Towards Christmas, many of our days were spent either at the guardhouse or finishing work on the platoon's Yuletide creation. Each of the two *pelotons* had to come up with its own creche, which was set aside in a locked room, under guard, and depicted some element of the nativity or of Legion life wrapped up in Christmas. Days and weeks were spent on this activity, including construction, electrics, painting and 'sourcing' of parts. It was an extraordinary focus of the resources of many on something of meaning to so few.

The preparation of the *crèche de Noël* was a Legion tradition to which only a minority of our number wished to be party. Those who did take part willingly appeared to be the brownnoses, the *élèves* craving the approval of NCOs and officers. No doubt the tradition had its worth in years gone by, but in the French Foreign Legion of the late twentieth century, the whole thing seemed to be an irrelevant anachronism.

If we were failing to get into the spirit of the occasion before, come Christmas Eve itself, a dose of the 'flu left many simply wanting to go to bed and stay there. But things had to be seen to be done.

We had sketches to prepare for the evening's celebrations – short spoofs or pantomimes about people or events from the course so far or from over the last year. Because many of the Legionnaires had raided the wine store, however, a number of them were already falling to the floor, drunk and vomiting. Intoxication aside, the nausea may have been induced by the overflow of shit and piss from the flooded latrine on the floor above. The excrement described a chocolate stain down the refectory wall, although someone had done a sterling job of camouflage with the careful positioning of a few Christmas trees and the liberal use of air freshener.

The subsequent dinner was not a happy affair. While the *officiers* sat at a high table and left the room to relieve themselves, we Legionnaires were forbidden to leave. This only marginally slowed the rate of alcohol consumption; although bottles filled with a golden liquid abounded, they remained untouched.

Late in the proceedings, *Capitaine* Megot, CIC's commanding officer, stood up and announced, '*Par ma Rolex, il est minuit. Selon la tradition, debout!*' (By my Rolex, it is midnight. According to tradition, stand up!) There was a collective groan in reply, and comments such as '*Quelle tête de noeud.*' We drank a toast to *le Noël* and the Legion, and then sang two Legion chants, with little enthusiasm.

This *Capitaine* Megot was universally disliked. As much as he extolled all to be *sportif*, he was was never without his *Gitanes* cigarettes, and in fact, no one had ever seen him run or march. There were rumours that he didn't even own a *sac à dos*. But then, who needed a backpack when you were driven everywhere in a Jeep?

On Megot's right sat the *Capitaine* Schpeck of 'shut your arses' fame, now most evocative of a recently sated Toad of Toad Hall after a Sunday roast beef. Maybe he did use too much skin toner. Like Megot, Schpeck was never seen running and he took great delight in belittling Legionnaires for not saluting him sharply or singing enthusiastically enough.

So much for my first Christmas in the Legion, then. Most of us got to bed around 0130, others as late as 0400. We had been told we could sleep in till 0700, but in reality Christmas Day began with the usual whistle blasts at 0530 and screams for us to get in place, standing next to our beds, for *appel*.

On 26 December, we were at Bertrandou, the CIC's equivalent of Bel Air and some 30 kilometres east of Castel, for a few days of combat training. Or in my case, with the plaster on my foot, a few days of sitting in the armoury guarding weapons while the others did the *parcours du combattant* flanking the farm.

After an hour or so, Bertoli, a Frenchman from Calvi, was sent off to the hospital for an X-ray. He was furious, threatening to bash the *adjudant*. He and Cheman, another of the many Frenchmen on the course, had been ordered by Raype to attempt the same obstacle at the same time. There had not been enough room for two and both men had fallen. Cheman reposed on a cot beside me, his ankle swollen to twice its normal size.

We headed back to Lapasset for New Year's Eve. My countdown to midnight was spent in bed, woken at the crucial moment by Bunt and a glass of champagne. He perceptively pointed out that I had quite a few New Years to go in the Legion.

The highlight of 1 January 1989 for me was to have my plaster taken off, though not without a moment of disquiet. The doctor wanted to apply a new one for another fifteen days. He only relented after much entreating from me and instead instructed that I was to neither run nor march.

Despite the direction of the Legion's doctor, I returned to Bertrandou anyway. There, I slipped my boots on gingerly, excited at the prospect of being initiated to the infantry tactics taught to the French Foreign Legion's *caporals*. This was more like it – at last. Some 400 metres from another farmhouse, along a leafy track and up a short but steep incline, was a plateau, around and across which we would now learn the tactical skills necessary to close with and kill the enemy.

Our platoon had been divided into groups, each consisting of roughly ten men and led by an NCO. Within each of these groups, there were three components: the command cell, which was the *sous-officier* along with his marksman/sniper; a four-man *équipe choc* (assault team); and a similar-sized *équipe feu* (fire support team). I was selected to command the last of these, as *chef d'equipe*, and supply fire support for my 'side', which was led by *Adjudant* Raype.

As we walked along the leafy track leading up to the plateau, the inevitable happened: the 'enemy' opened fire. Once they'd been located, I reported their numbers, type of arms and position to Raype over in the command cell, by radio. I ordered 'harassing fire', just enough fire to keep enemy heads down.

The *adjudant* called me, and the commander of the *équipe choc*, together to tell us that he would be leading an attack on the enemy position. He pointedly told me that I was to keep my eyes open to lend fire in support of this attack. Having had some previous experience, I felt confident enough – or perhaps foolhardy enough – to ask a couple of basic infantry questions. Did he wish to coordinate timings? I enquired. When was I to commence rapid fire, and then sustained fire, in support of his attack? And in the reorganisation after the assault, where was my team to go? It wasn't as if he'd given us any guidance on these points at all so far.

My questions were greeted with utter incredulity by Adjudant Raype. He just said, '*Mais t'es con ou quoi?*' (Are you an idiot or what?)

Spread out on the cold winter ground, I lay on my belly, behind my weapon, looking through the leafless undergrowth towards the enemy. Moments later I heard some scrambling about behind me in the bushes. Then, without warning, I felt as though my head was about to cave in . . . The *adjudant* was bashing my helmet with a chunk of wood.

Interspersed with more whacks to the head, our Portuguese leader outlined what was to happen during his assault. He would take the *équipe choc* to a likely place from which to attack the enemy. When he was satisfied as to the spot, he would lead his men from the front in a charge to the enemy position, all the while waving his beret. This would be the signal for us in the *équipe feu* to provide sustained fire. Once he had reached the enemy bunker, up on the higher ground, he would climb to its summit and again wave his beret. At this my team was to aim off, away from the bunker.

'*Tu comprends, tête de noeud?*' he asked finally.

I certainly did understand – I understood that at the Legion's school for its future NCOs, instruction in infantry tactics had not progressed far beyond those of the First World War. It was a complete joke, and at the same time, not remotely funny.

Another thing I learned that day was that *casques* (helmets) were good protection from the attentions of a wrist-thick branch, but they wouldn't necessarily save you from one hell of a headache later.

We returned to Lapasset and another *piquet d'intervention*. Although the day was quiet, with very little to do, and only one week to go now, I still found myself fed up with *poseurs* like Langer, another Frenchman, from the REP in Calvi. The ultimate teacher's pet, Langer liked to open *la grande gueule* (his big mouth) when surrounded by the course staff. If he were to come first on the course, I reflected, it would fully demonstrate the inability of Foreign Legion leadership to assess a man's character. After all, anyone who went out of his way to sit at the front of the class during the few lessons we'd received, yet for an exam was at the back of the class so as to better cheat, or who peeled off spots from the targets at the rifle range to give himself a better score, was a sneak and hardly leadership material.

On the medical scene durng those final days, Brillo, a Legionnaire from Spain, had his foot in plaster with a strained

Achilles tendon, while Cheman, in the aftermath of the Bertrandou incident, had his entire leg in plaster. Bertoli's arm had likewise been set, but more recently he'd had to return to hospital to have it rebroken and screws inserted. Apparently, the bones had begun to set incorrectly.

On Saturday, 21 January, and not before time, I finished the Foreign Legion's CME 88/10. Of the thirty-nine *élève caporals*, I came twenty-first. Not a bad effort, I considered, for someone with as little service as me, limited French and a foot in plaster for much of the time.

What did I learn? A few more marching songs and the fact that if this was the instruction one could expect from the Legion's premier training establishment, the Legion was in serious trouble. Not only did the instructors care little about whether their charges were well trained and tested, but the information presented was inadequate. Few people seemed interested in infantry developments anywhere outside France. All too often, questions from students to the staff met with the most self-condemning response of all: 'Je m'en fou.'

I wondered again if my expectations of the Legion were too high. I thought not. An Australian Army Reserve recruit, on a three-week basic course, received better training than this. I knew because I had both done the training and then been an instructor. On a Legion promotion course, it was quite reasonable to expect instruction on map reading, advanced tactics and calling in fire support. But we never did. Although most of the students spoke French, we were still treated as if we didn't need to know anything beyond the most elementary. If the Legion's recruit course was about indoctrination rather than education, the *caporal* course was not in fact confirmation of basic knowledge or instruction, but simply a test of endurance.

On an ice-cold morning just before we received our results, *Adjudant* Raype ordered us to form up on parade and told us what he thought of us. Because we'd failed to measure up to his very high standards (not that we had any idea just what these standards were), he had decided that ten out of the thirty-nine of us would not pass the course. In fact, it turned out to be another one of Raype's little jokes. Everyone, no matter how poor their results, did pass the course. Everyone was promoted.

And Langer came first.

13

MORE INSTRUCTION

Ne me casse pas les couilles.
(Don't break my balls.)

Once back with *1ère Compagnie* after the nine-week *caporal* course, I asked for weekend leave. A Saturday night would do. But Jakic, the *adjudant compagnie*, refused. He gave no reason; just an imperious and disdainful wave. He didn't even bother to shrug his shoulders.

A week after finishing the CME, I was made a *caporal* in the French Foreign Legion. At the conclusion of *1ère Compagnie's* morning parade, therefore, I had to present myself to everyone from the rank of *caporal* and above, as a formal demonstration of my new rank:

Caporal Mason
Nine months' service
1ère Compagnie
Section d'Adjudant LePeon

Newly named
À vos ordres, Sergent.

Along with my new rank, I was with the *2ème Section*, led by *Adjudant* LePeon, who'd been wounded in Lebanon while serving with the Legion. *Sergent-Chef* Solo, the trilingual Italian, was his deputy and there were two *sergents*, Redbach and LaFronde. Both of these *sergents* were French, overweight, and trouble.

Redbach was thickset, around 175 centimetres tall and with a voice permanently hoarse from screaming abuse at Legionnaires. One of his pet ways to humiliate recruits and new Legionnaires was to nod and ask them if they were *cons*, or idiots. LaFronde had blond hair and blue eyes, was shorter and fatter than Redbach, with bright tattoos of animals on his arms and chest. He thought himself a great joke teller, especially if it meant humiliating someone else.

As I had witnessed previously, the process of starting up a new *section* was inefficient and slow. It was characterised by yelling and screaming, and threats and insults. Everything was critically important, yet nothing was. There was no timetable, no priority and no coordination. It meant that there were forty new recruits running about the camp from the *infirmerie*, to cleaning, to issue of kit, to doing sport, in a constant state of anxiety that they might not be in the right place at the right time.

At night, after rollcall and following, at 2200, the familiar cry that always rang out throughout the *1ère Compagnie* building and across the *place d'armes* – 'Extinction des feux!' (Lights out!) – I would walk the quiet corridors and check the rooms. Sometimes I would hear snores or snuffling, sometimes I heard nothing at all. Sometimes I would see a glistening eye looking, unblinking, to the ceiling. It reminded me of the vulnerability I'd felt in their position, having just gone rouge and arriving here from Aubagne. I looked forward to getting away from Quartier Danjou, a place where too much time was spent on irrelevancies and where the barked commands of *caporals* and *sergents* filled the air from *reveille* to night-time *appel*.

So to Bel Air again, and running and marching through beautiful French countryside. I thought the standard was a lot lower than under *Sergent-Chef* Mahmood, who really could run. Even so, the footing proved too difficult for some; so difficult that the fat *Sergent* Redbach doled out a severe beating to one new guy who couldn't keep the pace.

Consistent with past practice, recruits were divided into three running groups according to ability. A Norwegian named Popp was incorrectly placed in the *première groupe* and suffered the attentions of *Sergent* LaFronde as well. It was just bad luck that he ended up in the wrong group, and that the *sergents* were feeling particularly enthusiastic that day.

Neither LaFronde nor Redbach could run very well. They carried the legacy of too much rich food at the *sous-officiers'* mess. It meant that when they found someone weaker than themselves, they had an excuse to stop running and deal out blows so as to encourage the others. The two combined to beat Popp so badly he walked about in a daze, not understanding how this could have happened to him. Later that morning when I saw him and his bruised face, I knew I was looking at a broken soul, something for which the *sergents* were responsible but cared nothing.

The other recruits in the *Section* had their own problems. A Frenchman named Little was so fat he was barely capable of shuffling 5 kilometres. During breaks in singing lessons, he had to run around the soccer field wearing a *sac à dos* filled with rocks. He was only permitted to take it off during sit-down class periods and while eating.

Moncan had even less good fortune and desperately wanted to leave the Legion. This was all very well, but he should have kept the idea to himself. The *sergents* were ruthless and unrelenting in their persecution of those who might 'infect' others. Moncan was not allowed to take his weighted backpack off or sit down even when eating. In fact, the only time that he didn't have to wear the thing was when he went to bed.

For some of the other would-be Legionnaires, watching the training and this treatment meant that their minds were made up very early. They deserted. Three English recruits hightailed it from the farm in the evening, on 19 February, at around 1800. They included Umnet, a phlegmatic ex-Guardsman who had left his unit in Germany, and Woodhen, formerly in Britain's Parachute Regiment. And so, true to Legion tradition, we *caporals* were out all night looking for the runaways.

I found myself posted at a dark crossroads, alone with a pick handle. I had ludicrous orders to give chase, catch and bash the three 'fuckings'. I didn't even have a radio. Later in the evening I was joined at my very cold post by Legionnaire Crocodile. He was a rather likeable Frenchman who told me that his job before the Legion was a mortician in a war veterans' home. Perhaps the nature of this work explained his eyes: the irises were small, black and, most disturbingly, appeared to not reflect any light at all – they were just black holes. I called him Crocodile because, like so many other Frenchmen, he had the most disgusting teeth; a financially strapped dentist's dream. Crocodile and I monitored the crossroads until we were relieved at 0430. It was some weeks before I learned what had become of those Brits.

Back at Bel Air, we had a new *caporal* named Bucoli, from Calvi. During the next few days, over coffee while the *sergents* taught songs, he told me that the Legion's Parachute Regiment lived in the past and was not a place he would recommend joining. He also said that LeCoq, among others from my recruit course, had deserted, having quickly found himself in a great deal of trouble. Bucoli didn't say what kind of trouble, and it didn't matter.

Caporals like Bucoli and I had to mount guard at the farm all night. The system devised by *Adjudant* LePeon could do little but exhaust us. According to the *adjudant*, someone had to be awake to monitor the recruits, the telephone and to raise the alarm in case of fire. One night at 0345, LePeon come downstairs to scream that I had to turn the light off because I was wasting the French taxpayer's money. I had the light on to read, as I knew that otherwise I'd fall asleep, despite my efforts with pins, clips and burning matches.

Earlier that evening, the *adjudant* and *Sergents* Redbach and LaFronde had returned from a regimental dinner in Castelnaudary. Redbach had been sick, leaving most of what I took to be a seafood dinner on the path to the staff entrance to the farmhouse. Next day no one heard him stir.

My next tour as *caporal du jour* was even less pleasant. During the course of the day, LaFronde had ordered a young Frenchman named Blede to wear his backpack as punishment for some infraction. Later, Solo asked me why Blede was carrying his *sac*, so I referred him to LaFronde. Not five minutes later, however, the Italian was back, calling me a liar and indicating that if I weren't most careful, he would see to it that I became familiar with the regimental jail.

There was no arguing with *Sergent-Chef* Solo, but I did broach the topic with LaFronde himself. The fat *sergent* didn't worry one bit that I and all the recruits who'd heard him give Blede the order knew he was a liar, nor that my position with the *sergent-chef* had been undermined. He just laughed and said, '*Mais je n'ai rien à branler avec tes problèmes.*' (I don't give a wank about your problems.)

Of course he didn't care, knowing full well that his rank made him unassailable. I imagined hitting him again and again – but what good would it do, other than make me feel better? Among other things, I would find myself in a concrete cell under the tender care of the Legion's jailers. I loathed LaFronde.

Unsurprisingly, given the quality of leadership, the *section's Marche Képi Blanc* on 1 March was a farce. We had been told to expect a distance of at least 50 kilometres at this, the first significant hurdle for the *engagés* in our charge. In reality, we marched and ran from Quartier Danjou to Bel Air – around 15 kilometres – and this at the instigation of our *section* leader himself.

Before hand, LePeon formed us up on the road outside Danjou and told the soon-to-be Legionnaires he was fed up with having to endure inconvenience for the likes of them. Just what the inconvenience was, he did not say. But then, with a change of tone and a sly wink, he became conspiratorial and the meaning was clear. He would not say anything to the officers if they, the recruits, did not either; and that way, we could all pull one over on those '*putains d'officiers*'. No one disagreed, and although the *section's* traditional rite of passage for acknowledging new Legionnaires was a lie, they all received their kepis.

With the *Marche Képi Blanc* out of the way and early spring in the air, I was only at the one-third mark of this, the first of my two sections d'instruction periods. But as much as I tried to focus on the future in stages, rather than an overwhelming whole, I hadn't counted on events that transpired on Tuesday, 7 March.

As *caporal du jour*, I was doing a one-week tour of duty, which included making the daily lists of *corvées*. And because our *section* was, that day, on regimental service duty as well, I also had to allocate men to the *ordinaire* who had not already been taken by the *garde 24* or PI details. Unfortunately for me, I was not aware of a major change in routine. The General Commanding the French Foreign Legion, no less, was to view a *section d'instruction* at Burnell, site of the old rifle range and obstacle course, and that *section* was to be ours.

Adjudant LePeon had briefed his *sergents* about the important event, but not the *caporals*. The upshot of all this was that LePeon was furious to see so few men in the ranks at morning parade. Legionnaires were hurriedly sent off to bring back others from their various services, while I sought an audience with the *adjudant*, to explain.

LePeon sat behind his desk. '*Mason, ne me casse pas les couilles*,' he began. (Mason, don't break my balls.) He then posed the time-honoured Legion question: '*T'es con ou quoi?*' I put it to him that neither I nor any other *caporal* was aware of the change, through written or spoken order. He had not told us or, to put a better face on it for him, perhaps one of the *sergents* had neglected to relay the message.

The *adjudant* was not impressed. All this was my fault. Apparently, I was very fortunate not to find myself before the *capitaine* on a disciplinary charge. From now on, he said, everything had to be *carre comme carre* – and in the air he described a square with his index fingers.

When I looked into LePeon's face and his mud-brown eyes, I saw nothing but resolute ignorance. I had never felt so angry or frustrated. He was an *adjudant*, I a lowly *caporal*; I had to be wrong. There was no court of appeal. He had the power, he owned my body, and I hated it.

LePeon gave himself away then – I was sure of it – with a narrowing of his eyes, as if, just briefly, he was acknowledging his own failings. My anger went inside, to the red-hot knot of loathing, and I knew then that neither he nor LaFronde nor Dober could touch me. I would always do what I thought was right and never become like them.

Thus empowered, I swallowed the lump of humiliation in my throat. After a firm '*À vos ordres, mon Adjudant*', I saluted with a resounding thwack of palm on thigh, did an about-turn, and left his office.

We did get to Burnell with the required number of Legionnaires to mount a series of demonstrations for *Général* Le Corre. One group was to throw practise grenades, another would tackle the obstacle course, a third would fire rifles, while two of us were to give a demonstration on anti-terrorist procedures in a Legion camp.

The other man in my team, *Caporal* Dandy, was short and freckled, with a red Asterix moustache to match his hair. He and I rehearsed the scenarios. The first one involved me playing the terrorist intruder and Dandy, the sentinel who confronts me inside the camp perimeter. He was to yell a series of warnings, increasing in urgency, until finally he'd cry out: '*Halte au large ou je vais faire feu!*' (Halt or I will fire!) At this point, I would scale a fence, attempting to escape, while Dandy simulated telephoning the guard post. It was pretty simple really.

The only scalable fence at Burnell turned out to be the front gate, barbed wire being much in evidence all around the perimeter fences. We rehearsed the activity twice and each time I pulled myself up the 3-metre-high gate without any great problem and then vaulted over the 20-centimetre spikes that sat on top. The two of us agreed we had covered every contingency.

The *général*'s car arrived and he was escorted, in turn, to the various demonstrations. Finally, in front of a standing *Général* Le Corre, his staff and the Legionnaires of my *section*, Dandy and I began our demonstration. Everything progressed as planned until I began scaling the gate. That's when it became clear that in our detailed planning, we'd neglected to factor in one participant's misplaced enthusiasm. Or put another way, Dandy's brain snap.

Instead of retiring to the imaginary guard post to make the telephone call, Dandy was suddenly running towards the gate. By the time he got there, I was on the point of vaulting from the top – until the idiot grabbed my ankle and began pulling.

'Dandy, what the fuck . . . ?!'

With my right foot in his grasp, the little *caporal* pulled me down onto one of the 20-centimetre spikes and drove it straight through my left thigh. The more he wrestled, the larger the wound became. I felt my flesh tearing. Yelling in French, then in English, and kicking with my right leg combined to finally produce the desired effect. Dandy let go.

Only then did I feel afraid. I looked down at my green-clothed leg and my flesh from which the wicked arrow-headed spike glistened and winked blood. I looked for bright red blood, knowing that if the femoral artery had been touched, I would be dead in minutes. There was none.

In that quiet, lonely space between fear and action, I made up my mind what to do. I was stuck but I wasn't going to stay up on that iron spike, on top of the gate. So, even as I felt other points sliding into my wrists, I took the weight from my left thigh and lifted and pulled it from the spike's sucking grasp. Just as I felt myself released, I fell to the ground on the far side of the gate.

Dandy opened the gate and ran to where I lay. He knelt over me, his freckled face grey, his eyes wide, and put his hand on my shoulder. I could feel him trembling. I quickly understood that he realised what he'd done.

We were not alone for long, though, and soon another Legion shambles ensued. As I began to slip into shock, I was aware of Solo screaming blue murder, Dandy sprawled in the gravel, away from me . . . I just wanted to tell someone I was allergic to penicillin.

Because there were no other vehicles, I was bundled into the *général's* car. The driver, a French *caporal-chef*, was not at all pleased. In an angry voice, he exhorted me not to bleed on the seat. I told him to fuck off.

Arriving at the regimental *infirmerie* at Danjou, there were no ambulances available. So I waited. Placed in a room by myself, I gave the wound a good long look. Having little or no feeling in my left leg, I began to feel sorry for myself; I sensed tears welling up in my eyes. Fortunately, the blustering, sometimes drunk *Adjudant* Renelli had not yet gone to lunch. As the camp's senior medic, with some twenty years in the Legion, this very large man, over 190 centimetres and 120 kilograms, took my case in hand. He marched breezily into the room, cleaned then dressed the wound, and gave me two injections, one anti-tetanus, the other morphine.

Transport was not to be had so Renelli argued for the use of the *général's* helicopter. The *général* gave his permission and I was soon on my way to an operating theatre at the military hospital in Toulouse. Like the driver before him, the pilot ordered me to not bleed in his helicopter, before inviting me to enjoy the flight. I told him to fuck off, too.

Once under local anaesthetic and the knife, I asked one of the surgeons how close the femoral artery had come to being cut. He looked up from the job, regarded me for a moment, and then held his right index finger and thumb together. '*Comme ça*,' he said. (Like this.) 'Feeling will return,' he continued, in English, referring to the nerve. 'It's not cut either. Given the size of the wound, you are very fortunate.'

Not fortunate enough to be working with Legionnaires who aren't complete idiots, I thought. I lay there in silence on the slab while the surgeons bent over the wound and stitched my flesh together.

One quiet afternoon in hospital I received a letter from Umnet, one of the deserters of a few weeks before. He wrote that all three had made it to Germany after forty-seven hours on the run. Even so, he was in a British Army lockup. I liked him and was grateful he had written to me. And I thought no less of him because he'd deserted; in fact, I felt a little sorry that he'd wasted his time.

After a week of eating and sleeping, I was sent back to Castelnaudary on Wednesday, 15 March. At the *infirmerie*, Dandy was there to meet me. As I hobbled down from the bus, the crutches under my arms clattering on the steps, he began his apologies. I asked him just one question: '*Pourquoi?*' He didn't know why. Excitement at having the *général* present or excessive enthusiasm, he wasn't sure. He put the tip of a finger to his temple and gave it a turn.

Poor Dandy. Even his red moustache seemed to be drooping. Any thoughts I might have had about hitting him evaporated; there was no malice behind his actions. Yes, I still harboured some anger, but it was far from the all-consuming thing I felt towards others here and had to guard so well. They were very different things.

The day after I returned, my leg became infected and I was admitted to the *infirmerie*. I saw the *capitaine médicine chef*, who 'as a last resort' prescribed antibiotics. He prescribed penicillin. I told him that I was allergic and that I'd informed the authorities in Aubagne of this. After expressing his outrage at the omission of such information from my medical file, and blaming me, he inscribed my allergic status in red pencil across the front of the file. The *médicine chef* then indicated that I would have to pay for any medication I received as the *infirmerie* did not have what my case required. I agreed and signed some kind of receipt. The following morning I woke with a headache, my tongue felt swollen and I found it difficult to breathe without gagging. It was obviously the drugs.

Despite feeling so sickly, one activity in the *infirmerie* immediately attracted my interest. We twenty or so patients were woken at 0600 and, as best we could, made our way on foot or wheelchair to the *salle de soins*, a room where drugs were given and temperatures taken. While we waited in line outside the salle, a medic appeared carrying a couple of thermometers and handed them to the two men at the head of the queue. Each patient inserted the appropriate end into his anus, waited until his name was called; whereupon the sick man would waddle into the room, extract the glass tube and present it for reading, while receiving his drugs in return from a second medic. The distribution of pills took but a moment, and so did the turnaround before the same thermometers were presented to people further down the line. There was no wiping of any sort, not even a quick rinse . . .

This couldn't be happening. I might've been feeling feverish and weak, but there was no way in hell I was going to slip one of those well-used temperature gauges in me. I refused the offer, pointing out to the two white-coated medics that even rinsing the thermometers under a stream of hot water wouldn't have protected us from a range of possible diseases. Where was the alcohol and paper towelling, for Christ's sake?

Neither man was too happy to hear this. I did what was appropriate for me: told each medic he could shove it up his own arse, and left the rest of the patients to their fate.

Thanks to big Renelli, my leg began to heal well and after a couple of weeks I was back at the barracks on light duties. I was to join the *section* on a trip to a military range to fire a number of weapons, including rockets and grenades. Before we left on 17 April, Solo made a point of reminding me not to forget the *section's caisse popotte,* the wooden box that contained all the necessary accoutrements for a civilised dinner in the field. For *officiers* and *sous-officiers* only, of course. The glorified picnic set included cutlery, plates, salt and pepper grinders and white tablecloths.

Among other weapons up at the range, we fired the 89 mm LRAC, the Legion's anti-tank weapon. It was during one such session that *Sergent* Redbach decided to teach the men a lesson.

We waited some 20 metres behind the LRAC firing line. From this position we could see the 'signature' of the weapon – the gases expelled from the rear of the tube, driving leaves, pebbles and dust into the air, and thus giving away the position of the firer. We could also hear the noise as each round exploded from the tube. Redbach ordered us all to remove the hearing protection from our ears. Only this way, he claimed, could we understand what noise in a real battlefield situation might be like.

To ensure compliance with his order, he walked among the men, examining their ears, although he did not remove his own protection, of course. By his own admission, he already half deaf. By the end of that day, it was pointless trying to give orders. None of the Legionnaires could hear anything other than the ringing in their ears. I wasn't sure what bothered me more: Redbach's arrogant, asinine ways or having to allocate a *popottier* to him and his fellow *sous-officiers* at mealtimes.

A week later, we arrived back at Quartier Danjou in time to complete preparations for Camerone, the day that celebrates death and sacrifice against all odds, and the glory of dying for one's *officier*. As the visit to the Legion's museum a year before had taught me, the ritual significance of the Battle of Camerone could not be overstated: it was the basis on which the legend of the French Foreign Legion had been built. Over at Aubagne this same day, in keeping with decades of tradition, *Capitaine* Danjou's wooden hand would have been taken from the crypt and paraded, just like a religious icon, before the entire *1er Régiment*.

Here in Castelnaudary, the *4ème Régiment* formed up in the town square and heard the recitation of the famous siege. All of us presented arms at the concluding eulogy, which was taken from the monument dedicated to Jean Danjou's men at the site of the battle:

Here stood fewer than sixty men
  against an entire army.
Its weight overwhelmed them.
Life sooner than courage
  forsook these soldiers of France.
30 April 1863

Camerone Day is the one occasion when everyone in the Legion celebrates the past and present as Legionnaires: *officiers, sous-officiers* and *soldats du rang*. Officially, it is a time to recognise that those in the Legion are different from the rest of society and to reaffirm the bonds each Legionnaire shares. The reality for myself and those around me on that last Sunday in April was very different, however. It was simply not possible to hide the lie behind these grand ideas of loyalty and brotherhood; the jollity and cameraderie was a facade, and a flimsy one at that.

After the parade in Castelnaudary, behind the booming drums of the regimental band and the flags and cheers of some of the local population, the entire *1ère Compagnie* was trucked to Bel Air. Here we set up tents and stood around bonfires till late at night, drank too much, sang Legion songs and formed up in our usual mafia groups and complained about the failings of the others. There was little movement between these groups, just as any *fraternité* with our officers and senior NCOs was almost nonexistent. They talked among themselves.

The following morning the company ran. A number of hangover sufferers in the company were in a bad way. One had to pity the unfortunates who had heeded the promise of the *adjudant compagnie* the previous night, a pledge that this would be a *footing*-free day. In the Legion it was often better to watch the actions of others rather than listen to their words. As a rule, *Adjudant* Jakic got hammered if and whenever he could, yet during the Camerone Day celebrations, he'd drunk very little. I alerted the new Legionnaires in my *section* to this, and while some ignored the warning, at least the others saved themselves from having to pay the penalty in the morning.

•

The loathsome *Adjudant* LePeon left the *2ème Section* not long before the completion of the fourteen-week period of instruction, having been hospitalised for surgery on his leg. His replacement was boozy *Adjudant* Jakic, and with him in tow, our Legionnaires took part in their *Marche Raide*. During the first week of May, we took to the same hills and tracks I'd covered twice before through the countryside of the Languedoc-Roussillion region.

Adjudant Jakic and *Sergent* LaFronde carried next to nothing in their *sacs*, just an opened (and therefore bulk-providing) sleeping bag and some food and water. Likewise a fellow *caporal fut fut* named Lieber, who took his lead from LaFronde. Me, I always carried what the Legionnaires did, and sometimes more. I took my lead from an army I knew. No NCO or officer in the Australian Army would ever do a Jakic, LaFronde or Lieber. I did it because I thought leadership and example were important. And I knew I was right.

Within a matter of days, Jakic's particular weakness would be displayed for all to see. It was during the *pot*, that ritual marking the completion of each training course, when the commander of the *4ème Régiment*, *Colonel* Seignez, directed that the *section* be presented to him by our *section* leader. We stood at *gardez-vous* in the white-walled room, looking at the Legion flame on the table described in small bottles of beer, waiting for Jakic to speak. But he was drunk again; he forgot which number *section* it was, how many people were in it, and slurred, stuttered and bumbled his way to an empty pause. Perhaps hoping to prevent a complete shambles, the *colonel* simply said, '*Merci, ça suffit.*' (Thank you, that will do.) An embarrassing moment for all.

That same day I learned that Tom and Hagar, whom I'd met on my first day at Fort de Nogent, had deserted. *Caporal* Wern, a Swedish friend who had taken the rapid-promotion route, had deserted too. The ranks of the reviled *fut futs* were thinning. I couldn't help wondering why the Legion bothered with the scheme at all. There was no assistance from within the organisation; indeed, some of the officers and NCOs in the regiment actively endorsed humiliating *fut futs*. It reminded me that I had no friends, or at least no one who would support me in public against these others. As *Sergent-Chef* Mahmood said, if I was set on staying, I had to harden myself to endure.

14

AUBAGNE AGAIN

Je veux rien faire du tout sauf me brânler les couilles.
(I'm going to do nothing at all except wank.)

It was 20 May 1989, my first anniversary in the Legion and a time to pause for reflection – except that Jakic was at it again. We were in Aubagne's Quartier Viénot where, in a change from past practice, the newly graduated Legionnaires of *2ème Section* were about to be presented to the *colonel* in charge of Legion personnel. The *section* was formed up in the sacred *salle d'honneur,* on the ground floor of the Legion museum.

The hallowed surroundings seemed to have been lost on our *section* leader, however. *Adjudant* Jakic had run into a few old friends at the *sous-officiers'* mess during *casse-croûte* and stayed on for a few drinks. He must've drunk a lot very quickly, because it was 1030 now and he could hardly stand up.

So, surrounded as we were by old battle flags, uniforms and medals of the Legion's heroic past, Jakic's salute wavered, he forgot his lines and with a familiar drunken mumble, failed to complete the presentation of the *section* in the correct way. The final embarrassing hiccup hung in the silence like the fragrance of alcohol. Just as Seignez had done back at Danjou, the *colonel* decided to end the torment. '*C'est bon*, Jakic, *c'est bon*,' he said calmly, his right hand held open, palm towards the floor.

The officer and his *aide-de-camp* then made a tour of the ranks. They asked the Legionnaires if their instruction had been what they expected and which regiments they wished to join. It was soon apparent that the *colonel* was not happy with the level of spoken French. He asked Legionnaire Herbert, a German, '*Tu parles bon français?*' (Do you speak good French?) After a long moment of indecision, of questing eyes begging for help, Herbert shrugged his shoulders and responded with a resounding '*Ja!*' This was too much, and the *colonel* asked *Adjudant* Jakic the crucial question: how many French lessons had his men received?

The *adjudant* was lost, not only because he had come late to the *section*, and not only because he was drunk. He was lost because he knew what everyone in *1ère Compagnie* knew: the men in this training *section* had received just three French lessons over the past four months. Jakic turned to *Sergent-Chef Solo* for help, who then leaned towards me and nodded to the *colonel*. I gave the information required. The Legionnaires had received sixty-four French lessons.

The *colonel* was still unhappy. The number was below that outlined in the recruit instruction program. He was obviously not aware that this was almost always the case. Nor that a great deal of discretion lay with individual *section* leaders, ensuring that there was no consistency of instruction between *sections*.

I wanted to step from the ranks and tell this officer what really happened on the recruit course at Castelnaudary, not to mention what I'd seen since as an *élève caporal* and now a *caporal* instructor. But I knew it would be no use. The institutionalisation of incompetence and lack of accountability meant that the *colonel* could ask all the questions he liked without there being any change. Unless there was organisational scrutiny of training – common testing, oversight, benchmarking – the same poor standard would remain.

A relatively conscientious commander like *Lieutenant* Hildebrandt, for all his faults, at least saw to it that there was plenty of running and marching, and some French language lessons. Leaders of the calibre of *Adjudants* LePeon and Jakic, on the other hand, could not have cared less. Consequently, any Legionnaires trained in *sections* led by LePeon, Jakic and the like arrived at the regiments woefully unprepared. Non-francophones were unable to speak French at the level assumed by their commanders; and for the most part, whether the new arrival was non-francophone or fluent in the language, knowledge of weapons was almost zero and certainly unsafe. It followed that because these Legionnaires were poorly trained, their receiving units treated them badly. This further compounded the desertion problem: poor training and poor leadership meant people voted with their feet and walked out the front gates of Legion regiments never to return.

The reason I knew that *2ème Section* had 'received' sixty-four French lessons was because it was me who prepared the report for submission to the authorities in Aubagne some days before. Neither the *adjudant* nor *Sergent-Chef* Solo wanted to spend time doing the paperwork, so, on the second floor in the *section* office of *2ème Section* at Danjou, I was handed the forms and told to 'approximate' the directives from Aubagne.

After voicing my lack of enthusiasm for the enterprise, both were amazed; open-mouthed, incredulous. Jakic's line was that the administrators over in Aubagne knew nothing about what the job of training recruits actually entailed, and besides, this was how it was done throughout the regiment. As for Solo, he pointed to the sheets of paper and said matter-of-factly, 'Just get on with it. The system is fucked.'

It felt like I was fiddling the books, like I was part of a small conspiracy. And the conspiracy had undermined my responsibility towards those who were supposed to be trained. I felt compromised, diminished. As I handed the bundled documents to the *sergent-chef,* he said in a bored voice, 'It's okay, you'll get used to it.'

Wednesday, 31 May 1989

Dear Mother,

I'm in a hotel, actually I'm being very generous when I call it a 'hotel' – but it is cheap – in Paddington, London. I have a room to myself, time to think, to go jogging and to read. In all, very good for the soul.

This brief repose has been at the discretion of British Immigration authorities. You see, I had a deal of trouble getting into England. Leaving France was fraught with all the old difficulties. On the train to Calais, for example, I flashed my identity card and my Legion permission slip. The policeman on the train was good enough to inform me that such documentation would not be adequate to depart France. I agreed with his advice and simply carried on . . .

Once aboard the ferry to Dover, an English fellow came up to me and asked, 'You a Legionnaire?' Upon replying in the affirmative, he laughed, telling me that he owned a bar in Orange, home of the Legion's cavalry unit. He reckoned he could spot a Legionnaire a mile off. It could not have been hard, given my haircut, sides two millimetres and three millimetres on top, or the military bag that I was carrying.

Dover at last. This is where my troubles really began. I joined the European Nationals queue and when I arrived at the passport control booth, the fellow asked, 'What's that?' I replied with a simple: 'A European military identity card.'

His response was a snort and a 'Oh, you're one of those! Wait over there, please.'

. . . I was escorted into a little side room. This is the sort of room that exists in every airport of the world. From these rooms, there are those who look on disconsolate as others pass through Immigration. In this room, I was interviewed by a very pleasant but unbelieving British Immigration officer.

After more than two and a half hours of questions, of being told, 'Look, I am sorry, but I don't believe you; I know you are either a criminal or a deserter', I thought it more than likely I would be turned around and sent back to France with just two pounds in my pocket. I thought of the law I knew and the telephone calls I would make before they could send me off. It is not at all pleasant, feeling legally vulnerable. But I wasn't leaving without putting up a fight.

As things transpired, this affable fellow returned after one of his interminable phone calls and reports to his 'superior' to inform me he was going to let me into the country. But as he put it, he felt somewhat uneasy 'facilitating your junkets to Britain'.

Having had my past confirmed during his phone calls, he was very interested as to my reasons for joining. I tried to tell him that I feel driven to move, something of a nomad setting myself difficult tasks and never being afraid to look. He thinks I am very odd.

Got myself into London and met up with Brett D, who offered to put me up till my credit card came through. He is a wonderful

friend; someone on whom I can rely. He offers to help when
he knows he does not have to. What a far cry from most of my
comrades in the Legion!

Love,

David

Yes, I went on leave – and for almost three weeks. This granting
of leave came as a complete surprise, and according to Jakic,
was a reward for assisting him in Aubagne. I wondered why
I had to be rewarded for something that made me feel less
than I thought I was. It was as if nearly everything I did in the
Legion left me deflated or degraded and while others knew it,
they valued and repaid silent compliance.

By 5 July, I was back at Bel Air. I sat looking out of the window
on the first floor, listening to a tape of Dire Straits' 'Money
for Nothing'. I was in a new *2ème Section*, led by *Sergent-Chef*
Adler, soon to be promoted to *adjudant*. He had served as
second-in-command to the mad *Adjudant* Raype on my *caporal*
course. The *section's sergent-chef* was Mahmood, from my own
instruction, who told me he was off to French Guyane after
this *section*. The other *sous-officiers* included *Sergent* Mistral, a
Martiniquan who often said that if anyone wanted a problem,
he was a problem – '*92 kilos de muscle*'; and the rat himself,
Sergent LaFronde. Among the new recruits there were a number
of Brits, including Raleigh, a short, tattooed, former Royal Marine
who told interesting stories about Prince Edward's failed effort
to become a Royal Marine.

I had a double guard as Lieber was away having his nosed
fixed. He'd been head-butted by *Caporal* Hemming from
another *section* in *1ère Compagnie*. According to Hemming,

it was all a dreadful misunderstanding. 'Why can't all these bloody foreigners speak English proper?' he concluded. Lieber was gone for three weeks.

Another *Marche Képi Blanc*, another *Remise Kepi Blanc*, more guard duties and another desertion; that just about summed up the first month or so. Ordinarily quiet and thoughtful, Kentara, a Polish Legionnaire, deserted. He bashed his *binome* over the head, rendering him paralysed, and escaped with a carving knife. He reportedly halted a car driven by a woman with her baby and demanded she take him to Spain. He was cornered and captured near Narbonne, to the south-east of Castelnaudary. The news we had from the *compagnie* was that he would be sent to a French civilian jail and then back to Poland, never again to be allowed into France.

The Poles in the *section* were very agitated, concerned that Kentara's behaviour might reflect badly on them. Like Kentara, most of the Poles, Czechs, Hungarians and Romanians joined the Legion to get French citizenship. Who cared about five years of humiliation when social security was on offer?

In response to this agitation, and concern over new Legionnaires who were what he called *'trop sensible'* (too sensitive), *Sergent* LaFronde ordered me to beat the daylights out of anyone who got out of line. Unfortunately, this view was entirely inconsistent with a directive from the *chef de corps*, *Colonel* Seignez. This latest directive included instructions that no *caporal* was to force a Legionnaire to do pushups; no *caporal* was to inspect the locker of a Legionnaire except in the presence of a *sous-officier*; and any *caporal* who struck a Legionnaire, except in self-defence, would go to jail. Dober and Kronk wouldn't have stood a chance. As was so often the case, though, in practice all this was ignored. There appeared to be a complete dislocation between what regimental headquarters wanted, and what happened in the *compagnies*.

A few days later, we returned to Danjou and I saw what could have been written as a comedy script. An English Legionnaire from one of the other *sections* in the *compagnie* had broken his leg. He was sent to the hospital at Toulouse to have the leg X-rayed and plastered, before being bussed back to Castelnaudary. This was all entirely routine.

I became involved as I saw him receiving a kicking from a *sergent* outside the *infirmerie*, just as he descended from the bus. I ran over and asked what the problem was. The NCO replied that the Brit was a malingerer. The other man was groaning with pain and angry that no one would listen to him. He couldn't walk, even with both crutches, he said. Because, despite the X-ray and his protestations, despite arguing with French doctors and nurses, plaster had been applied to the wrong leg.

The Englishman was trembling with suppressed rage now. I helped him to his feet and then to the top floor of the *infirmerie*, where I put him on a bed. I made sure he went back to the hospital the following day to have the correct leg plastered. I explained everything to the *sergent*, who just shrugged his shoulders. '*Je m'en fou . . .*'

Every time I walked out the front gate of Quartier Danjou, I felt a weight lift off my shoulders. I felt free for a moment of the scrutiny of every action, of the screaming and humiliation of myself and others. I could relax a little. I had weekend permission starting on Saturday, 22 July, and that's just what I intended to do.

To escape Castelnaudary itself, I planned to take the Saturday afternoon train to Toulouse. At Castelnaudary's station, the

Police Militaire waited, ready to catch any deserters, and they carefully examined my leave pass and my uniform. Thankfully, they failed to check in my green bag; had they done so, they would've found civilian clothes, which were forbidden to Legionnaires with less than five years' service or under the rank of *sergent*. On the train were a number of NCOs and officers, perhaps going to visit their families. As for me, I was going to Toulouse for sex.

Dropping my gear in a hotel room not far from the Gare de Toulouse-Matabiau, I changed into jeans and a leather jacket and then walked around the corner to the red-light district. For as far as I could see along the street, there were girls. Good-looking ones, too, with warm smiles and very short skirts. After a while I settled on one. We agreed a tariff and, arm in arm, her thigh against mine, her high heels striking the cobbles, we walked towards her room. As we talked, the subject soon turned to work – to my work.

Abruptly, she stopped and asked whether I was a Legionnaire. I said that yes, I was. At that, the girl gently took her arm from mine. She looked at me seriously and told me that, like all the other girls on this street, she did not take Legionnaires. Why not? I asked. Legionnaires always hit them, she replied, and worse if the girls didn't agree to do certain things.

Apart from the immediate issue of my thwarted lust, I was at once appalled and amused. Appalled that a group of men could consistently behave so badly over a period of time that the reputation of all was tarnished. And amused because those very same men would always find their desires thwarted. I wanted sex; I wanted the pleasure and the intimacy, if just for a moment. I had no female friends in France, and on the limited leave I got, there was no chance of making any. I had to go without, and instead brought a bottle of wine to wash down an evening meal of steak and *pommes frites*. It was part of being a foreigner in the Legion. I was asleep well before midnight.

My next solo trip away from Castelnaudary was in early September, when I was on leave in Montpellier, the capital of the Languedoc-Roussillon region. Along with Paris, it's my favourite city in France, a city of warmth and light. The *Place de la Comédie* in front of Montpellier's opera house was a great place to watch some of the most beautiful women in France. And it was a wonderful spot for a lonely Legionnaire,

Just short of finishing a long afternoon jog back to the hotel, I was distracted by a passer-by. It was Legionnaire Miller. Or more accurately, ex Legionnaire Miller, who had deserted from the Infantry Regiment at Nîmes, having completed instruction with *2ème Section*, under *Adjudant* LePeon. I wanted to talk and find out how he was, but Miller couldn't wait while I had a shower. He was on his way to work as a waiter, the job he'd had before he joined. Just as we were parting company, though, he thanked me for helping him with *Caporal-Chef* Le Balm.

I laughed, remembering the day well. In line with my duties as *caporal de semaine*, I'd made arrangements with Le Balm, as manager of the *compagnie* club, where it was possible for *compagnie* members to buy beer, cigarettes and coffee, to supply him with a worker if he needed one, to help clean up at closing time. That evening, from a line-up of the twelve *corvée* workers at my disposal, he chose Miller. I should've known better.

I allocated the rest to cleaning the company offices, corridors and latrines until shortly before *appel* at 2200, when they all returned to their *sections*. It was then that I wondered what had become of Miller.

I mounted the steps to the *compagnie* club to a rising sound of chairs and tables being scraped, and a subdued but emphatic, '*Non! Non!*' I tried the door, but something heavy kept it closed. After pushing and kicking at the door, at last I could see into the room. Young Miller was being chased by a very aroused Le Balm, whose face was red from drink and lust, his trousers about his thighs and the swollen head of his cock bouncing against his flabby belly. I pushed open the door until I could enter the room, thereby creating an exit for Miller.

Le Balm stopped his chase. After telling Miller to get back to his *section*, I advised the amorously aroused *caporal-chef* to pull up his pants and that I'd be informing the *sergent de semaine*. He opened the palms of his hands to the ceiling, shrugged, and said, 'Mason, *je m'en fou!*'

At least Miller was grateful.

I returned to Quartier Danjou on 7 September, a few weeks before leaving the regiment; just in time for *2ème Section's Marche Raide*. My fourth such trek again traversed the Cathar route south towards the Pyrenees. On this occasion, rather than marching with a *sergent*, *Adjudant* Adler had me accompany him, to save him from getting lost. From the very first day we had a problem with Legionnaire Vermeil.

Vermeil was a Dutchman who wanted to give up, but Adler had other ideas. Having slowed the column down yet again, Vermeil complained about his feet, the weight of his *sac* and the fact he was hungry. At last the *adjudant* took matters into his own hands. He took a piece of cord and tied a noose around the Legionnaire's neck; the other end he attached to his own pack. Thus, like a goat to slaughter, Vermeil was led for more than four days. He marched over 100 kilometres looking at the back of the *adjudant's* head. At each halt he was tied to a tree, just like a dog.

It must have been humiliating for him, and I wondered if it was hate that kept him going. I knew a bit about that myself. I watched him closely and at night I made sure he was fed and watered. Days after the *Marche,* I'd watch him rubbing his neck, his face closed to scrutiny, showing nothing other than the shadow of humiliation, and perhaps the knowledge that the shadow would fall on him wherever the memory of those few days followed him in the Legion.

At the conclusion of the *Marche Raide*, the end-of-course clean-up, the *pot* and the speeches, on Friday 29 September we headed back to Aubagne. As the train pulled out from Castelnaudary and headed south-east, we soon passed Quartier Capitaine Danjou on our left, separated from us by the long, straight Route de Pexiora. I took a long final look and felt slightly sick. The buildings and the grounds were well tended and neat, but inside, where men had volunteered for service and committed themselves to training, their lives and intelligence were wasted and discarded. I had waited, watched and actively searched for instructors who were serious about training Legionnaires. It was easy to find NCOs who were adept at breaking a man down; at reminding him he was a fool, ignorant of the tools that made him useful to the Legion. But it was impossible to find one who would inspire a man to embrace the Legion, its principles and its mystique. Castelnaudary was not a place I liked, and I made a commitment never to return. Life in other regiments would tell me if there was anything to the Legion's much-touted *honneur* and *fidélité*.

And I was pleased to be heading to Marseilles and Aubagne. The innovation of having the recruits go to Aubagne to be interviewed by Legion personnel was a vast improvement on the previous process. A year ago, when the new Legionnaires were interviewed at Quartier Danjou, I knew more than a few who were intimidated into not asking to be let go, to go *civil*. After all, once the visiting officer had left the Quartier, there was no one to protect the hapless Legionnaire from vengeful *caporals* and *sergents*.

By early October I was in Quartier Viénot, sitting at a table in the building that housed the *1er Régiment's* administration company, *Compagnie d'Administration de la Legion Étrangère*, the CAPLE. I had made it through the *caporal* course and both periods of recruit instruction; all of the small stages on the road to my future were now completed. Although there had been times over the last year when I'd wondered why I kept going, I never seriously contemplated deserting. And the longer I stayed, the less likely I was to desert anyway. Time in the Legion meant time invested, and I wasn't going to throw it away.

With Legionnaires Krisson and Raleigh of my previous *section*, I would be heading to Djibouti, in the Horn of Africa, with either the October or the November detachment. There, I knew, protecting France's interests in East Africa, was the *13ème Demi-Brigade de la Légion Étrangère* (13 DBLE), the French Army's only permanent 'half-brigade'.

The day before, Saturday, we'd taken a train from Aubagne into Marseilles, and across from the station set up in a bar and ordered three litre glasses of beer. It was wonderful to tip the fluid down our throats and embrace the freedom, however fleeting, of being able to relax and enjoy a sunny afternoon in the oldest city in France.

The next night I was on *piquet d'intervention*, which was a very different experience from the traumatised goings-on at

Danjou. The various *corvées*, including sweeping, mopping and emptying garbage bins, were performed by the numerous inmates of what was a very small brick-and-stone jail next to the guardhouse. Initially, I thought it remarkable that there could be so many men from one regiment in jail. In fact, less than one third of the inmates were from Aubagne, the rest being deserters from other regiments. There was one man who had deserted from the Legion a decade before; he'd been travelling through France with his wife and family, had his passport checked and then found himself a day later with a very short haircut and a forty-day residency in the cells at Viénot. Obviously the Legion, and French authorities, kept good records when it came to deserters.

At the morning administration *rassemblement* on the small gravel parade ground to the rear of the CAPLE building, I was allocated to work with red-haired, sun-blotched Legionnaire Keyman from the English Midlands. With our arms in cold greasy water scrubbing pots, he told me that he had just been kicked out of *1ère Compagnie* of the REP for beating the *caporal de semaine* with an axe handle. 'He was a bloody wanker,' Keyman reasoned. 'I'll be fooked if I take shit from anyone.' He was off to Djibouti, possibly in my detachment. I liked him immediately. He'd been in the British Army and was direct, frank and forthright. I wondered how the next two years in Djibouti would treat him – or rather, how would he let it treat him?

Raleigh was selected for the October detachment and Krisson and I were to follow in November. We had no idea why it had turned out that way. Generally though, this had worked out well, for if I made it back to France in two years, I'd be doing everything I could to get back to Australia. After all, a Legion Christmas, as I had discovered, was not much fun.

And so, because I was held back, I formed up with the rest every morning on the gravel behind the CAPLE building. Our company commander – and the possessor of the most extraordinary eyebrows I'd ever seen, like index-finger-fat caterpillars crawling across his brow – was *Adjudant-Chef* Torral. It was he who allocated Legionnaires to the various tasks around the quartier, his speech peppered with generously rolled 'r's. I was often sent off to the *poste de police*, as a guide and escorter of *punis*, those in jail who had to be interviewed and processed out of the Legion. Most of the time I lay on my back, on a dirty woollen Legion blanket atop a mouldy mattress with stains in its middle, thinking about the future.

I met *Caporal* Dave Darley during lunch in the Malmousque mess while I was on a few days' leave in Marseilles. He had almost finished his long leave after returning from two years in French Guyane. Dave's background was pretty colourful, to put it mildly. His parents were English and worked for some years on the island of Bougainville in Papua New Guinea. He was schooled in Queensland and later attended Sandhurst before seeing service in Cyprus. Why he left the British Army went unsaid and unasked. He'd also worked in Australia for a while and later as a tourist bus driver from South Africa up into Kenya. Dave Darley must have had a connection with just about every member of the Brit mafia, so he was a man to know.

He joined the Legion at the age of twenty-eight and was now, according to him, thirty-four. He looked much, much older. In fact, the lines around his mouth, the grey that bristled on his scalp and the way his gaze seemed to always be resting on the ground made him look like a tired, broken man.

Dave asked me for 200 francs and I gave it to him. He had no money after his two years in the 'green hell' of French Guyane, having fallen in love, by his own admission, with a Senegalese 'bar girl'. For the last hundred days of his leave, here in the south of France, he had spent all the money he'd saved overseas on this girl. When I met him, he was particularly upset. The previous night they had argued while he was babysitting her son, she having just returned from servicing a client.

'What the fuck am I supposed to do?' he ranted. 'I love the bitch and I thought she loved me. I don't mind that she's a whore . . . But she doesn't want anything to do with me now. She called me a "typical fucking Legionnaire" who spends all his money on women, leaving nothing for the future. I told her I'd spent it all on her because I loved her – what else was I going to say?'

It sounded like she didn't want to hear what he had to say, and I told him so. Whatever he said to this girl, with logic like hers there was nothing he could do.

So at lunch, over a carafe of acidic red wine, with Legionnaires around us clattering cutlery on plates, eating bread and greasy lentils, and laughing too hard at poor jokes, Dave and I sat in silence for a moment and reflected on the reality of being alone.

I was doing much the same thing later that day, while contemplating the Château d'If from my bedroom window at Malmousque, when there was a knock at the door. I opened up and was confronted by the sight of a man I loathed. Fat, blond-haired and animal-tattooed – it was *Sergent* LaFronde.

He was in Marseilles to pick up some new recruits for Castelnaudary and had sought me out, he said. Sitting on the end of my bed, he took great delight in telling me that there had been another *fut fut* deserter: Lieber, of lightweight *sac à dos* fame. As he blew his lips and smirked, I loathed him afresh;

him and his staccato laugh. I loathed the roll of fat that lolled over the top of his too-tight green combat pants. Even more, I loathed the way he took pleasure in seeing other people fail.

With barely controlled glee, LaFronde then told me that in a few months he was off to Tahiti, for two years of sun and, to quote: 'Mason, *je veux rien faire du tout sauf me branler les couilles*' – basically, he was going to do nothing in his island paradise except wank.

There was no justice. Just disappointment – disappointment that a man such as LaFronde could remain in the Legion to rot it from the interior, when too many good men abandoned it as a lost cause. Well, I thought, there was no reason to leave it at that . . .

As we both sat on that bed, I told LaFronde that if ever he and I were the same rank, I would beat his fucking brains out. He blinked as if he didn't understand. I told him to leave then, as I had better things to do with my time than speak with him. He blustered, blew out his cheeks and backed out of the room like the coward he was.

15

AFRICA AT LAST

Baisez les nyahs *si vous voulez, mais mettez la capote.*
(Fuck the *nyahs* if you want, but wear a condom.)

I arrived with Krisson and the other reinforcements at Djibouti-
Ambouli International Airport, just south of Djibouti city, on
the evening of Wednesday, 8 November. It was hot, humid
and very different from the air-conditioned warmth of Paris'
Charles de Gaulle Airport where we were shepherded away
from flickering screens announcing the imminent fall of the
Berlin Wall. As I stepped off the plane, I sucked at the wet air
and realised that my return flight out of Djibouti would be in
two years' time. For a moment, the humidity was like a warm,
damp, suffocating glove over my face.

To say that France had some history with this part of the world
would be something of an understatement. The first French
incursions into the Djibouti region came with explorations in the
early to mid nineteenth century. At that time, France negotiated
rights on the Somali coast around the Horn of Africa, but it
was not until 1883 in the context of the European scramble for

the so-called 'last continent' that French interests there turned to annexation and ownership. By 1887, a series of treaties were concluded between her and most of the local rulers of the Gulf of Tadjoura, the strategically important basin between the Red Sea and the Indian Ocean. By then, French dominance was established and in 1896 the region became French Somaliland. In 1888, construction commenced on the port of Djibouti, and a railway to connect it with Addis Ababa, in landlocked Ethiopia, was completed in 1917. Even today, Djibouti remains the main port for Ethiopian trade.

During the Second World War, French Somaliland was the scene of conflict between German-backed Vichy French forces and the Free French – a fact that few in the Legion knew, or if they did, cared to discuss. What happened in France in general and in the Legion in particular was played out across Africa. There were Legionnaires who fought for Vichy France in support of the Axis powers, as there were others fighting with the Allies against Germany under the Free French banner. Indeed, the only Australian artilleryman to ever receive the Victoria Cross did so in 1941, fighting Vichy French Legionnaires in Syria. The ignorance of (or indifference to) embarrassing details about France's loyalties in the Second World War was no different from that concerning a divided Legion during the same conflict. According to Legion history, or at least the only history I ever heard, there was no Vichy France and no Free French Legion; just *la Légion*. If it made the telling of history and glory much simpler, it also made it far easier to digest.

Closer to the present, French Somaliland became a territory within the French Union in 1946 and was renamed the Territory of the Afars and Issas, after the two main ethnic groups in the country, in July 1967. Ten years later, on 27 June 1977, it became the Republic of Djibouti, a small country by African standards (just 23 200 sq km), with a population of just 400,000 people, more than 70% of whom lived in the city, the rest were nomads moving across the country with sheep, goats and camels. Since its independence in 1977, and much to the despair of ethnic Ethiopian Afars, the government had been led by President Hassan Gouled Aptidon, an Issa. In a difficult and volatile corner of the globe, French military forces, including the Legion's *13ème Demi-Brigade*, had been invited by the President to stay. This met the interests of a fledgling and fragile Djiboutian government, vulnerable to attack from within and from outside. Most pressingly, they were vulnerable to attacks from three Afar groups that later, in 1991, formally merged to form *Front pour la Restoration de l'Unité et de la Démocratie* (FRUD), those ethnic Afars who felt themselves disenfranchised by the Issa leadership of the Djiboutian President. The Afar groups were active in the shanty towns outside the city and were training in Ethiopia and in the west of Djibouti.

Also, the French Government was keen to to ensure its foreign policy interests were protected in what it characterised as part of the French-speaking world.

We descended the aircraft steps to the tarmac, patrolled by rifle-toting French Air Force ground staff, but once into the airport building, the Djiboutian *Gendarmerie* took over. They wore green uniforms that hung loosely from their skinny, coal-black bodies. The whites of their eyes were red and they spat a green vegetable mess, the ubiquitous 'qat', onto the tiled floor as we walked by. As I was to learn, the amphetamine-like drug was chewed by nearly all the males over twelve in Djibouti, and had been grown for use as a stimulant for centuries in the Horn of Africa and on the Arabian Peninsula.

We were shepherded through Djibouti customs, where pencil-thin men in khaki slouched against walls, their pistol belts hanging low and loose, like misplaced gunslingers from a B-grade western. After being loaded onto a bus, we were taken on the short drive to Quartier Monclar, the Legion's home in Djibouti.

At last, I was with the French Foreign Legion in Africa. What a wonderful ring those words had. They resonated inside me. This was my choice; at last I was with an active Legion unit, one that was patrolling the deserts under the African sun.

Through the main gate, where a *caporal* in green fatigues and kepi saluted, we turned right, then were dropped outside the office of the *Compagnie de Commandement Appui et de Service* (CCAS), and from there escorted, our bags over our shoulders, to the *chambre des passagers*. The room stank of shit, due to a blocked toilet, which the most junior in the detachment, Krisson, was set to unplugging and cleaning, his fist down the hole. The only fan in the room didn't work, so the thirteen of us new arrivals slept that night on damp mattresses, trying to fight off the myriad mosquitoes that whined around our ears and sought to suck at our glistening foreign flesh.

Next day we had a tour of Djibouti city and the countryside. First though, at 0900, we were presented to a *commandant*, the head of regimental security. He went to great lengths to inform us of the activities of *nyahs*, the local women, and also the word that was most used when referring to prostitutes.

With hands on his hips or pointing at one of us for emphasis, he said, 'A *nyah* will do anything to part you from your money. She will tell you she loves you. She will tell you she carries your child. She will ask for presents for herself, for her family or to pay a bribe.' At this he paused, before pursing his lips and

adding, '*Baisez les* nyahs *si vous voulez, mais mettez la capote.*'
(Fuck the *nyahs* if you want, but wear a condom.)

There were no available white women here, we learned.
They were married to diplomatic personnel or members of
the French military. There were no single girls over sixteen,
all sixteen-year-olds and older being educated back in France.
Therefore, any unattached female was jailbait. Just to make
things perfectly clear, the *commandant* said that if there were
any singles, they were for *officiers* only. And then he smiled.
For the likes of us thirteen reinforcements, there was no choice
but to slake our lust on the locals.

We were then loaded into a minibus and driven north into
town. There was poverty everywhere, through which steered
the odd Mercedes driven by a very dark pair of sunglasses with
more in the back seat. The white population occupied the newer
buildings. The Europeans were mainly French, either military
personnel or people serving the military and connected with the
French Government's commitment to the country. The town
smelt, a hot, sweet, rotten smell; a place about to be abandoned,
if not one that should already have been.

There were men with black hair piled high on their heads,
daggers with angled blades thrust into their wide leather belts,
and thick, roughly woven, bright-white cloth thrown over their
shoulders. They strode tall, disdainful of the crowd, while the
townsmen in torn jeans looked upon our vehicle with narrowed
eyes, awaiting their main chance. When I turned my head to
watch them as our vehicle passed, some spat into our wake. I
remembered what the head of security had said; that there were
many people who wanted the Legion out of Djibouti and that
we should never be drunk in town on our own. The women
were wrapped in long colourful robes of reds, blues, oranges
and greens. They did not deign to see us.

We drove through the Place de Menelik on a brief circuit through the city centre. The place was named after Emperor Menelik II of Ethiopia, who not only doubled the size of Djibouti's giant neighbouring state during his reign from 1889 to 1913, but defeated an Italian Army. This was the commercial centre of town. From the Place de Menelik, we headed south down Rue Éthiopie, a street flanked by bars including the Bar la Lune and the Bar Marseilles. Even in the weakened light of daytime winter, there was not much to tempt.

At the bottom of Rue Éthiopie we turned east and drove past Hamoudi Mosque, the main mosque in the city to which the Islamic faithful were called to prayer. It was painted white with two horizontal blue stripes described along its walls. Through its only entrance, men passed, their dark skin contrasting sharply with the brilliant white, their prayers hidden from the road. Hamoudi Mosque's tall white minaret dominated Djibouti city's skyline; when I looked up, its lines were sharp against the clear deep blue of the mid-morning sky.

Just 100 metres or so along a potholed road we turned left again to find Djibouti's main market, the *Grand Marche,* on our right. Men in crisp white robes and turbans, or in dirty blue jeans and T-shirts, sold everything from pots and pans and cloth, to ivory, cheetah cubs and Ethiopian swords; indeed, almost anything one might desire, much of it unobtainable or illegal elsewhere in the world. The sellers sat in shaded dark stalls covered in colourful awnings of red, gold and yellow, chewing or talking as they worked beads through their fingers. The minibus slowly rolled along parallel to the 300 metres of stalls, and I watched a young man in bright blue shorts spit a green mess onto the road just as a tall, proud looking figure strode by, wooden comb in the hair piled on his head, a white robe thrown over his shoulder and leather sandals slapping the dust at his feet.

Once clear of these small Aladdin's caves, we motored on past the Djibouti's optimistically named Olympic Stadium – although, from the look of the old concrete, flapping iron and bleached flaking paint, I doubted whether any Olympic events would ever be held there. Soon we were passing through the suburb of Gabode, where many of the French military housed their wives, and on to the road to Arta, Ali Sabieh and Dikhil, out to the west. Along with the road east to Loyada on the coast and the Somali border, and the one north towards Tadjoura and Obock, the road to Dikhil is one of Djibouti's major arteries, if not the major one, as its designation as N1 attested. It eventually feeds westwards into Ethiopia and the African continent.

Leaving the city, we passed a shanty town set up on the right-hand side of the road. This was Balballa. Shelters of cardboard, tin or whatever came to hand were homes to hordes of refugees and displaced people, stretching towards the horizon. Thousands of small plastic bags, having become snared on garbage, fluttered in the breeze like so many colourful damaged birds. There was a sweet acrid smell of burning polymers and other things; and by the roadside, small mounds of smouldering rubbish, of plastic, shit, offal, and vegetable that had been collected and lit. Beyond Balballa, there were more plastic bags: some caught by the sparse undergrowth or around rocks, others that appeared to ride in the air. In that monochrome brown landscape, these bags were suspended in the sky like exclamations of colour.

Soon, after 30 or more kilometres on a narrow strip of bitumen, the road entered a land of clean, dark brown and started to climb. To our right was the turn-off to Arta, home of the *compagnie tournante*, a company doing a four or sometimes six-month tour in Djibouti from 2 REP. Also at Arta were the

French Ambassador's summer residence and the weekend retreat of President Hassan Gouled Aptidon, whose benign image, I'd discover, was pinned, plastered or glued on the wall of every shop, stall and brothel in the country.

Our minibus followed the main road, as all the while we sightseers looked way down over our left shoulders to a dried riverbed, a wadi, or more often in this part of the world, a *oued*. From the debris I could see, the *oued* in flood must have been devastating. Not far beyond the intersection with the Arta road was a descent, followed by a short, sharp climb up to Oueah, at 40 kilometres from Djibouti, home to the *Escadron de Reconnaissance*, 13 DBLE's armoured reconnaissance squadron.

Before the escadron's Quartier Brunet de Sairigné was built, there had been no buildings here. Just dust, rocks and wandering goats. Now there was a petrol station and many small rock huts, occupied by the local population. These people gathered around the *quartier* in the hope of securing some work, or in the case of the women, providing sex for money to the Legionnaires.

Continuing our journey west, we passed the turn-off to Lac Assal, Tadjoura and Obock, some 15 kilometres from Oueah, before making our final stop, at the Grand Barra. The view on arrival was breathtaking: a plain some 30 kilometres long and 20 kilometres wide, the whole thing bleached-yellow dust. The Grand Barra was apparently the catchment area for the hills that encircled it. After a few minutes, during which some among us were clearly unsettled by this great expanse of nothingness, we returned to the bus and started on the return trip to Quartier Monclar.

Although the tour was short, it made a deep impression on me. I admired the people for their independence and pride. And I loved the country for its raw purity and limitless sky and space.

•

Once back at Monclar, we were *quartier consigne*, which meant we were restricted to camp for the evening. Next day, we had to present to the commanding officer of the regiment (or, in this case, the half-brigade). It was now that we would discover where we'd be posted during our stay in 'the *Treize*', short for *treizième* – as in 13 DBLE.

Appearing before the commanding officer, like any superior in the Legion, was a highly structured and ritualised activity. An *adjudant-chef* briefed us on the necessary etiquette when entering *Colonel* le Flegg's office: first, knock and ask for permission to enter; then, with kepi on head, enter and halt four paces from the *colonel*'s desk; salute the regimental flag, situated on the wall, behind and to the left of the *colonel*, and then salute the officer himself. What followed was the normal presentation, with the added challenge of having to compete with a rattling air conditioner. This time, though, I concluded with the French equivalent of: 'Newly posted to the 13th Half-Brigade of the Foreign Legion. At your orders, *Colonel*.'

Apart from this, I said nothing to *Colonel* le Flegg, and he didn't ask me anything. He read from a piece of paper on his desk and posted me to 13 DBLE's sole combat company, *3ème Compagnie*. I got the distinct impression that he would have much preferred to be at home. At one point, he held a hand up to his red-bearded mouth, to camouflage a yawn. Krisson was affected to the *Escadron de Reconnaissance* at Oueah. I supposed I would rarely see him.

The following day was Saturday, 11 November, and because of the morning parade to commemorate the conclusion of the First World War, those of us posted to the *3ème Compagnie* did not pass *rapport capitaine*, (report to the *3ème Compagnie capitaine)* until late morning. I presented myself and stood before *Capitaine* Rocky for no more than two minutes. He introduced me to *Lieutenant* Dallas, my new *chef de section*.

Dallas was very plump of face, in his mid twenties, and stiff and formal with the *capitaine*. Evidently, he had not long been in Djibouti. The telltale sign of an *ancien* in the combat company is a leanness of body, skin tight against the bones of the face, any excess having been melted off by exercise and the heat. I had seen these men already in the last day or so, and some of them I knew. They walked purposefully around the *quartier* in shorts, with black socks rolled over the tops of their boots, short-sleeve green shirts and green berets positioned so that the badge of the Legion flame sat over their right eyes.

On leaving the audience with the *capitaine*, *Lieutenant* Dallas took me to his office in a building, 20 metres from the *3ème Compagnie* headquarters that he shared with the other *section* commanders. Here he informed me that for the next week or two I would be doing the driving course for vehicles and trucks. At the conclusion of the brief interview, I saluted and he waved me away, directing me to the *3ème Section* barracks, across the *place d'armes*. I was to set up in *Caporal* Potter's room.

So, on 11 November 1989, I was affected to *3ème Section*, *section tireur d'élite*, *3ème Compagnie*, 13 DBLE. I was in Africa with a combat company of the French Foreign Legion. This had to be the Legion I was searching for.

Just ten days later, it had become clear that all was not well in the *section*. In the military, there would always be comments as to how much better the previous commander was and how poor the new one may be. Thus it was with Dallas. Most of the *caporals* said they wanted to be transferred to another *section*.

This included Rovery, an English *fut fut* almost blind in one eye who had learnt the eye chart off by heart; Schnebel, a German *fut fut*; and Wanger, a loud-mouth Frenchman kicked out of the job as chauffeur to *Capitaine* Rocky because he was unreliable. When asked where they might go, heads were shaken and shoulders shrugged. They were gasbagging. All three arrived at about the same time, over one year before.

The only one who said little on the issue of command was Potter. A veteran of regiments in Guyane and Nîmes, he was the *plus ancien* of the *caporals* and Legionnaires in *3ème Section*. The Frenchman had a large rectangle with a Legion flame in the interior and 3 REI inscribed underneath, tattooed on his left thigh. He knew that when a new officer arrived to command a *section*, he would go out of his way to impose his will on its men.

Of course, it was difficult for someone in Dallas's position, where many of the men had been there for well over a year. The most important thing to remember was that a young *officier's* future was contingent upon his performance with his *section*. There would be no transfers and the first few months would be difficult for all.

So it was that we had constant reviews of equipment, double checks on clothing sizes, fitness tests and the seemingly never-ending weapon checks. On paper, the daily routine was gentle enough: *reveil* at 0445, *appel* at 0500, and at 0600 *commence travail* (start work), which was ordinarily a run; *soupe* at 1200, *sieste* until 1515 and *rassemblement* at 1600; then work till *soupe* at 1800. This 'full' day was scheduled for three days of the week – Saturday, Monday and Wednesday. Sunday, Tuesday and Thursday were officially half-days, finishing at 1200, when one could sleep, do some sport or, more ordinarily, go into town and take a *nyah*. Friday was the one day off a week; if you did not have guard or were not out on terrain. As was so often the case, the daily routine was but a model. In our case, there was little correlation between the 'official day' and our existence.

Because we got few afternoons off compared with other French military in Djibouti, who didn't work at all in the afternoons, many Legionnaires preferred to spend the evening inside the camp. Here they could visit the foyer, which opened at 1900, or the *bordel*, which opened at 2100. The foyer was similar to that at Quartier Danjou except that the prices were much inflated and it was located next to a very popular open-air cinema.

Not to be confused with a Legionnaire's description of life under French command, the *Bordel Militaire Contrôlé* was a brothel run by a *caporal-chef* and staffed by four *nyahs* and a Legionnaire acting as medic. The job of managing the brothel in Djibouti was one of the most highly sought after positions by *caporal-chefs* in the Legion. Not only did he get his monthly pay of almost 23,000 French francs (5,000 Australian dollars), which he needed not touch during his two years there, but he received some of the profits and no doubt plenty of backhanders in the course of his business.

The *nyahs* were selected by the brothel manager from among the hundreds who plied their trade in town. They were, according to the *caporal-chef,* examined weekly by a doctor in the camp, and all the girls were *propre* (clean), he assured me. I wondered how it was possible to be protected from the endemic neglect of *capotes* by Legionnaires and the threat of *SIDA*, or AIDS. Then, why would he care – why would he want to discuss matters that would adversely affect his profit?

In the *bordel* we paid three times as much for a beer as we did in the foyer at Monclar, just 100 metres away. Out the back of the brothel was a small beer garden, which was usually the preserve of the Brits. Here, one could, while consuming a very cold beer, observe the business of military-controlled prostitution in practice. If you wanted one of the *nyahs*, the procedure was simple enough. Go to the *caporal-chef* at the bar inside and point out the girl you would like. Pay him 3000 FDJ (around 25 Australian dollars) – a discount on town prices, which were 5000 FDJ – and he would give you the torn-off half of a numbered raffle ticket, colour-coded to the girl. Then, approach the girl with your ticket and, assuming your number had 'come up', she would escort you outside, past the beer garden, to the medic – the *infirmier du jour*.

The *infirmier* sat behind a small table at the entrance to a narrow corridor off which ran the girls' rooms. The *nyah* would walk straight through to her very small room, while the Legionnaire had to present himself for examination. *Infirmiers* got this service instead of such things as *garde 24* or *piquet d'intervention*. There was never a shortage of volunteers, for in the course of its execution, it was possible to make money.

There was much snapping of rubber as the *infirmier* donned his glove. In various states of arousal, Legionnaires exposed their muscle for examination while the medic lifted folds of skin and exposed them to ultraviolet light. Then, after pursed lips and shakings of head, negotiations took place along the following lines, with the *infirmier* leading the discussion:

'What the fuck is that thing there?'

'What thing?'

'That thing. It looks like a festering sore.'

'Where? Oh that . . .' often said with surprise. 'I've never noticed it before.'

'Well, you won't be doing any shagging here with that thing.'

'Aw, come on! What's a little spot anyway? Can't we just keep it between ourselves? What if I . . . ?'

And here, a hand into a pocket, and a few crumpled notes passed. If the Legionnaire was without a visible infection he would be straight through to pleasure. The *infirmier* always gave each man a condom, but its use was not compulsory; it was always possible to go 'bareback' for a negotiated fee with the *nyah*. It was as if many of the Legionnaires suspended belief, or didn't care that they were exposing themselves to HIV. There were times, in fact, when I thought men had sex without condoms simply to thumb a nose at Lady Luck, for they were with the Legion in Africa and any luck that came their way was their own. This was a madness I could not share. Perhaps because I was older I always tried to balance luck on my side.

Into the second week of the *Instruction Élémentaire de Conduire* (IEC), the driving course, my view of the French Army was being tested. There were eight Legionnaires and some twenty French Marines on the course, most of whom were National Servicemen, posted to Djibouti for nine months or so. For the most part, these National Servicemen were not happy to be in Djibouti, and they demonstrated their dissatisfaction by arriving in the morning unshaven, with various gold and silver chains about their necks. Most, and in this they were similar to Legionnaires, were either hung-over or still drunk from the night before. In the heat of a morning parade, the stink of old sweat and alcohol saturated the senses.

In the afternoons on our half-days, I sat on my bed in *chambre* 13 and wrote up my diary while the others in the room slept. In the bed opposite mine was *Caporal* Potter. Next to him slept young Legionnaire Drabble, who'd needed his parents' permission before being able to join the Legion. The seventeen-year-old had been in Djibouti for some four months, having arrived straight out of instruction. Fortunately for the young Frenchman, Potter had taken him under his wing. The next bed was occupied by Nabok, a Polish Légionnaire *1ère classe* and formerly of the Legion's Cavalry Regiment, 1 REC. By his own admission, Nabok was in Djibouti to make some money and, at the end of five years, get French citizenship. He was often yelled at by the Frenchmen, especially the French *caporals*, who liked to humiliate someone from a country even less well regarded than their own.

Normally asleep in the bed beside the Pole's was Kapper, a Turk who had outstayed his time in Germany, but at that moment he was in the regimental *taule* (jail), with his Turkish friend Legionnaire Amir. The last person in the room was a Frenchman named Dalby, another *première classe*, whose bed was opposite Nabok's. Dalby was an *ivrogne* (drunk), taken out of the *officiers'* mess, where he worked in the kitchen, and put into this *section*, not because he was a drunk but because he reportedly bashed a *caporal-chef*. It was okay to be an *ivrogne*, but not to hit a superior.

On the final day of tests on the driving course, we were returning east, back towards the city. It began to rain and over the radio came word that the wadi at Ambouli, the usually dry creek bed that separated the refugee shanty town of Balballa from the city, was flooded. We stopped at the side of the road, at which point one of the *caporal-chef* instructors declared, to no one in particular, that he wanted to buy a goat.

We built a small fire and, as the temperature had dropped a little, Legionnaires and locals alike were soon gathered around. In the course of the subsequent negotiations, De Olimop, a Portuguese *caporal* from my own reinforcement detachment, asked one of the tribesmen if he fucked the goats he looked after. The man looked at De Olimop with an expressionless face and moved a few metres away. Some of the Legionnaires began laughing their hard laughs and declared the man a *'putain singe'* (damn monkey). Suitably encouraged, De Olimop decided to further amuse himself. He proceeded to demonstrate how one heated French Army rations, simply by throwing an unopened can into the fire. Before the can of beef exploded, I rescued it from the fire and assured the local men that it was best to open the can before consigning it to the flames.

Not be outdone, De Olimop went on to offer his theory on why it was that, in his opinion, Djiboutians were all savages. With his hands in the pockets of his green shorts, he tilted his head back and laughed. The tribesmen, in their cast-off clothes scavenged from the occupying French troops, stood about with eyes downcast, not even looking at one another. Their faces were empty.

Consistent with observance in a Muslim country, the Friday was a day of rest for the local population. So, knowing this, on Thursday night I went into town to take my first *nyah*. I took her from the Bar Mic Mac, around the corner from the Bar Marseilles on Rue Éthiopie. As soon as I walked into the bar, I was met by beautiful black girls who ran their hands all over my body. The music was loud, the lights strobing across the walls.

Because Legionnaires with less than five years' service had to wear uniforms into town, the girls knew from looking at my uniform what I was: as a *caporal* without ribbons or brevets, I could only have been a *fut fut*. And since I wasn't as skinny as the other Legionnaires, I had to be a new arrival. That made me doubly attractive to them. After all, a Foreign Legion *caporal* earned a small fortune, and while the girls were content to have paid sex, they much preferred to have one Legionnaire set up a small apartment and keep them, and thus their family, for the two-year duration of his posting.

I had to buy Amina two drinks at 1000 FDJ each (about 8 Australian dollars) to keep the patron of the bar happy. Later, she took me to a narrow dirt street just behind the *Grand Marche*. She smelled of sandalwood, her skin was very black and soft, her body very supple. Here was the promise of pleasure. I told the taxi driver to wait for me in the alleyway.

In her squalid room, the bed was a filthy mattress, raised off the dirt floor by planks of wood and covered by a piece of cotton that moved with our bodies. The walls were thin plywood and cardboard, plastered with pictures ripped from magazines, of places she would probably never see – the Eiffel Tower, the Empire State Building and the Statue of Liberty among them. Michael Jackson performed 'Thriller' on a cassette player and although there was an overhead fan, its action was lazy and we were both quickly drenched in sweat. Amina didn't look at me; she looked at the ceiling.

As I put myself inside her, I realised that she'd been 'cut', a victim of the appalling practice of female genital mutilation. At some time in her past, probably when she was little more than a child, someone had cut off her vaginal lips and her clitoris, doubtless with some rusty old blade. Fucking her was how I imagined fucking a fistful of warm raw minced meat.

I paid Amina the going rate of 5000 FDJ and then caught the battered green taxi back to camp. Once back in the *3ème Section* block, I took a shower to rinse off the sweat and sluice away some of the guilt I felt for myself, and some of the sorrow I felt for her. Like all the women working in the bars across town, Amina was being exploited.

I had sex with other girls in Djibouti. They were all bar girls, from Somalia, Kenya and Ethiopia. Some had skin that was shiny coal-black, others more like warm cocoa, but always their eyes were dark, with shadows inside. Some smiled, some did not. I never beat them, refused to pay them or attempted to humiliate them. After sex, some of the girls asked me to share coffee with them and their family, as if I were a guest.

No matter the number of times Amina caressed my leg in the bar, or whispered encouragements to me in that cardboard hut, there was no mutual desire on her part. Of course not. I knew the money I paid might help her and her family get away from Djibouti some day. I also knew I was in Djibouti for two years. What was I to do for those two years, during which I could be killed or die from some endemic disease? This was no moral alibi, I realised. It was selfish; a shit of an excuse and a pathetic rationalisation. But it was the best I could come up with that night, and it nestled inside me beside the others I lived with.

16

JOYEUX NOËL AND A BLOODY NEW YEAR

Il n'y a rien qui change. Quelle bande de cons.
(Nothing changes. What a bunch of bastards.)

Christmas was soon fast upon us. On Saturday, 23 December, to make way for a bar, all the members of my room moved out, beds, baggage and all, to a *chambre* next door. It meant for a crowded few days but importantly, the bar would serve all comers for two days from the following day. According to *Caporal* Schnebel, the German *fut fut*, this was a means by which the *section* could raise money to pay for incidentals such as soft drinks and ice when we were in the field.

I was helping Schnebel stack beer in ice behind the bar when he reminded me why it was that all the *soldats du rang* referred to our uptight *section* leader as 'Dallas': because, like the hugely popular American TV series of the same name, with him everything was a major drama. The *sous-officiers* hardly appeared to hold him in high esteem either. They being *Sergent-Chef* Postnoz and the two *sergents*, Carrion, my own *chef de groupe*, and the man known to all as the Fat Indian, from Mauritius.

In contrast, Christmas Day 1989 was distinctly low on drama, but certainly warmer in temperature than mine the year before. At 0800 I sat on my bunk and looked through the door to the *place d'armes* and the flagpole on which the *tricolore* hung limp. The *3ème Compagnie* barracks were set about the parade ground in the shape of a letter U, with the open end out to the west. There, grouped together in white, single-storey buildings, were the four *sections* in the company: *1ère Section* specialised in explosives, *2ème* in amphibious work, *3ème* were the marksmen while the fourth one was a *section commandement*, which included an 81 mm mortar team, radio men and office personnel. The company offices were just beyond the southernmost building, under enormous plane trees. Sitting on my bunk I could feel the cool air on my shoulders, stirred by the overhead fan.

The Christmas Eve festivities had been in equal turns predictable and unpredictable. First, there were the sketches, which, like those at Castelnaudary, were not very funny at all. Then came the dinner, the contents of which, to be fair, we could never have predicted. A far cry from our routine fare of lentils and bread, we were presented now with turkey in a rich, sweet sauce with vegetables, cakes to follow, and all of it washed down with plenty of red wine.

During the course of the meal, everyone received a *cadeau de Noël* (Christmas present) from the regiment, this year's being a tracksuit. No sooner had the distribution of presents taken place than Dallas began to *chant* – which in this context meant to lead into a Legion song. He was all *voix basse* and authority. Given that he was new and so young, he had to be seen to be doing something. We all joined in.

Highlights of the evening included the awarding of *caporal* stripes to Poobelle, Berka and Embisill, a trio of whom I was already doubtful. All French, they'd been busy brown-nosing and displaying ever more creative efforts at sycophancy, or wheedling their way out of work details. The three did not lead by example or teach the younger, more inexperienced Legionnaires the tricks to survival, or even how to be soldiers. Instead, I came to know them as a chorus of poisonous men, who belittled others to appear greater and more important to the *section* leadership. These men believed they had always, and only, to look up to their NCOs. Me, I believed that a *caporal's* job necessarily involved showing respect towards the men also; those who looked to us for help and leadership. Sadly, it all seemed rather too close to life back in Castelnaudary for my liking.

The evening's greatest surprise was that Hovellet – the Wolverhampton man of Caribbean descent I'd known from my first *section d'instruction* – was awarded his *première classe* stripe. Unlike attaining the rank of *caporal* or *sergent*, such an award was not a formal promotion, but rather, a distinction. It could only come after a minimum of one year's service with good conduct. In effect, though, being made Légionnaire *première classe* was indeed a promotion because pay increased as did the man's relative status.

In Hovellet's case, the element of good conduct had been absent for some time. Because he'd gone to Corsica and the REP (from which he was ejected, after serving less than one year), he refused to do much work here, preferring to concentrate on the *nyahs* in town. He often claimed that, because he was black, everyone was against him. This was a view not entirely without basis for, despite it appearing to welcome men from all over the world, the Legion was notoriously racist, and remains so, certainly against black Africans. The result was that there were very few black men in any of the Legion's regiments. Hovellet, however, did himself no favours, and by his own actions created further problems for himself.

Once the promotions were distributed, songs sung and the tables cleared, we were given permission to retire to our rooms to lock away our prizes. Then, at 2200, the *chambres* were cleared of personnel and locked. With little alternative, everyone drifted to the various bars that had been set up by each *section* for fundraising purposes and as sites for the dubious concept of socialising between *officiers* and Legionnaires.

Along with Camerone Day, Christmas Eve was perhaps the most dreaded and loathed evening of the year. According to tradition on this Yuletide celebration, the Legion's officers would remain at the bars with their men until dawn. The idea was that, given the emotional nature of Christmas and the memories it brought of family and home, an officer needed to assert himself as a paternal figure, if not surrogate father, to the Legionnaires. After all, wasn't one of the Legion's mottos '*Legio Patria Nostra*' (The Legion is our Fatherland)?

So a very odd thing would happen. The very men who for the entire year – and indeed that very morning – called Legionnaires *mongols*, *crétins* and *bons pour rien* (good-for-nothings) now went out of their way to buy us drinks. This was the way *officiers* of the Legion bonded with their charges. Even the most unsophisticated among us would shake his head at the hypocrisy of it all. '*Il n'y a rien qui change*,' I heard someone declare that night. '*Quelle bande de cons*.' (Nothing changes. What a bunch of bastards.)

With Christmas Eve being more about duty than celebration, therefore, we hoped to achieve something rather more meaningful the following night. On Christmas Day, the Brits had dinner at the Arta Restaurant in town. Gungie Whyte, a Scot who had served in the British Paras and then at Calvi with 2 REP, and Bonnie, a West Indian Scot, had worked hard on organising this event. It was a traditional Christmas dinner, with turkey, lamb, dumplings and all the trimmings. There was even a specially imported Christmas pudding. We tried tuning in to the Queen's Christmas Address but weren't able to pick it up at all on the radio.

I gave a speech that Gungie and Bonnie had asked me to prepare. I chose Rupert Brooke's 'The Soldier', because of its resonance with all English-speaking soldiers away from home:

If I should die think only this of me:
That there's some corner of a foreign field
That is forever England. There shall be
In that rich earth a richer dust concealed;
A dust whom England bore, shaped, made aware
Gave, once her flowers to love her ways to roam,
A body of England's breathing English air,
Washed by rivers, blest by suns of home.

And think this heart, all evil shed away,
A pulse in the Eternal mind no less
Gives somewhere back the thoughts by England given
Her sights and sounds: dreams happy as her day,
And laughter, learnt of friends: and gentleness,
In hearts at peace, under an English heaven.

The next day, a Tuesday, I took my first *garde 24* in Djibouti. And what a civilised affair it was.

Guard duty in Djibouti was very different from the trauma-tised service at Castelnaudary – mainly because people knew their job and did it. Here a Legionnaire could not just say he didn't understand, and thus expect the *caporal* to take the blame.

Like the guard at Castelnaudary, the relief took up the *garde 24* at 0600 and was replaced at 0600 the following day. Unfortunately, this meant that instead of relaxing or even sleeping, we had a full day with the *section*, at the rifle range, on a *footing* or whatever. This made for some difficult Legionnaires and a very tired *caporal,* who had been awake at his post from 2400 till 0600, having secured at most two hours' sleep.

On New Year's Eve I went into town, where I planned to meet up with a few of the boys at the Bar Saigon for a game of pool and to see in the New Year. The taxi dropped me at the Place de Menelik. From there could I walk down Rue Éthiopie and through the fruit and vegetable markets to the Saigon. Little did I know then that an event was about to occur that would follow me through my years of Legion service.

Just as I reached the Bar Marseilles, I met a French Marine with whom I had completed the driving course. We agreed to a drink and we made our way into the bar. Once we were set up and had brushed off the usual dark, insistent hands, I asked why it was that there were no submarines based at Djibouti, given that the Horn of Africa dominated the shipping route into the Red Sea and thus the Suez Canal. He laughed; the answer was really quite simple, he said. The Gulf of Tadjoura was too clear and not deep enough to hide a submarine.

It was twenty or so minutes before midnight, and time to go. Outside the bar as we shook hands, something seemed to catch his attention, over my shoulder. '*Regardez ça,*' he said. '*Quelqu'un a tombé.*' (Look at that. Someone's fallen over.)

When I looked for myself, over towards the Bar la Lune, I realised that this was no drunk. The body was twitching as if it was going into shock.

We ran 20 metres to where the body lay and as we arrived, three Djiboutians who had gathered there ran off. The figure on the spit-splattered footpath was a white male in civilian clothes. Flat on his back, he had an open gash over his right eye that, for all its size, bled little. His eyes were open but he could not see. When I spoke to him, he began to rave.

I took off my kepi, gave it to the Marine and told him to run to the Place de Menelik; when he saw a *Police Militaire* vehicle, he was to attract attention by waving the kepi. I told a passing Djiboutian to go into the Bar la Lune and phone for an ambulance.

On New Year's Eve, on Rue Éthiopie, Djibouti's busiest street, I saw Legionnaires, including Poobelle and Berka, walking by on the other side of the road. They all ignored me as I tried to wave them over; none of them asked if I needed any help. Maybe they thought I was doing a fine job, or they just didn't want to get involved.

The injured man stopped breathing. I wiped away the blood from his mouth, hoped he didn't have AIDS and, as best I could, formed a seal and breathed air into his lungs. Soon he started breathing again. I took his pulse: it was over 140 and accelerating. I started talking, then shouting at him while searching for identification. This I found in a back pocket and it identified him as a Legionnaire. I then moved my hands between his back and the ground and found blood. As well as the wound above his eye, he had been stabbed in the lower back, into a kidney.

All this took a matter of seconds but at last I was able to communicate with him. I asked who had done this to him. His response was, '*Un ami.*'

A friend? That didn't sound right, so I asked again. '*Amir*,' he said this time.

I double-checked: '*Légionnaire Amir le Turk?*'

'*Oui, oui. Légionnaire Amir, 3ème Compagnie.*'

I asked him why and his response was no surprise. '*Une pute – ma nyah. Il veut la prendre.*' (A prostitute – my woman. He wants to take her.)

By this time a small group of people, mainly Djiboutians, had gathered. Some stated it matter-of-factly: the man would die. His pulse was racing. His breathing was becoming more shallow and rapid. All I could do was talk to him, slap his face and prevent him from sliding into unconsciousness.

At last, the Legion's *Police Militaire* arrived, as did an ambulance. I told them all that had happened and they let me go on my way. By the time I got to the Saigon, it was well past midnight and those I'd wanted to meet up with had left, either too drunk to continue drinking, or having selected a *nyah*.

A day later I was called to the office of the *Police Militaire*. The connecting door to the interior of the building opened from the inside to reveal Marino, Amir's accomplice, and Amir himself. Cuffed and seated, they were giving some account of themselves to a *caporal-chef*. They stopped talking and turned to me, their eyes narrow and hard.

Marino elevated his chin and said, 'We know you, Mason. We know who you are and where you come from. One day we will find you and kill you.' He drew a line across his throat with a finger from his cuffed hands. Amir's brown bullet-shaped head nodded; the Turk flared his nostrils and gritted his teeth so hard I could see the ripple of muscle up his cheek.

I walked past them to the next door and, before closing it, turned to them both and said, 'Anyone who cuts someone from behind is a dog. *Adieu.*' I had no idea how they knew I was involved.

I spoke with *Adjudant-Chef* Sanders, the senior NCO with Legion security. Again I recounted all that had happened. He told me I had saved the wounded man's life, that I had done a fine job and that he would recommend me for a medal. The Legionnaire was now in a coma and on his way back to France. Both Amir and Marino would be dealt with by the authorities back in France, their crimes too serious for a Legion prison. The *adjudant-chef* went on to say that those Legionnaires who had walked by without lending a hand ought to be given a beating. Their failure was just as serious, and a long way from the spirit of the Legion. Sure, I knew that too. It was far removed from the spirit of a lot of things.

17

GOLFERS AND BARBECUES

Nul à chier.
(Not worth shit.)

On Wednesday, 4 January, almost half of *3ème Section* was allocated a week of guard. We were sent to Douda, an area south-east of the airport, to do what we called a *garde antenne* – the occupation and protection of a communications site with five large antennas. This centre provided the French military with communications to France and naval elements in the Indian Ocean.

The facility was set on a small rise that was once a fortified post. There were trenches and bunkers here that had been built by the French before the Second World War. A fence some 3.5 kilometres long surrounded the facility. We overlooked the airport to the north, with Djibouti's city skyline beyond; the sea to the east, where the rusted hulk of a tramp steamer lay on the beach; a squatters' camp and the makeshift Djibouti golf course to the south; and to the west, part of the Douda ammunition dump, which was patrolled at this time by members of the *Armée Nationale de Djibouti*, the AND.

Four hours off duty and two on for the entire day; my post was a watchtower that faced south. Just before sunrise one morning, I climbed into the tower as usual. The sun was rising over the Gulf of Aden, the giant expanse of water between the Horn of Africa and the Arabian Peninsula, and I could see people leaving their makeshift huts to squat in a small gully not 50 metres from the base of my tower.

Not long after sunrise, a flash of light caught my eye. Was it the glass on a sniper's telescope reflecting the sun's rays? I brought the binoculars to my eyes and directed my gaze to the spot . . .

No, it was just a lone golfer stroking his ball through the basalt rocks and thorn bushes of Djibouti.

The guard was quartered in air-conditioned wooden huts, also home to the multitude of mosquitoes that bred in the overflow of the septic tanks and in the air-conditioners. I shared a room with Bonnie, who had served with the British Army's postal service during the Falklands War. Taking off his shirt to display a recent scar that ran from his breast bone to below his navel, he told me he was stabbed by some Arabs near the Place de l'Opéra, in Marseilles, near the Old Port. He had gone to a prostitute and, as he put it, 'mid-stroke' found himself set upon by a group of thugs intent on separating him from his wallet. Fighting back meant being stabbed, and he lost his cash anyway. He wanted to learn 'Waltzing Matilda' so I wrote down the words for him.

We lay on our bunks and talked about the way the world viewed us Legionnaires. 'No one likes us, mate,' Bonnie said in his Glasgow accent. 'Getting pissed, fucking and fighting

– that's all people think we're good for. That's the legacy our predecessors have left us.'

A week later, I was in a wadi 5 kilometres inland from Arta Plage, some 40 kilometres west of Djibouti city on the Gulf of Tadjoura, watching a small Afar encampment. Years before, I had read British explorer Wilfred Thesiger's account of his expedition to this region in 1933–34. He described the people he'd encountered as tall and proud. The men castrated their enemies and wore additions to their clothing that told the world how many they had killed.

Whenever the Legion went into the field, however, these tall, proud men were viewed as nothing but the fathers and brothers of the prostitutes in Djibouti. For Legionnaires, this view was reinforced by the fact that we rarely saw young women in the Afar encampments. The work appeared to be done by old women and very young children.

We were in the wadi having marched all night from the *Escadron de Reconnaissance* base at Oueah to get here. *Lieutenant* Dallas had told us – and this was the first time I ever heard him give any indication of his plans – that we would march to a night location and establish a lookout post. The post was to be relieved at some point during that same evening by other troops. In fact, there was no night location and no sign of any other troops. Maybe the *lieutenant* got lost.

We'd left Quartier Brunet de Sairigné on sunset. Dallas simply took a bearing from his compass and marched. The rest of us in *3ème Section* followed in single file. There was no allowing for the terrain; we didn't go around hills, we went over them. We negotiated the dark, the ascents and descents, the rocks that rolled from underfoot and the thorn bushes that tugged at our *musettes*, clothes and faces, all as best we could. In less than an hour the *section* had fragmented into small groups and people were spread out across the terrain, yelling, cursing and crying out in complaint. The *section* had descended into a rabble while, up at the forward group, Dallas maintained a stubborn silence.

To his back, and within definite earshot of their men, *Sergents* Carrion and Fat Indian called him an idiot, '*nul à chier*' (not worth shit) and much else besides. When finally ordered by Dallas to retrace our route to regain contact with the others, the Fat Indian made no effort to hide his lack of respect from the officer himself. '*Putain ça me fait chier!*' he replied. (What a bitch – this is giving me the shits!)

Equally hard to fathom was the fact that Dallas continued to say nothing; he appeared to examine his map more closely now, even though it must've been near impossible to read in the dark. Then he pulled out a plastic compass and looked off into the distance. Meanwhile, the Fat Indian was spluttering with anger, yelling at Legionnaires as he pushed or punched his way past them on his way to the rear to join up with the stragglers.

Hours later, towards 0200 and after the climb and descent of three more ridges, we came to a dry watercourse that led to the sea. Dallas followed it and we followed Dallas. We had little choice; not only because he was our commander, but because he was the only person with a map. If Afars had set an ambush to kill us, it would have been an easy thing to destroy a Foreign Legion *section*.

Finally, we descended into a large wadi, through which ran the sole vehicular track to 13 DBLE's commando training centre at Arta Plage, and we stopped. To my great satisfaction, Poobelle was loaded onto a passing vehicle: *malade*. I doubted he was sick. More like he'd just had enough and decided to take the weakling's way out.

The sun came up and most of us tried to get some sleep in the shade, but even an hour after sunrise, it was already too hot. No one was happy, there was no banter. Dallas did not share why it was we'd stopped at this spot, nor when we would be picked up. Even when in the field with a combat regiment, it seemed, Legionnaires were still treated as ignorant and pathetic things that could not be trusted with such basic information. For some of us, though, I had to admit that this was probably the right approach.

I sat on a rock, the sun warm on my neck, and watched the others. I had been with *3ème Section* for two months now and I already knew that I would never truly belong with many of these characters – Wanger, Berka, Hovellet and the like. I could be with them in time and space, but I refused to share their wilful ignorance and self-representations that they were better than they really were.

Rather than dwell on this, I looked around me, to the clear blue sky and the wadi walls, like stained red ramparts, that reminded me of Monument Valley in Arizona or the Kimberly in Western Australia. At the head of the wadi was a small encampment where some Afar tribespeople had settled for a time. All either old women or young children, they were camped on gravel that, almost uniquely for this area, carried grass sufficient to feed their small flock of fat, Roman-nosed, floppy-eared sheep. The four flat-topped dwellings, perhaps 3 metres in diameter, had internal frames of wrist-thick sticks, the outsides covered with matting woven from local grass and, occasionally, a blue plastic tarpaulin.

The tribespeople stood and watched us, their hands over their eyes to protect themselves from the sun's slanting rays, their bodies wrapped in fabrics of primary colours. From where I sat, I could see the women's uncovered faces and make out their fine straight noses and defined features.

I looked back to where my *section* was lying in the shade. Unlike the nomadic group further along the wadi, they rested in the darker places, like tired lean lizards in their dirty green clothes, their movements sluggish. I smiled ruefully and reminded myself that only a few months before I had chosen to stay.

Hours later we were trucked back to Quartier Monclar and my first tour as *caporal du jour*. If this first experience was any indication, it was likely to be a very long two years. I had trouble with the French *caporals*; Poobelle and Berka were very much the sycophantic snivellers and Wanger was a truly obnoxious fellow. All three were busy reporting the apparent failings of the new *fut fut* to the *sergents*, particularly to Carrion, a Frenchman, my group leader.

Along with five years' service, Wanger wore French parachute wings, a detail that most took to mean he'd been in the Parachute Regiment at Calvi. Wanger's wings, however, were due to his having served previously with a French Army parachute regiment, although he was the last to dissuade anyone from assuming he was an ancien of 2 REP, of course.

The post of driver to *Capitaine* Rocky, much sought after by the French as it required no guard duty or the usual *corvées*, had once been Wanger's. He'd committed some misdemeanour and, for his sins, now found himself in our *section* and not at all happy about it. He had a wife in town and, in front of as extensive an audience as possible, ostentatiously asked *Sergent-Chef* Postnoz and the *sergents* if they would like to join him and his wife for dinner at his apartment.

Wanger was wiley, duplicitous and sneaky. He was short, with bleeding tattoos on his arms and a gaze that never seemed to settle for long on one thing. This gave the Frenchman an air of shiftiness he was never able to displace. He seemed to spend most of his days planning how to avoid being responsible for anything. As he lived in town, he was rarely present in the evenings, so upon his arrival in the morning, whether it was his week as *caporal du jour* or not, he'd yell for the sake of it – just to let everyone knew he was present. He insulted, kicked and derided Legionnaires for anything they did, his pet phrase being '*bande de branleurs*' (bunch of wankers). I never heard a constructive word from Wanger, in fact, and he did nothing but destroy morale.

I was now *chef de chambre*, in charge of a room and its occupants. These included Selker, a brown-nosing German; *Caporal* Berka, due to finish his two years in Djibouti in just a few months, during which he'd continue to as little as he possibly could; and Kit, a Légionnaire *1ère Classe* and the son of a Vietnamese refugee to France. A recent arrival from Nîmes, who owed his lack of promotion to falling asleep while on guard duty in Chad, Kit was already fed up with the *section* and wanted to be transferred to somewhere '*tranquille*'. The last man was Leeman, who'd been part of my first *section d'instruction* at Castelnaudary, under the poisonous LePeon. As often as they could, these men caught a cab into town, got drunk and had sex. It was all they could do with the time and money they had. It was also what everyone else did.

On Thursday evening that week, however, Dallas ordered compulsory attendance at a *3ème Section* barbecue, to be held just ouside the barracks. Rather than going into town to start the weekend early therefore, we all had to stick around.

By 1700 we'd waited half an hour and there was still no sign of Dallas. Even in such a short period of time, the *section* had broken up into its constituent national and language groups, and so it remained for the rest of what became a very tedious evening. There were plenty of free beers, although, as usual, we'd actually contributed to the costs at payday.

When he did put in an appearance, neither Dallas nor the *sous-officiers* went out of their way to talk to the Legionnaires in anything less than a dismissive, patronising manner. Tension filled the air, for there was no such thing as a social get-together here. During the course of the barbecue, out of his earshot at least, derision of our *chef de section* was quite open, with the NCOs again being accomplices to the undermining of morale and authority.

That *Lieutenant* Dallas and other officers even tried a social evening was simply a sop to the notion that all Legionnaires were brothers. It was an idea that people talked about, this bonding, but everyone knew that there was nothing to it.

That Thursday gathering was due to last just two and a half hours. Come 1900 hours, we couldn't get out of Quartier Monclar quickly enough. Dallas never again tried to hold a *section* barbecue.

18

PATROLS, ANNIVERSARIES AND UNREST

Demerde toi!
(Do it yourself!)

In the final week of January, *3ème Compagnie* left Quartier Monclar to take part in a patrol lasting around fourteen days. The company did the so-called *tournée du nord* at least twice a year, travelling north around the Gulf of Tadjoura to Obock, and then west out to Balho, near the Ethiopian border.

For much of the time, we sat in the back of open trucks as we made our way over the rough and dusty dirt tracks of the region, all the while, the fine, talc-like dust entering our pores. Yet we were forbidden from wearing the one item of issue kit that could have kept the stuff from our lungs: the *cheche*, a 2-metre length of cotton worn about the neck or as a form of Arab headdress. Under strict instructions from the *capitaine*, berets were to be worn at all times, and anyone caught wearing his *cheche* would be charged. Thus in less than half an hour, we were covered in this fine white dust and our lungs wore the lining of the track.

At the conclusion of a week of patrolling, we arrived at the foot of Mount Garbi on Thursday, 1 February. As usual, neither Dallas nor the *sous-officiers* deigned to confirm where we were. It was simply march where you were told. Having discussed this with some of the Brits, I'd learned that every year at this time, elements from the demi-brigade and the REP's *compagnie tournante* marched to the top of the 1688 metre mountain and assembled for a ceremonial parade. The annual parade was held in memory of the twenty-seven Legionnaires killed here on 3 February 1982 while on a training exercise. In bad weather, their twin-propeller transport had hit the side of the mountain, around 100 metres below the summit, killing all on board. Saturday, therefore, would mark the eighth anniversary of the disaster.

In the hour or so after we arrived, we selected a camp site on the edge of a wadi some kilometres from the summit. From where I rolled out my sleeping bag, I watched as two lean black men packed up and moved off, their camels in tow behind them. *Capitaine* Rocky had selected a position not far from that of the cameleers, leading them, it seemed, to make a swift departure. As I watched them, I understood that we shared at least two things: the difficult environment and suspicion.

Before first light, we set off for the summit of Mount Garbi. Along with rifle, rounds, rations, sleeping gear and the other things that went with living in the field, each Legionnaire carried at least 9 litres of water in his *sac à dos*, including a 5-litre container, carried on the orders of Dallas. In total we carried more than 30 kilograms on our backs.

After an initial march to the base of the mountain, we began our ascent. Leading from the front, Dallas chose to ignore a clearly discernible track 200 metres to our right, which Rocky took, but we followed Dallas. It was straight up. The march quickly became a movement upwards on all fours, sweat dripping off noses, some forty men grunting and groaning, clambering over the fractured basalt boulders as best we could.

Hovellet and Gatley, another Brit in the *section*, began to fall behind, eliciting a cry from some of the others: '*Putaines Anglaises!*' The ability to keep up on marches was one of the most important elements of being a Legionnaire; if you were weak on a march you had no respect from others. Worse still, from my point of view, the humiliating comments were coming from Frenchmen, usually the weakest in the *section* – at least until the arrival of more Poles, who, as national stereotypes go, seemed to consistently underachieve in the Legion.

Arriving at the shoulder of the mountain, about two-thirds of the way up, those of us at the front paused and waited for the others to catch up. With the chance for a brief rest, we took off our packs and, as usual, stood them upright in one line, one against the other. The view across the country below was glorious and I stood there, with rifle slung over my shoulder, hands on hips, looking out across a land of red and bleached green; a land whose severity, and the challenge that imposed, made it all the more attractive.

I was roused from my reflections by Dallas, who ordered me to retrieve his map case from the outside pocket of his *sac*. As I did so, the whole pack toppled over, forcing me to stand it upright again. It was almost empty. I handed him the map case.

Dallas had inserted the standard length of foam matting, so giving his *sac* a neat and regular form, as all we all did; the difference was he hadn't then filled it with the necessaries that would've brought the overall weight up to about 30 kilos. His came to 5 kilos, no more – just sleeping bag, wine *sac* full of water and perhaps some food.

Dallas moved off to read his map and I looked at the *Sergent-Chef*. '*Quoi?*' he demanded with an upward tilt of his chin. I said, 'There is almost nothing in his *sac*.' He looked at me for a moment, at the sac and then at Dallas' back, shrugged his shoulders and said, '*Je m'en fou.*'

I was furious and felt that old knot of hate inside me flame. Sure, I'd seen the same thing from the likes of LeFronde, Jakic and Lieber in the Training Regiment, but this was the real thing – a French Foreign Legion combat regiment. If an officer in the Australian Army ever did such a thing, he'd have been deemed unfit to lead. In the Legion it was a different story. One did as one wished, apparently with disregard, indeed disdain, for one's own men.

We reached the summit around 1500, and not long after, watched the arrival of two Puma helicopters, bringing water, rations and extra gear for the officers, and parade uniforms for all. We then moved over to the memorial. I sat in the sun and even in February it was hot. At this altitude though, the air was cooler and even the breeze had a freshness to it that gave you a shiver. I thought it meant a cold night, something very different from what we were used to.

The memorial sculpture was surrounded by a square of whitewashed rocks. In a concrete slab, 2 metres square, was set a vertical triangular slab over 2 metres high, like the tail-fin of an aircraft. On the fin was an inscription dedicated to those who had lost their lives. Below the memorial, some way down the mountain, I could see Legionnaires of the *compagnie tournante* among the wreckage that still marked the site of the crash. Most of our *section* went down the slope to join them, but Weng, a newly arrived Legionnaire, and I stayed and sat on the step of the memorial, enjoying the view and musing on whether anyone inside the aircraft could have survived the impact. I hoped not.

A couple of minutes passed and a cry carried up to us. Weng and I moved to the edge of the slope and were witness to a scene reminiscent of the Kubrick movie *2001: A Space Odyssey*. Someone had found what appeared to be a human thigh bone and was brandishing it over his head, while a squabble was taking place around him over who would get to keep the relic. Above the commotion, I heard one voice calling out clearly, 'Jesus, all I want is a fucking skull!'

That night it grew cold very quickly and the *section* camped just a few metres below the flat-topped summit. As we were preparing our meals, Menke, a Portuguese *ancien* of 2 REP, asked if he could borrow my cooking stove and a ground sheet for himself and his compatriot, Da Silas. In packing their gear, they had decided they could do without such fundamentals. '*Demerde toi*,' I replied and added a 'fuck off' for good measure.

Even if we hadn't received explicit instructions as to what to carry up, why do without sleeping kit on top of a mountain? So here were a couple of anciens begging gear off a maligned *fut fut*. I had no time for them. If they couldn't get it from anyone else, they'd just have to eat cold food and be cold and wet from the dew overnight. They did and they were. I set up my sleeping gear next to Gatley, who looked very tired. I made him a coffee and as the sun went down, I was glad I'd brought my woollen jumper and balaclava.

Next morning we changed into parade greens and formed up into a U-shape around the monument. Once the fog and cloud had cleared, the unmistakeable beating of helicopter blades could be heard. The aircraft soon disgorged its cargo of senior French *officiers*, who took station before the memorial. There was a short speech detailing the bravery of these men who had given their lives in the service of France. Then we presented arms, the clarion sounded *Aux Morts*, the Legion's Last Post, and there was much saluting.

With the parade over and dignitaries and uniforms seen off in the helicopter, we made our way down the mountain. In a race to the bottom of the slope, I watched Embisill lean against some rocks, which then toppled and crushed a finger of his right hand. He cried out and blamed the falling rocks on a recent addition to the *section*, Legionnaire Grean.

So, at the bottom of the first descent, *3ème Section* formed up around Embisill. Dallas declared that he would have to be taken off the mountain by helicopter. Why this was necessary was not evident; after all, Embisill could still walk. The *section* was ordered to give up all remaining water and rations to *Sergent-Chef* Postnoz and Embisill, for who knew how long they would have to wait for an aircraft? No one but me had any rations, so I dutifully surrendered them with some of my remaining water.

We carried on in groups, with Menke having a hard time of it. He kept stumbling, all the while complaining that he had to carry the machine gun. I offered to carry it, along with my own weapon, and he gave it up willingly. Menke carried on marching, a dark, sullen look on his face.

As we drew closer to our camp and the trucks, he suddenly wanted the weapon back. I knew his game. I refused, keen to wait until we were within earshot of the rest of the *section*. When that moment came, I handed it back and said, loudly, that if he ever again surrendered his weapon for somebody else to carry, I would shove it up his arse. No one said a thing. Carrion turned and narrowed his gritty grain-brown eyes on me for a moment but, like the rest, stayed silent. Menke fumed, puce-faced. I was learning that in part at least, a Foreign Legion *caporal* survived by asserting his right to humiliate others.

This may have been wrong, in the sense that it was a naked exercise of power, but it was right for where I was; and I had learned in Castelnaudary that aggression definitely had its uses in the Legion. For me, it was easy for me to rationalise. I was sending a message, being consistent and not tolerating those who would take advantage of me or anyone else.

Late in the afternoon, more than two hours after we had reached the vehicles, the *sergent-chef* and Embisill strolled in, sharing jokes and smiling. There had been no helicopter, but nor had there been any need for an evacuation.

On our return to Quartier Monclar, the men of *3ème Compagnie* found themselves doing lots of guard duties. On 15 February, I was to find myself yet again on PI duty; it was the fourth time in a week.

As usual upon our arrival in the *salle d'alerte*, we turned over the mattresses, invariably damp from the occupant of the night before, and checked the mosquito netting for rips. From my bag, I then pulled out the first *Newsweek* of fifty-two, ordered on a pay-later scheme. I was craving some international news, and I'd had to wait three months for it until today, the reason being that *Newsweek*, like *Private Eye* and other publications, was always put to one side at the company office.

Over at the *bureau de semaine*, sheltered by the giant plane trees just south of the U formation of barracks, *Sergent* Munez had been putting all my mail into a box stashed under the counter. I'd confronted Munez in his office, where a number of other NCOs stood about killing time, drinking coffee and gossiping. I asked for my mail. He said there was none. Politely,

I asked again, directing him to the box in question. His face grew flushed and he told me to *dégage* (piss off).

He put his face close to mine now, and repeated the direction. In reply to my asking a third time, he began to rave, calling me an '*intellectuel de la gauche*' (a socialist) and a *bon pour rien*. Even so, he picked up the box and tipped it onto the counter, the contents spilling out and down onto the floor. I thanked him, picked everything up and walked out. We never saw eye to eye after that.

A socialist? I don't think so. Over in the foyer, less than 200 metres from where we slept, just beyond the *ordinaire* located behind the company offices, the television played video porn – but there had to be things other than drinking and fucking, surely. I wanted to connect with the rest of the world, yet with the Legion in Djibouti, you were entirely removed and isolated from it. Your world shrank and the only thing that was important was that shrunken-down version of a world. This didn't seem to bother others much, I noticed.

Because they felt they no longer participated in the world, went the logic, why bother to follow it? The world did not care for them; they were being cared for by the Legion. Men spent two years in Djibouti with no idea of what was happening elsewhere. For example, this being late February 1990: author Salman Rusdie had been forced into hiding after having a fatwa issued against him, Nelson Mandela had just been released from prison, and the former Eastern Bloc was tumbling by the week as countries followed East Germany's lead – all these era-defining moments would've passed me by in *3ème Compagnie*, 13 DBLE, had I not gone against the grain and sought out news. *Chef de Corps Colonel* Le Flegg and his *officiers* did nothing to provide information or access to information for their Legionnaires.

If you wanted to read anything apart from the Legion's *Képi Blanc* you had to go out of your way to find it. This was in keeping with the Legion's goal of integration, which meant displacing a man's fears and failings with the ideals of the Legion, which were, put most simply, obedience and sacrifice. If you deprived a person of information relating to the outside world, what alternative did the man have? Over time, he had nothing but the Legion in his mind and in his heart and soul. *Sergent* Westway, the Gestapo man back at Aubagne, had said that, and he was right.

Perhaps it was just as well I was being kept so busy. I spent an additional week doing *caporal du jour* as I replaced Berka, who was missing at *appel*. He got twenty days in jail, but what did he care? When he got out, he got his *solde* and at least one night of leave so he could 'decompress' from the stresses of jail. And he was going back to France soon anyway. For some reason, the Legion never took away a man's pay, but instead gave him up to forty days in prison for the most minor infractions. No one cared that such lengthy stays in jail impacted on the *sections*, meaning more and longer duties for all.

After finishing up that week as *caporal du jour*, on Thursday, I quickly changed into the necessary *tenue de sortie* (walking-out uniform) of kepi, khaki short-sleeve shirt, shorts, long socks and black shoes, and caught a taxi into town and the Bar de Paris. This bar was off limits to Legionnaires so I liked to go there, and I liked the lack of pretence about the place. No dark lights or spaces to hide a face. Instead, there were very bright lights, a concrete floor, a lazy overhead fan, very long zinc-topped bar, and, for a toilet, a single hole in the floor. The only problem was that it sold East German beer, which gave me the most bloody awful hangovers.

That evening I met an American yacht owner, aged fifty or so, head lolling on his neck, with two *nyahs* draped about him. He had blue eyes and salt-and-pepper hair stuck to his head with sweat. Each *nyah* had a hand in one of his light-khaki trouser pockets and an arm around his bright red, orange and yellow tropical shirt.

'Hey, give me a hand, son,' he said. 'God damn it, these girls are beautiful, aren't they?'

I nodded, he was right about that.

'I just wanna take 'em home and play with 'em all . . . That tells me I'm too far gone to give a damn.'

He was right about that too, and the girls knew it. They were trying to get him out of the bar and into the street. His legs were rigid, though, like those of an unwilling dog being dragged to a bath, meaning the move towards the exit was abruptly halted. He put his hand into a shirt pocket and pulled out a wad of US dollars. The entire bar froze, as sweat-shiny black faces turned and eyes rounded in wonder. It was probably more than any of them had ever seen at one time or ever would. A heavy-bass Bruce Springsteen hit played.

I made the American put his money away and offered to buy him a drink. Taking a seat up at the bar, we were set upon by his two companions, and soon almost every other girl in the bar. Slim black hands found their way into our pockets, warm thighs pressed on ours, dark lips pressed into our necks and hot tongues into our ears. He tried to offer me some cash, a sort of retainer to deliver him to the port, but I refused any payment. Then, much to the outrage of the women, I half carried him out to a waiting taxi.

'You cannot enter the port, you're with the Legion,' the driver said, quite correctly. The authorities knew they'd probably steal something or, more likely, steal themselves away, so we were officially prohibited from the fenced-off section north-west of the city.

The taxi pulled up to the manned gate at the entrance to the port area and the two of us got out, the guard taking a close interest in my presence. I told him I simply wanted to escort my very drunk friend to his vessel. I asked the driver to wait and then turned back to face the Djiboutian and his AK-47. At that moment, we caught the Yank urinating very noisily against a wall, his legs splayed, one hand against the wall to support himself. Urinating in public was just not done in the city; it was regarded as a gross affront, the height of disrespect. The American, however, was beyond caring.

After yelling a report of the incident to his colleagues, some 20 metres away, the guard's eyes grew wide. He licked his lips and seemed ready to beat the transgressor with his rifle – this called for immediate action. I took a 5000 FDJ bill from my pocket and pressed it into the nightwatchman's hand, asking simply that the American be allowed beyond the gate to find his own way to his boat.

Thankfully, the guard nodded, and the last I saw of the drunken sailor was a stagger as he swayed off into the distance under the bright lights of the port, his shirt billowing like a colourful sail in a tropical breeze. I got back into the taxi and went back into town.

At the Bar la Lune, on Rue Éthiopie, a *nyah* presented me with a portfolio of references from her previous lover, an officer in the French Marines. She just sat down next to me when I went to order a drink and, as if selling real estate or a share portfolio, opened her plastic binder to reveal a number of signed notes and letters. One letter claimed she was clean and reliable, and not given to liaisons with anyone but the man taking care of her. I thanked her for the offer, but declined.

She shrugged, her breasts dark round grapefruits heaving in her designer frock. Into my ear she said: 'You are a good one. You do not hit, hurt, or humiliate the girls. There are few like you.' Then she walked away.

In the last week of March we were back on the Gulf of Tadjoura's southern coast, at the *Centre d'Entrainment Commandos d'Arta Plage*, or CECAP. We were there for three weeks, to earn our commando brevets, by doing hand-to-hand combat, demolitions (although, only *sergents* and above got to set charges) and ambushes (but only in the Legion sense).

We camped in three mechtars, or open huts, with corrugated-iron roofs and concrete floors, and slept on camp beds. I was in a group with Kapper, the Turkish-German guest worker who'd escaped a cycle of poverty by joining the Legion; Selker, another German, and one of the brown-nose brigade; and two Englishmen, Hovellet and Mum. The last of these had earned his nickname from fellow Brits because he walked like a woman and complained far too much. Mum had blessed his otherwise unremarkable body with a number of very aggressive tattoos, including, on his calf, a paratrooping Legionnaire, and skulls on his chest and arms.

Hovellet, on the camp bed across from me, was writing a letter to an old girlfriend who had just told him she had AIDS. For a black guy, he was almost pale. I watched him looking off into the distance, silently mouthing the months since he'd last had sex with her, trying to match this with his most recent AIDS test. I remembered that, just before coming on the course, he'd had a number of injections to clear up a lingering sexually contracted infection. The effect of the infection was so bad that he had to wear cotton swabs in his underwear, to soak up the dripping.

The commando course was not without its challenges. The physical ones were easy, but the mind games could be draining. There had been trouble between Hovellet and myself for some time, and behind my back one day up at CECAP, I heard the words '*fut fut*' uttered in his unmistakeable Midlands accent. Although he and I had finished our instruction at about the same time, I was a *caporal*; he was not, and not likely to be for some time. Most of his problems were due to his own stupidity and envy. But any snide remarks from a Brit (or anyone unless they carried a superior rank than you) had to be dealt with quickly.

So, during the afternoon siesta, I invited him out to the open field where the hand-to-hand combat training took place in the mornings. We stood toe to toe. His nostrils flared and I felt my heart rate increase to pulse in my ears. I was calm and rational, though. I told him that if he wanted to have a go at me he could, and I invited him to take the first swing.

After considerable yelling, his voice becoming hoarse and higher-pitched, Hovellet cracked: 'I hate this shitbag outfit and I want to get the fuck out!'

For some reason, I was now the confidant of this man – he was disillusioned and simply wanted to desert. The tough news was that we were in Djibouti, a place from which some tried to escape, but few ever did. A part of me ached to punch him, to revel in the bright-white, raw power of violence. This was a feeling that came to me often now. It came when I was dealing with stupidity, when rationality was not enough, or too much for some people. But I knew there was a kernel of truth in what he said.

'You don't have a problem with me,' I replied. 'You have a problem with the Legion. That is a personal problem. Sure, it's something we can talk about, but your problems become my problems when your behaviour affects me and my position. Understand?'

He nodded because he knew very well what he'd been doing.

'If you want to, Hovellet, we can fight every single bloody day, but I will never give up. Anyway, I don't think this would be very healthy for either of us. Do you?'

We looked at each other for a moment. We were not friends, nor did we even shake hands. He said, 'Yeah awright . . . Fuck it. Let's go get some kip.' So we did.

Because *Sergent* Carrion was off on a course to get promoted, our group was saddled with a *caporal-chef* from 13 DBLE's transport section. This fellow was physically unfit and knew next to nothing about *combat*, even French *combat*. He stated quite openly that he'd volunteered for the group-leader role just to score a commando badge. It would look good with his transport badge. Sometimes the Legion was indeed just like the Boy Scouts.

In the course of those few weeks, we paddled inflatable boats in the Gulf of Tadjoura, we marched, we did the water commando course, we fired our rifles and we killed a goat to eat. For the most part, we slept very little, but we were not tested on anything except a short, simulated, unarmed attack. To achieve your Legion commando badge, you just had to go along with the crowd.

In mid April, as a relief from the tedium of *garde* duty at Quartier Monclar, the *3ème Compagnie* went on terrain with a group of new *lieutenants*, who were out on a tour of Djibouti from France. We were to show these fellows how things were done in the Legion. For us, it meant another weekend of leave lost, along with any chance of getting away from company leadership for a while.

We carried out a motorised tour to Lake Abbe, in the far south-west of the country, on the border with Ethiopia, and then a short march beyond the salt lake. Not surprisingly, vehicles became bogged down in the difficult terrain. Most surprising, however, was *Capitaine* Rocky – jumping in to lend his troops a hand, shirt stripped off his back, shovelling mud. There was a degree of shock among the Legionnaires present, more than a few of whom pushed berets to the back of their heads, arranged sunglasses on noses, and simply watched. Ordinarily, our company commander contented himself with yelling abuse and ensuring that everyone wore a beret. This sudden bout of esprit de corps was just a cynical show for the new *lieutenants*. Even Dallas didn't sink to such hypocrisy. In fact, he looked embarrassed.

Days and hundreds of kilometres later, we were marching up from Lake Assal to the ridge that looked down on the Ghoubet, the most westerly point of the Gulf of Tadjoura. From that high ground, we could see how remarkable Lake Assal is; at some 157 metres below sea level the lake it lies at the lowest point in Africa. Arriving at the ridge, we were told there would be some wait before the arrival of trucks to take us back to the Quartier. So I sat down to contemplate the view and the geography of the Rift Valley and set to brewing up some coffee.

As the water came to the boil, Dallas looked over and said to one of the other *lieutenants*, '*Votre café arrive*.' He then made to take the canteen of hot coffee from my hand. My response was a terse 'Now, we don't want to start the young *lieutenant*s on bad habits do we, sir?', spoken in French, of course.

Like all his fellow officers, *Lieutenant* Dallas believed that we *soldats du rang* were their possessions. They lived under the misapprehension that we would give them anything and everything they wanted, no matter the inconvenience or the sacrifice. Dallas looked hurt.

It was fitting that the anniversary of the Battle of Camerone was just around the corner. Back in 1863 in southern Mexico, the Legionnaires had been surprised at breakfast, outnumbered, called on to surrender but refused; they'd protected the bodies of their *officers* with their own, saving the last rounds for a determined bayonet charge. And, to conclude, the three who survived did so because of the actions of a Mexican officer, who reportedly declared, 'How can I refuse anything to men such as you?' Great stuff. French officers loved it, especially the parts that dwelled on dying gloriously and Legionnaires giving their lives for them. I knew of no anglophone, or indeed any thinking man out here, who would have even dreamed of it. This was the point, of course: Legionnaires were not supposed to think and were discouraged from doing so. They were supposed to respond only with the heart, and their hearts were with the Legion and its embodiments, *les officiers*. What a difference there was in mentality. French officers could not understand, and *les fuckings* certainly would not.

The Camerone Day celebrations that year saw the beer warm and the wine cheap, bitter and nasty. But this failed to inhibit most of the luncheon diners in the shade of camouflage nets from eating and drinking to excess. It was a prelude to the events that took place in Djibouti city later that evening.

I went into town to get out of the quartier for a while, but there was something wrong, something violent in the air. The Muslim period of fasting, Ramadan, having just finished, the local people wore confident smiles and carried themselves more proudly than usual. No problem at all in that, but to then have a horde of Legionnaires, drunk and amorous, descend on the streets of the capital did not make for a pleasant evening. I went to bed.

In early May, *Capitaine* Rocky ordered that there would be *appel* at 0100 every morning. According to the *capitaine,* there were two reasons for this. One was an outbreak of violence in town between elements of the two main ethnic groups, the Afars and the Issas. Some five men had been killed and twenty wounded.

The other reason was the fighting currently taking place on the Djibouti–Ethiopian border. Doubtless, the two were related, but an analysis of the military and political situation was beyond most Legionnaires, and our company commander was probably incapable of giving it. The fighting resulted in the deaths of twenty Djiboutian soldiers. We didn't know the number of Ethiopian or Afar civilian casualties, nor did anyone particularly care. Was it a prelude to war? I didn't think so; it was too bloody hot to be having a war.

From my discussions with local taxi drivers and over beers at the Bar de Paris, I was aware that the locals viewed their government as being under the control of Somali Issas, and that it was a cause of great frustration to Djibouti's ethnic Ethiopian Afars. The Afars wanted, among other things, a share of political power, to make decisions for the future of their own ethnic community, which included the teeming thousands in Balballa. The ruling government wanted nothing of the sort, so a small insurgency took root and grew so strong that it challenged the AND.

Notwithstanding the nascent civil war, our footing continued unabated. Morning runs were very, very important. They were used not only to keep fit, but to demonstrate one's superiority over others and our enthusiasm for sport. They commenced just after *rassemblement* and saw us running 5, 10 or many more kilometres. We would run out the main gate, turn left along the potholed road into town, past houses or buildings with iron gates, and then make a tour of Gabode, across the Djibouti–Addis Ababa railway line, in front of the French Marines' base, and then back to Quartier Monclar. We ran on tarmac, dust and gravel, and through the throat-gripping stink of rotting offal, shit and burning rubbish.

During these morning sessions, I used to think we were running from something. Perhaps it was self-knowledge. But was it also the fear that the Djiboutians we ran past, squatting to relieve themselves amid the dust and decay, might one day stand up and spray us with bullets?

19

SUMMER MADNESS

Il veut me prendre la tête.
(He's playing with my mind.)

On Monday, 12 May, *Lieutenant* Dallas called all the *caporals* to his office. He spoke with each of us individually, then as a group. Apparently, we weren't doing our jobs properly; we were losing control of the Legionnaires and something had to be done. When I asked for specifics, the *lieutenant* was unable to elaborate. The implicit message was that we had his permission to bash Legionnaires. Dallas would be blind to bruised and bloodied faces.

This was particularly ironic in light of *Capitaine* Rocky's little chat to the company just a week before. He'd said that any bashing of a Legionnaire by a *caporal* would find the man responsible placed in jail for an extended period.

I had considered such mixed messages before, particularly while attempting to fathom the random approach to discipline and punishment dished out at Castelnaudary. Now, as a *caporal* in a combat regiment, I had the chance to set an example and

During Operation Godaria with surrendered Ethiopian weapons.
TOP: Inspecting a wrapped pistol. BOTTOM: Surrendered weapons in cases.

TOP: Some of the many different surrendered weapons. An anti-aircraft gun (*left*) and a rocket-propelled grenade launcher (RPG) (*right*).
BOTTOM: Playing the fool with the weapons stash.

TOP: A river of refugees just kept coming during Operation Godaria.
BOTTOM: We provided what medical care we could.

TOP: Feeding the Legionnaires meant peeling a lot of potatoes.
BOTTOM: During Operation Godaria, running to a helicopter for water resupply.

TOP LEFT: The author at the front gate to Quartier Amilakvari, Arta, in Djibouti.

TOP RIGHT: Learning how to fire a rocket-propelled grenade at the range near CECAP, Djibouti.

LEFT: In Sardinia during NATO's Operation Dragonhammer.

TOP: The author in parachute rig preparing to jump, Corsica.
BOTTOM: Jumping over Camp Raffalli, Calvi, Corsica.

TOP: At Djibouti receiving basic instruction on diving.
BOTTOM: During Operation Iskoutir, in Djibouti, volleyball was the *section* sport.

LEFT: Marching in the hills behind Camp Raffalli.

BELOW: The sentinel: a Legionnaire alone with his thoughts and his future, Quartier Amilakvari. It was on the area's highest ridge, which extended west, dominating the terrain south of the Gulf of Tadjoura.

ensure that things were set out as clearly as possible for those in my charge. First, though, I needed someone to do the same for me. Either bashings were allowed – always for a valid reason, of course – with each incident reported to a *section* leader and handled professionally; or, bashings were explicitly wrong and an abuse of power. In the latter scenario, the *caporal* would be responsible for his actions, since the premise was that by bashing a man, he'd failed in some way to communicate what he wanted of the victim. He had lost control and resorted to violence.

As things currently rested in *3ème Section*, neither Legionnaires nor *caporals* knew where they stood and Dallas won no matter what happened. Was he not seen as someone stamping his authority? Perhaps even a 'hard man'? After all, the exercise of violence and, more importantly, the threat of its exercise were determining factors in the social relations between Legionnaires and ranks above them.

There were many men here who understood little else but the power of the fist, boot or knife. A failure to exert control using one of these methods was often seen as a weakness in a *caporal*. Besides, what else was there as a sanction? To be put in jail, while somewhat inconvenient, was hardly severe. Access could always be had to alcohol and the Legionnaire's *solde* remained intact.

Fundamentally, though, just as in the Training Regiment, there was still no one line, no consistent approach to the issue. But then, this was entirely intentional, I realised. The product of miscommunication regarding discipline through violence was precisely what the Legion wanted and demanded of those in its ranks: fear and unthinking obedience to orders.

I might have known the answer to this particular riddle, but it hardly made the challenge of trying to be a professional soldier any easier. And neither did events over the next couple of weeks.

On a day in early June I was abruptly banished to participate in *garde antenne* down at Douda. Two things happened that may have been related. The day before, Tuesday, when walking by me on the parade ground, Dallas told me I was to pass *rapport capitaine*. I asked him why, to which he responded with an irritating '*Tu vas voir*' (You'll see). He and I knew that when you hadn't requested a *rapport* and one was set down, it almost invariably meant you were up on a charge.

I asked around in the *section*, and no one could shed any light. The French have a splendid phrase that sums up this state of affairs: '*Il veut me prend la tête*' (He's playing with my mind). Dallas was playing the games that were played too often in the Legion. I wouldn't find out the charge until I was actually standing in front of *Capitaine* Rocky, ready to receive my punishment.

Come Thursday, 7 June, while in Monclar getting the lunch rations to take back to the *garde*, I learned that I was indeed up on a charge, the crime being that the packs kept on shelves in the back room of my *chambre* were badly arranged. *Sergent* Carrion had apparently remarked on the arrangement to Dallas, who in turn paid a visit. To give him his due, our *section* leader was in a quandary: his *sergent* wanted me in jail but there was nothing concrete to pin on me.

Carrion was of the old school. He believed all Legionnaires should endure a life, if not short, then at least brutish and nasty, in order to desensitise them to what was required. He believed in beating and humiliation; I did not, so he didn't like me at all. In discussions with other Legionnaires, he called me a 'soft intellectual'. A much more significant factor was that I was different. I wondered whether to treat Carrion's comments as a compliment.

Before heading back to Douda, I learned a far more important piece of news. That same morning I had been sent off to Douda, my friend Gungie Whyte had been killed and Legionnaire Weng had lost an eye in an incident at the mortar range, beyond Oueah. According to another Brit who was there, Caporal Thurley, the events unfolded in the following way. The *3ème Compagnie's* 81 mm mortar *section* was firing live rounds at a target while, some kilometres away, the 120 mm *section* of the CCAS was practising on the same target. That was the plan, at least, until one of the CCAS teams fired at the *3ème Compagnie* position in error. According to Thurley, our 81s had just ceased firing and most of the *section* had returned to their truck for a coffee when three 120 mm rounds came down near the tubes, killing Gungie instantly and badly wounding Weng.

How such a thing could've happened on a range, with all the checks that normally took place, and who exactly was responsible, was not clear. The likelihood of an inquiry was remote. The Legion looked after its own – or rather, it did not. Gungie Whyte was a bloody good lad, and more than that, he was a friend to many. Everyone, especially the Brits, would miss his smile, sense of humour and willingness to help his mates.

At 0220 on Wednesday 13 June, my final morning on *garde antenne*, I finished a poem about Gungie. It might not have been much good, but it summed up the way I felt.

The Day They Killed Caporal *William Whyte*

Caporal *William Whyte* was a Scot –
From Dundee he came.

He'd been in the Paras
And fought in the Queen's own name.

He joined the French Foreign Legion –
Determined he signed on.
He did his first five years
Then decided to carry on.

In Djibouti we met –
A wink and a nod 'like 'ken'.
A worldly gnome's smile and
He'd sup another cool green Heineken.

We lost William Whyte on a long dusty range.
The mortars it was and a radio lark.
One-twenties raining seven heads of death
That blew his life apart.

After they killed William Whyte
The Colonel as his want
Spoke and he cried,
To the ranks of green and red and képis blanc.

The Colonel, his mask comical and sad
Addressed his Legion's cool silent stare.
He said – and who didn't believe?
'Caporal Whyte, he died like a Legionnaire.'

But we of the Thistle and Union Jack –
The land of the Southern Cross beside,
Of the Orange, White and Green
Can never forget how William Whyte, he died.

Once I'd returned to Monclar, a few of us got together to make sure Gungie's coffin made it back to his family. Each of us contributed what we could to avoid what would have been a highly unsatisfactory final resting place for this great Scot.

The alternative was burial in the Legion's cemetery in Djibouti, and I knew the place – a godforsaken wasteland filled with anonymous dusty mounds. It was only on the sacred day of Camerone, when a guard was mounted and photographs taken, that the dead were honoured with the addition of their names. Each year, before the guard was in place, prisoners were trucked in and made to hammer a white wooden cross into the ground at the head of each mound. Which wooden cross to which mound was of no concern. The Legion's indifference meant that this was not somewhere we wanted to leave Gungie. He belonged with his family and the glens and green grass of Scotland.

Because we had so few *caporals* in the *section*, *Caporal* Lafaible, a Frenchman who was with me on the *caporal* course in Castelnaudary, was transferred to *3ème Section*. Lafaible formerly held the cushiest job in 13 DBLE: as *garde piscine*, looking after the regimental swimming pool, just 50 metres or so from the foyer. He had his own room, video and no camp guard duties. What a life for two years. An English speaker, he was very pissed off at having to join us in the combat company. 'I will be out of that *section* before anyone notices I am there,' he said on hearing the news.

According to *Sergent* Fat Indian, Lafaible had brought his girlfriend out from France to Djibouti. She got herself a job in the Bar Flamingo, another one of the bars just off Rue Éthiopie. Serving drinks and then, later, serving on her back, she earned money beyond her wildest dreams. As the only white woman in Djibouti prepared to sell her body, she charged enormous amounts for her pleasures. So Lafaible was not happy, either at being with us or with his girlfriend.

As for me, I was just happy I didn't have to pass *rapport capitaine* after all. Nothing was said. I just never had to turn up. Instead, with *garde antenne* over, I prepared to head out on patrol again. We were gone for two weeks this time, out in the sweltering heat of summer Dikhil and the Ethiopian border.

We returned to Quartier Monclar on Thursday, 14 June to make a discovery that really did piss me off. *Chambre* 14, my room, the room I shared with Selker, Berka, Leeman and others, had been ransacked and robbed. This was despite there being Legionnaires next door and Selker in the area for much of the day in question. He had stayed back from patrolling as he was doing the *garde piscine* course. His brown-nosing had finally paid off.

As Selker put it, on the evening the robbery took place, he locked up the room and went out on the town; then, having taken a girl, he returned in the morning to find it in a shambles. None of the Legionnaires in the next room heard anything at all, which I found rather surprising. After all, the contents of the lockers were strewn together in a pile in the centre of the room with the lockers on top of the mess. The place had been turned upside down.

I entered the room, with Dallas, Carrion and the Fat Indian behind me. The *lieutenant* was the first to speak. 'It must have been a fucking nigger,' he declared, his name for a Djiboutian.

Initially, I didn't know what to think. Sorting through the mess, I found only two of my things missing: some cash and my Australian passport, secured on my trip to the UK the year before. Everyone in the room had had money stolen, even Selker.

My Walkman remained, as did Leeman's CD player, watches and all manner of things electronic and valuable.

Dallas argued that the thief must have climbed up the barbed wire outside, forced open the window to the back room, climbed into the roof after removing a ceiling panel, and then dropped into the main room, having removed another ceiling panel. It took me less than ten seconds to see the flaws in this little scenario. So I put it to the *lieutenant*, with all due respect, that any man capable of climbing the barbed wire at night and crossing open ground to the barracks, and back again, had the balls of a Legionnaire. He would've known that getting caught meant a death sentence, that was for sure. The Legion handed over any locals who broke the law to the Djiboutian authorities, who dealt with them very harshly.

And there were other questions unanswered by the *lieutenant*'s theory. How did the thief know that the room was empty? If he was a local, would he not have taken every valuable he could find? And why place a stool under the panel he had removed and escape that way, when he could've used the back door, which opened from the inside? Finally, why was there no disturbance of dust up there in the roof compartment? On this last point, Dallas made a great show of climbing into the roof to look for evidence, an act that achieved nothing except to demonstrate the extent of his ever-expanding waistline and to evoke in his men a nervous anticipation he'd fall through the roof.

Dallas and his two *sergents* looked at me now in silence. Until at last the *lieutenant* spoke: 'You are a real Sherlock Holmes, Mason . . . So who was it then?'

Of course, this I didn't know. More than likely it was Selker, working with one or all of the fellows next door. 'I can't be sure,' I replied.

'Right,' said Dallas. 'It was a nigger. You have a problem with that?'

And of course, this was the crucial point. Carrion and the Fat Indian visibly tensed. 'No. I understand.'

They had me over a barrel. They knew I could not take the issue any further. There was no proof. Plus, I would face jail if I admitted to Legion security that I had a passport. Unless someone was caught red-handed, the investigation of the *chambre* 14 robbery created too many problems for everyone.

As Dallas was leaving the room, he turned and said, 'Oh, since you are so intelligent, you can take the *bureau de semaine*.' In other words, after a fortnight of patrolling, I'd just been consigned to a tedious week of sitting and sleeping in the company office, rather than being outside doing sport, drinking beer or sleeping. Carrion, ever the fair-weather crony, curled his thin lips and his smile was a sucking wound.

Come the start of July, the heat across the coastal plain beside the Gulf of Aden was sweltering. The only good pieces of news were that it didn't get much hotter than this, and in 13 DBLE they at least took steps to allow us some respite. In the early part of the month, the *3ème Compagnie* tents were set in the Forest of Day, at an elevation of some 1500 metres, inland from the Gulf of Tadjoura's northern coastline. Over a period of a few weeks, the entire regiment would be rotated through the camp as a relief from the heat on the coast.

Getting to Day (actually pronounced Die) involved plenty of the usual unnecessary drama. As *caporal du jour*, I had to oversee the packing of cases, including the ever-important *caisse popotte*. On the evening before departure, we got to bed at 2300, only to then be woken up two hours later. At 0230 we were at the military area of Djibouti port, loading trucks and ourselves onto a 30-metre landing craft. As tired as we all were, word soon came from *Capitaine* Rocky that no one was to take off their webbing, in an attempt to use it as a pillow. After all, we didn't want to give the French Marines the wrong impression, did we? The *capitaine* though, retired to a small cabin and slept.

Alone, away from the shadow forms trying to catch a wink of sleep on the deck, I stood and leaned on the side of the vessel as it turned out of the port, past rusted container ships flying Panamanian flags, and headed north. From the starboard bow, I watched the sun rising and thought of Henry de Monfreid and Arthur Rimbaud, men who lived the thought that real life was 'elsewhere' while travelling in this part of the world. Rimbaud I'm sure would certainly have appreciated the view. I remembered his poem 'A Season in Hell', particularly the line: 'It has been found again. What? Eternity. It is the sea mingled with the sun.'

After arrival at the port of Tadjoura, we loaded ourselves into the trucks and headed due west into the interior, for Randa and then the Forest of Day. The contrast between the bare semi-desert and dusty ridges we'd inhabited since November and this verdant land was extraordinary. The Forest of Day, while only some 15 square kilometres, was a place one might have expected to find in the pages of Tolkein's *Lord of the Rings*. It was possible to walk to the edge of the escarpment, which dropped thousands of feet to the coastal plain, and look south-east over the purple and red ridges to the blue of the Gulf and the horizon.

The trees of African juniper were reputedly hundreds of years old and not to be touched for firewood. They reminded me of fig trees but with far coarser trunks, twisted with age and the difficulty of surviving in this land. At this height, the days and nights were markedly cooler than at sea level. I learned much later that nearly 90 per cent of the forest had been lost in the last two centuries, and much of that in the last fifty years, coinciding with the visits of the French military.

Our *section* had been allocated three tents. One was set aside for the NCOs and another for the majority of the *soldats du rang*. The last tent was reserved for Dallas, along with those of us doing a course over the next week, as well as Wanger, now serving as *3ème Section* medic, and young Drabble, who had become Wagner's lap dog.

I was fortunate to be among those signed up for the Stage 12.7, or .50 calibre machine-gun course, and therefore in the less-crowded, third tent. My only problems were the proximity of my canvas cot to the *lieutenant's* and the medical checks.

Caporal Schnebel presented himself for medical attention one day with the words 'Ma bite me fait mal' (My cock hurts). Not a pretty sight, his penis was a mass of putrid pustules. The German had long delayed seeking medical help, hoping the altitude and cool air would help, but it obviously hadn't.

There were a dozen of us doing the Stage 12.7, Leeman, Keyman, Hovellet and Lafaible, among them. From the start, our instructor, *Sergent-Chef* Reed, outlined what would be required. There were to be written and practical tests, as well as a series of hillside marches carrying the heavy Brownings. I stood in the rank behind Lafaible and watched him tremble. He raised his hand and, in a quivering voice, explained that he was not a volunteer for the course, he was sick, and it would be better if he left. The *sergent-chef* looked at him and blinked. We didn't see Lafaible for the remainder of the course.

Reed was an Irishman and approached his job in a manner closer to the British or American style. He cut out the yelling, screaming and intimidation that marked the usual Legion training. In short, he was the best instructor I'd yet seen in the French Foreign Legion. And he had one habit that particularly amused all his students.

Each morning we would go for a run, following him up burnished brown, rocky hillsides and along dry creek beds, before stopping every so often to perform a range of arm exercises. Then, to provide the legs with a different stimulus from pounding along the tracks, he'd lead us on star-jump exercises. What *Sergent-Chef* Reed would not do, though, is don underwear, preferring to 'allow me bits to breathe', as he put it. And breathe they did – the head of his cock appearing from his shorts at regular intervals, mid jump, like some inquisitive snake. Combined with the earnestness of his instruction, it made many of us curl our mouths and smile.

As Reed had promised, we twelve *stagiers* with our four 12.7 Brownings marched. We marched with bulging *sacs* weighing 25 kilograms, rifles and one machine gun between three of us. As a *chef de batterie* (crew chief), I took the tripod and the siting mechanism, while Keyman and Leeman, my team members and both competent lads, shared the body, the barrel and some fifty practice rounds. In all, we each carried over 40 kilograms.

After the first short march, distances became longer, until eventually we were gone for two whole days. We became familiar with the weight and after each short rest we could prepare ourselves mentally for the loads we had to carry. At day's end, we'd be wet with perspiration, our shirts and shorts a dark green colour, soon replaced by salty tidal marks once the material dried out.

During the course's exams, I noted with interest the French instruction pamphlet on the machine gun, particularly a line on page 89, paragraph 126: 'The weapon is normally transported on vehicles or on the backs of mules.' Indeed, we were mules.

•

On Monday, 16 July, after a march to waiting trucks, we were driven back to Quartier Monclar and the stifling heat. The day after our return, I was dispatched to the *infirmerie* to report on Lafaible's medical condition; in effect, to spy. Aware that the reluctant ex-pool cleaner was a complete slacker, Dallas said he didn't believe the word of a '*toubib*' (doctor) and sent me to assess the lie of the land.

Despite it being early morning, I found *Caporals* Lafaible and Rovery in with the medics watching a video, eating chocolate and drinking beer. Rovery, the English *fut fut*, had reportedly hurt his knee up at Day but, like the supposedly *malade* Lafaible, he looked very happy indeed. Lafaible confided in me, 'I'll be going back to France soon.' When I asked how, he and Rovery laughed and offered me a beer.

Once back before Dallas, it was obvious he simply wanted an assessment from me that would reinforce his own views. Lafaible may well have been a shifty, lazy bastard, but I preferred to deal with him myself. And Dallas had been doing some shirking of his own. He'd become so fat now that he no longer took part in the painful but exhilarating early-morning runs with the *section*. After the morning parade, he would excuse himself and take off for a frolic in the swimming pool. He began to look like a sated water rat. Aged just twenty-five or so, he had no medical problem; he was just overweight and couldn't keep up with the rest of us. And he probably couldn't see what a hypocrite he was either.

'Difficult to say, sir,' I said in response to his questions about Lafaible. 'The doctor is probably the only person with all the information.'

The *lieutenant* pursed his lips and sent me on my way.

I was happy to leave, but I was happier to get the hell out of Monclar and down to Rue Éthiopie. As soon as a free evening presented itself, I went into town for a girl. I wanted – no, I ached for – the touch of another person. Even if I paid for her time and her body, perhaps for a moment I could convince myself there was more to the world than the Legion.

I met Fatima in the unassuming Bar de Paris. A tall Ethiopian woman, with shining black eyes, evenly spaced, gleaming white teeth, and hair plaited into fine knots over her head. Aside from the local languages, she spoke English, French and Italian. She wanted to be an engineer in the United States but somehow had to finance the dream.

Outside in the rotting night air and the dust of Djibouti city, one of the ubiquitous battered green taxis was ready to take us away. We slid into the back, across the slimy plastic that covered the seat. Fatima had an apartment at the Plateau de Serpent, in the respectable north-east of town, and a few minutes later I was inside the building, her hot hand in mine, leading me up bare wooden stairs to her room.

There was a single bulb hanging from the roof, and as she moved around the room to light candles, she seemed to dance in shadows against the wall. I stood foolishly, in khaki issue shorts, shirt and long socks, watching her. She flipped a switch on a radio that sang songs of Ethiopia while I undressed, laying out my uniform to preserve the creases.

She lay on the top of the bed, her body long, naked and very black. Below her was a multicoloured Ethiopian-woven cloth covering the bed like a quilt. I pulled the condom from my shirt pocket, rolled it on, and moved between her thighs. She neither wrapped her arms around me nor spoke. Instead, while I moved inside her, her arms were stretched out behind her head and she watched my face intently, a quizzical look that was more knowing and amused than uncertain or fearful.

At last, when I'd finished, she rolled away from me and pulled some of the filmy cloth to her breasts and covered her thighs. I pulled the ridiculous rubber thing from me, tied the end into a knot and threw it under the bed. Then I paused, wondering how many others had done the same thing. So I looked. And there, on the dusty wooden floor, were clumps of them, like multicoloured dried foreskins, each one abandoned and left to speak for a spasm of pleasure.

I thanked Fatima, paid her, and offered her a lift back into town. I never had sex with a *nyah* again.

By early August, the dearth of *caporals* in *3ème Section* was becoming critical. Rovery and Lafaible were still in the *infirmerie*, their fourth week there. Wanger was in the *bureau de semaine*, after which he'd be returning to France, Gatley had been transferred away from the company and Potter was in prison. That left just Schnebel and me.

As if we didn't have enough guard duties, one more appeared. Someone had been stealing clothing from the *sous-officiers'* washing line. As a result, a new *garde* was placed at the clothesline, equipped with infra-red headsets, rifles (but no rounds) and pick-handles. So it was that eight men from the internationally revered French Foreign Legion spent long nights on their bellies, guarding underwear.

It was fortunate then that I found myself at Douda, this time guarding Djibouti's ammunition dump, a task that was certainly preferable to the regular kit and material reviews over at the regiment. Why, I wondered for the thousandth time, was there such a priority placed on these reviews instead of on weapons training, life on terrain, and combat skills? Many of the newer Legionnaires would never even set eyes on the Legion's light machine gun during their time in Djibouti. But they'd get the message all right that the presentation and review of light bulbs, blankets and brooms was more important than combat efficiency.

That was life in the *quartier*.

Another reality was the fact that we'd heard nothing official about the war in Kuwait, where Operation Desert Shield had been under way since 7 August. No announcements from our officers, nothing about the implications for Djibouti or our possible role in the conflict. It was extraordinary. At night I listened to the BBC World Service on my small radio and followed what appeared to be the most significant war in decades. In Djibouti, the Legion carried on as if nothing was happening.

Next up on our badge-collecting summer was the *Stage Tireur d'Élite*, the course for marksmen and snipers. So, along the familiar N1 road we were trucked to Ali Sabieh, a southern Djibouti town of a few thousand people, flat-roofed, whitewashed stone and brick buildings, and dusty streets. Close to the town was a base formerly occupied by *3ème Compagnie*, 13 DBLE. The camp had an unsealed airstrip and access to the railway link from Addis Ababa to Djibouti. Like the other former Legion outposts at Hol Hol, Dikhil and Obock, this one had been handed over to the AND at independence in 1977.

We set up our tents at the rifle range next to the AND base. Unfortunately for a marksman course, there were problems with the rifles. We were not using the FRF1 rifle, the standard *tireur d'élite* weapon, nor were we using the FRF2, the weapon that was to replace it. Instead, we had semi-automatic MAS rifles, weapons we would never see again after this course. Worse was the fact that there weren't enough to go around, so we had to share one rifle between two men, meaning that the rifle had to be adjusted to the requirements of each firer after every shoot.

Every time one of us missed the cardboard silhouette during the various shoots – at 200, 300 or 400 metres – we had to walk up 'the 673', a steep rocky hill next to the range, so called for its metric height above sea level. We'd fire five rounds, check the target for hits, and if one round had completely missed, up the hill we'd go. Some men were up and down that hill five or six times a day.

If the weaponry situation wasn't farcical enough, the night navigation exercises took Legion incompetence and bloody-mindedness to a whole new level. The first was an exercise on the southern side of the Grand Barra, the huge yellow-dust plain I'd visited by bus on arrival in Djibouti. There were three teams, led by Thurley, a Frenchman named Buffons, and me, and the exercise required that each team reach a number of checkpoints over a distance of some 25 kilometres. It was clear that Buffons could not read a map and was a danger both to himself and to those he led. With temperatures of a least 25 degrees Celsius at night, daytime temperatures near 45 degrees and very limited water, the consequences of incompetence could be fatal.

That's not to say we were given the appropriate instruction before hand, of course. *Sergent* Carrion took the one-hour seesion on navigation, which offered plenty of theory on scale and distance, but no practical application. Out of the twenty-eight men doing the course, only five could read a map, and fewer a compass.

A week or so later, the teams were out all night. This exercise, Dallas insisted, was designed to test our ability to set up an observation post at a designated point. After being dropped off at 2100 hours, we had less than eight hours to get to the position and dig in.

My team reached a hill next to the railway line, which I knew was fairly close to our designated point. I scaled the hill and, despite the pitch-black night, I could see one of the trucks not 500 metres away; lights were on and someone was using a gas stove. The hill we were after was just beyond the truck. At that moment the Fat Indian came on the radio.

At the end of our brief conversation, I turned back to my team members and said there'd been a change of plan. With the map spread out on the ground between us, and a mini-torch in my hand, I showed them where we ought to have been, and then explained that we'd just been ordered to construct the observation post where we were now, by the railway line. I selected the sites and the men began digging. There was no time for sleep.

In the pre-dawn light we settled down in our positions and waited for *Sergent* Fat Indian to arrive and carry out an examination of the observation post. It was fine, he said – a shame, though, that we were on the wrong hill. When I reminded him that he was the one who detailed our position, he simply laughed. It got worse.

Later in the morning, at the debrief back at the range, Dallas told us that we had only just met the standard, and it was unfortunate that some men couldn't read a map. 'Even those who believe they are the best map readers can get it wrong,' the *lieutenant* added. 'There is no excuse, Mason.'

After we'd been dismissed, one of the others on my team came over, shook his head and said, '*Quelle bande d'encules*' (What a bunch of arse-fuckers). He was dead right about that.

A few nights after this, the night exercise involved reaching a series of designated checkpoints, at each of which we'd recieve instructions on to the next one. All the while, teams had to march and stay alert for 'the enemy' – the Fat Indian and Carrion, somewhat fittingly – who would be trying to capture us. Another order from the *lieutenant* was that if we saw a green flare, we should rally to it immediately. Teams were issued with red flares, so that, if someone was injured, we could use the flare as an alarm and help would come to us.

Some hours later, having cleared the last checkpoint, I was leading my team south along the edge of the largest wadi in the area, towards our final objective, a well only 8 kilometres away. With a healthy advantage so far, we'd be first home and get some much-needed sleep. About 3 kilometres out, however, a green flare appeared almost a kilometre south of the previous checkpoint. Of course, we turned back.

Over an hour later, we arrived to find *Sergent-Chef* Postnoz and Potter waiting in a vehicle. The idea of green flares only being used to rally appeared to be news to Postnoz; he'd just been firing off some 'spares'. He radioed Dallas for confirmation. After a few crackled exchanges, the *sergent-chef* signed off, '*Merde*,' he said.

Postnoz put my team into the truck and drove us east for a while, parallel to our proposed course, before dropping us off beside a track in the still darkness. Unfortunately, the road on which we'd travelled was not on my map, nor from the terrain was it possible to determine how far south or beyond the well we were. I explained the situation to the team. Should we blunder about looking for a reference point and risk being taken by one of the vehicles seeking to capture us? Or follow this track to what I believed to be a village on the edge of my map and then get to the well by a sure route? A route certainly not covered by the *lieutenant* – an outflanking manoeuvre.

I chose the second option, although it cost us two extra hours of marching. At 0100, we crossed a wadi; in the distance now was a luminescence on the horizon, the small fort that dominated the little village of Ali Adde. The four of us approached the fort with its large wooden gate and crenellated towers. 'Anyone there?' I shouted.

To the sleepy AND guard, we must have been an unusual sight. Four men with rifles, dressed in *goulie* suits – camouflage outfits made from old combat greens and strips of sandbag sewn on the outside. The sentry called his superior and I was invited into the fort.

The ground inside the fort was paved with brick, the internal walls a white that lent the air an opalescence, like being under the sea. The *chef de poste* was a tall man with very high cheekbones, and his eyes laughed when I shook his hand and asked the way to the well. This was a man I could trust.

Taking out my map, I pointed to our present position, our goal and a *chamelière* (camel track) that provided an easy route between the two. I wanted to know where the *chamelière* began. We had only to continue 500 metres north from the fort along an unsealed track, he replied, and from there the *chamelière* headed west.

Before we left, the *chef* invited us to fill our water bottles. He and I shook hands and he said, '*Bonne chance*.' I didn't think he was necessarily referring to this night's march. I thanked him and, before turning away, we held each other's gaze for a moment. What would the future hold for him and for me?

An hour or so later, we found ourselves the only team to reach the well, the only team to respond to the green flare, and the only team to get at least a little sleep. During the course of the morning, most of the others were picked up by vehicles. It would take until early in the afternoon, however, before

Buffons' team had been located. The four of them were tired and dangerously dehydrated. They had drunk all their water early on and got themselves lost, but instead of waiting under a tree, they'd carried on marching. Buffons had no idea what he was doing.

Later, Buffons came into the accommodation tent and told the assembled *stagiers* that he'd been thrown off the course. And not because he couldn't find the well, but because he gave the *lieutenant* a piece of his mind. He could lie to us and himself if he wanted, that didn't matter. The real problem was that he was sent out with other men even though he was unable to read a map, and Dallas knew it.

As always amid the frustrations that accompanied all aspects of Legion life, there were some moments during our time on the *Stage Tireur d'Élite* that shone through and made the challenge worthwhile. Moments of connection, realisation, that transcended the circumstances in which they occurred.

The first was when, two weeks into the course, and more than a little fed up, I decided it was time for a drink. One of the Brits volunteered to come with me on a beer run, so we made a plan to make our way to the *gite d'étape* (rest house), 3 kilometres from the range camp along a dry wadi.

We dropped into the narrow wadi after *appel* at 2200 and passed underneath the AND watchtower at the old Legion base. After an hour or so, we arrived at the *gite* to find its gate locked and the nightwatchman reluctant to let us inside. Some gentle negotiation and the sight of our FDJs however, soon saw us leaving the place with a case of beer each.

Walking back along the sand of the wadi bed was thirsty work, and we decided to have a couple of beers while striding along. We must've been noisier than we thought, because we woke the Djiboutian guard in his watchtower. He challenged us, all the while cocking his weapon with a snap of spring and metallic parts. It was best to be frank.

'We're Legionnaires, going back to camp at the range.'

'Why don't you use the road?' This was a very good question, and there was uncertainty and an element of fear in his voice. He was alone.

'This is part of a test for our course, and vital for survival in the Legion – the bringing in of beer undetected.' At this he laughed and told us to go on.

The soldier's bond. Across the world, and no doubt across time, men in uniform understand life in the ranks. When you were in the ranks, you did what you could to make things better. After all, if you didn't, no one else would.

Another special moment, though far more profound, occurred during one of the interminable exercises around Ali Sabieh. That's when I saw something that motivated me to do something years later.

It was early morning, and I lay just below the crest of a ridge, scanning across the Djiboutian border into Ethiopia. Dark sharp rocks pressed into my hips as I watched tall, too-lean men with coarse white cloth around their waists and daggers slid into wide leather belts. Tilting back my beret, I leaned further into the rubber eyepiece of the telescopic sight. I felt the rubber form a seal and when I moved a little I felt the soft suction. I was bound to the weapon and it seemed to be an extension of myself; my brain, my eye, the telescopic sight and the round that it carried in the chamber.

Emaciated men moved between camel thorn trees, leading camels with ribs that threatened to spring from their hides. One man had wiry black hair and obsidian black eyes rimmed with red that spoke of too many days in the bright hard light and windblown sand. When he grimaced, which he did every few paces on his plastic sandals, he exposed a wide gap in perfect-white front teeth. The men carried AK-47s across their shoulders; the camels carried weapons on their backs. They were bringing rifles into Djibouti to supply those ethnic Afars who felt themselves disenfranchised by the Issa leadership of the Djiboutian President.

I marvelled at the life led by these men and their camels, moving across a country pitiless to the weak and the ill-prepared. It was a place where people died too early, from tripping a mine, from the lack of a few drops of water or from a bullet like the one I had chambered. I wondered at the toughness of such men, in a land that was hard and intolerant to weakness. It was watching them that inspired me to another adventure – I wondered what it would be like to walk across Australia with camels of my own.

I watched the men move off through the waves of heat and between the camel thorn trees, then radioed back to Dallas. Later, I wrote out on a piece of paper the route I thought I'd take across Australia – across the heart of the continent, from the most easterly to the most westerly point – and slipped the small page into my pocket, where it seemed to glow with promise.

It was Friday, 7 September, but there was one more exercise to complete. Dallas told us we would be dropped into the desert on the Djibouti–Addis Ababa train. All trains had stopped running due to 'terrorist' activity, and we found ourselves back at Quartier Monclar instead. Rather than trains, trucks would drop us off at the required locations. Some of the Legionnaires went into town to drink and have sex the night before, which I was sure was an unwise move. I doubted there would be much sleep over the next few days.

And yes, the final exercise was largely as expected: lots of observation posts, changing of orders, marching and firing of weapons. All of it done in small teams with very little sleep.

At the conclusion of the stage, and following the final parade at Quartier Monclar, Legionnaire loudly blamed Legionnaire for their own poor shooting. Each man claimed the other had made too many or too few adjustments to the rifle once it had been handed to him for use. What should have been a shared sense of achievement at the award of our *tireur d'élite* badges was instead disappointment and resentment. We fragmented into our small mafias, the only groups on whom we could rely.

20

NUMB

Comme toi, j'ai souffert.
(Like you, I have suffered.)

Immediately following our return to Quartier Monclar, I was allocated to the *bureau de semaine* yet again, it being the *section's* turn once more to provide a *caporal* for the week. Walking back from the *ordinaire* one day, during a rare foray outside the company headquarters, I looked across the *place d'armes* to witness *3ème Section* on parade and *Sergent* Carrion giving a beating. Drabble was the hapless victim, the teenager and former room-mate of mine.

Carrion wore shorts and a singlet, so I could see the tattooed colour of Jesus Christ reaching down his arms. I knew that crucified Christ lay tattooed on the *sergent's* back, from his neck down to the base of his spine. Below Christ's feet were the words *Comme toi j'ai souffert* (Like you I have suffered). A crown of thorns extended to the base of Carrion's neck and the words ran in a swathe above the swell of his buttocks. Even from where I stood, I could see a bead of sweat, like a tear, trickle down his back.

The *section* was at *gardez-vous*. From his place in front of the men, Dallas stood motionless, watching Drabble being bashed and kicked. This was Carrion's way of exerting authority and control. Like *Sergent* LaFronde, he used to say, '*Il faut un coup de stress*' (It needs an injection of stress). Just typical of Carrion to have selected young Drabble as the recipient. He never fought back or indicated he was prepared to stand up for himself. Pick the weak and make your point.

Once the beating was complete, the *section* was dismissed. Men left the scene of the humiliation, exposing a lonely body there on the gravel, knees to chest, sobbing. Life in *Lieutenant* Dallas's *3ème Section* continued to consume the weak. Likewise, the presence of *caporals* continued to be a rarity.

Schnebel had been taken from the field, a victim of sexually transmitted disease. He was immediately admitted to hospital and placed on an antibiotic drip. Rovery was still laid up with a bad knee, his pal Lafaible was gone – deserted. I understood his parents had come through with the money necessary to pay his way out of the country.

Potter had been transferred to *Section Commandement* as a mechanic, while Wanger had done his two years and was now in France, which was no great loss. As for the incompetent Buffons, he was in jail, paying not only for his sins, but also for the appalling standard of Legion instruction. This left Thurley, recently transferred to *3ème Section*, completely on his own.

Me, I'd just had word that I was moving on at the end of the week, transferred to the company's newly created *4ème Section*. *Lieutenant* Tallyman, the *chef de section*, told me that a directive had come from Aubagne. Because the quality of the fourteen weeks of instruction at Castelnaudary was now deemed so poor, Legionnaires were required to do more training once they reached their regiment; so, to better prepare them for integration into their new *section*s and to better serve the regiments, there was now a training *section* in Djibouti and in French Guyane. Nothing similar for mainland France and Corsica, but here in Djibouti, it meant that new arrivals would do three months in *4ème Section* on top of the period they'd endured at Castel.

Lieutenant Tallyman used to work at 13 DBLE headquarters. His staff now included *Sergent-Chef* Amrak, newly arrived from Castelnaudary; *Sergent* Mex, formally of 1 REC; *Sergent* Mistral, the self-annointed '92 kilos de muscle' I'd known while in Adjudant Adler's *2ème Section*; and a *maréchal-des-logis* (the cavalry's equivalent of a *sergent*) named Dumont, usually over with the Escadron de Reconnaissance, but here to do a component of his *sergent-chef* course.

There was only one other *caporal*. Like me, Krapski was a *fut fut* from Castelnaudary. Even though he was Polish, and my experience of them generally indicated that they made very poor Legionnaires, I waited before passing judgement. I need not have.

On the last Thursday in September, at the conclusion of another week in the *bureau de semaine*, I stayed the night in room 25 of the Hôtel Plein Ciel. This hotel used to be the place to stay for overseas visitors to Djibouti city, but since the opening of the Sheraton at Plateau de Serpent, the Plein Ciel had become the weekend playground of Legionnaires down from the escadron and Quartier Monclar. Its main advantage for Legionnaires was that the hotel management allowed them to bring in *nyahs* overnight.

That evening, as I was enjoying a quiet beer on the verandah of the Historil bar, next to the Air France offices just off the Place de Menelik, I saw something that went a long way to explaining the myth of the Legion. Dallas, in the walking-out *tenue* of an *officier* of the *Légion Étrangère*, Kapper, Rovery, Kit, Jeanet and Renoir, were all sitting around a table having a beer and sharing a joke. It must have been very amusing. The only reason they were together – French, Brit, Vietnamese, Turk and African – was for the benefit of the photographer from the French magazine *Paris Match*. This was the first and last time I saw Dallas in public in uniform. It was also the first and last time this group associated socially. I supposed this sort of exposure would be good for the *lieutenant* and possibly for Rovery, who was looking for promotion to *sergent*. For the Legionnaires present, they would've had little choice – but it looked so good for the camera.

Keyman soon joined me as planned, and together we watched in silence for a moment. 'Fook, I hate this bullshit,' the straight-talking Midlander muttered. 'Won't people ever realise that this place is shit and not what it seems?'

I told him I doubted it; certainly not while the French continued to go out of their way to sell the Legion as best suited their wider aims. Could it not be a model for a future United Nations force? went the theory. And, since they had the experience, weren't the French best suited to directing such a force? At the same time, any ex-Legionnaire who criticised the Legion had to be discredited as a malcontent, a sensationalist or even as lacking in the requisite *honneur*, *fraternité* and *fidélité*. In other words, the French spin doctors had the public relations sown up.

Keyman and I walked across the Place de Menelik to the similarly named hotel, where downstairs, Gatley's Djiboutian girlfriend worked as a barmaid. As we crossed the place, a twelve-seater minibus marked *Gendarmerie Djiboutian* braked to a sudden halt some 10 metres beyond us. The side door slid open and a Djiboutian *gendarme*, dressed in khaki with a blue cap, sprang from the vehicle. He brandished a pistol towards a woman walking by, who, judging by her boob tube, micro-mini and high heels, was most likely a prostitute on her way to work.

I told Keyman to wait and watch. The *gendarme* demanded her passport, but she had none, of course. The women who worked the bars as prostitutes were almost all illegal immigrants from Ethiopia or Somalia. She was duly bundled into the bus with two other women and perhaps eight *gendarmes*. With a plume of exhaust smoke, the bus took off at a terrific pace down Rue Éthiopie.

An hour later, as we sat outside the bar at the Hôtel Menelik, we watched the same three women being pushed from the bus. Although quickly confirmed as illegal immigrants, they weren't expelled from the country; after all, who would pay for their expulsion and where would they go anyway? Instead, they were probably raped and robbed, before being returned to the streets.

The women picked themselves up from the dirt and, with all the dignity they could muster, dusted themselves down, arranged their short skirts and continued along Rue Éthiopie. From the back of the minibus, the Djiboutian *gendarmes* shook their fists, whistled and cheered. Keyman and I continued drinking. It wasn't long before Keyman said he wanted a *nyah* for the night and left to make his selection among the bars. I stayed for another gin and tonic, and then returned to the Plein Ciel for an early night.

Next morning, on my way to breakfast, I walked past Keyman's room to find the door slightly ajar. I pushed it open to the sound of groans and the sight of my red-haired, freckle-skinned friend behind and between the blue-black thighs of a young *nyah*. I watched his arse cheeks move as his cock, looking like brie cheese with a long blue vein, slid in and out of her purple-plum anus. Behind the curtain of black hair and shame that hung over her face, I could see her eyes, glazed in pain and humiliation. She looked at me, I at her, and there was nothing to be done.

Keyman looked up. 'Want some?'

'No thanks mate,' I said and made to leave.

Before I reached the door, Keyman called out again. 'It's true you know – if you punch them here . . .' And he gave the girl a short, sharp punch to her side, just below her rib cage. '. . . their guts'll spasm around your dick.' He groaned with delight, then grinned through his freckles at me. I turned, closed the door, and went downstairs to coffee and a croissant.

Sometimes, and too often, Legionnaires took what they could. We hurt others as people hurt us, because if you weren't a Legionnaire you were less than we were. Many of us thought we were victims of a capricious system, a system that was uncaring, arbitrary and hurtful, so we imposed our world on others who were, for whatever reason, unable to fight back. In hurting the world around us, and making the world fear and sometimes hate us, it brought us together as men separate from the rest. It was shameful and ultimately not worth much, but it made us feel stronger and better about ourselves.

When I look back on that moment at the Hôtel Plein Ciel, and think of the girl's eyes behind the dark curtain, I wonder that I did not try to do something to help her or at least tell Keyman what I thought. I know now why I didn't; I was numb to the hurting around me. It is something you will rarely see in yourself, especially when you're numbed over a period of time. When you are surrounded by others in the same position as you, self-knowledge of the change will elude you. Twenty years ago, when I was in the Legion, numbness came when there was too much for me to feel for too long. When I was exposed to things that could move me, I was either detached, insensate and indifferent, or so profoundly moved I would cry, my soul sobbing in sympathy for the pain around me. My responses had become binary, with no gradation of measured reaction. It took me years to relearn that the rest of the world does not think this way, and the relearning cost me dearly in friends.

Later, I was outside, sitting at a table sipping my coffee, when a *gendarme* approached, his thumbs inside his pistol belt. He asked for my *carte d'identité*. Was I not aware, he asked, that all the whites had been called to get off the streets?

An hour or two after this, I found out part of what had happened. My going to bed early the night before may have saved my life. Half an hour after I'd quit my post outside the hotel bar, a highjacked taxi containing a number of *terroristes* threw a grenade onto the terrace of the upmarket Café de Paris (not to be confused with the no-frills Bar de Paris), killing and wounding a number of people. The café was less than 5 metres from where I'd been sitting.

So that was Thursday, 27 September 1990 – the night of the Djibouti city bombing. Back at Quartier Monclar that afternoon, I learned from the guard at the front gate that a number of grenades were thrown into at least two bars, but only in the Café de Paris had the terrorists remembered to extract the pin from the grenade. In the quartier, there was much movement. We were on alert. According to rumour, the attack had been variously linked to the FRUD movement within Djibouti, a military movement on the Ethiopian border, or the call by Saddam Hussein for all good Muslims to fight the unbelievers.

There was no address from *Colonel* le Flegg, *Capitaine* Rocky or our own *lieutenant* to outline what was going on. According to more rumour, terrorists had penetrated the frontier between Ethiopia and Djibouti, looking to bring down the Djiboutian Government. These same rumours told us that other French forces in Djibouti had already been sent to the border to deal with incursions. For us, we had our *sacs à dos* at the end of our beds and rifles in our rooms. We were ready to go at a moment's notice. Where or why or what we might do, we weren't so sure about, because we had no information on which we could rely.

After a month and a half of high alert in the camp, two Hungarians, Meckler and Markic, were absent at *rassemblement* one morning. Everyone in *3ème Compagnie* assumed the two were off in town enjoying the fleshpots. Or had they been taken by FRUD kidnappers perhaps?

Two weeks later, Meckler and Markic were out of jail, having been very lucky and having got off very lightly. Their efforts at desertion reflected the utter ignorance that they, indeed most in the unit had with respect to the Horn of Africa. The Legion did nothing to inform its men of geography. It was impossible to forget that whenever we went out on terrain, we were never told where we were going. When I asked, the response was always, 'Pas besoin de savoir' (No need to know).

In any event, over a weekend in mid November, Meckler and Markic changed into civilian clothes and took a taxi south to the Somali border at Loyada. Their intention was to get a train, bus or car to Mogadishu and present themselves to the Hungarian Ambassador there. Little did they know that Somalia had begun to fracture into warring factions and was tearing itself apart in the lead-up to a brutal civil war. Unless they were prepared to ride camels across heavily mined and lawless country, there would be no transport. Moreover, Mogadishu was over 1000 kilometres from Loyada, so even if they could get a cab, it was sure to be an expensive trip.

Instead of a drive to the Hungarian Embassy in Mogadishu, these two adventurers found themselves in a minefield marking the Djibouti–Somali border, near a customs office, and were fired upon by Djiboutian soldiers. The deserters were forced to retrace their steps, the Legion's *Police Militaire* were called, and Meckler and Markic were whisked back to Quartier Monclar and a stay in jail.

Apart from the need for freedom outside the camp perimeter fence – usually through the more appropriate medium of leave rather than desertion, it must be said – money remained close to the hearts of all. I passed *rapport capitaine* around this time and put to *Capitaine* Rocky a request he said was extraordinary. I had quite a sum in the *Caisse Nationale d'Épargne*, the CNE, where all Legionnaires' pay was kept, and I wanted to send it back to Australia. All I wanted was a cheque in French francs.

I stood at *gardez-vous* in Rocky's office, in front of his desk. The *capitaine* sat and was flanked by *Adjudant* Cognac and *Lieutenant* Tallyman, both standing. After I'd told him my request, Rocky looked up to me and asked, '*Ah* Mason, *tu es un pédé, non?*'

He was asking if I was homosexual – Legion mind games again. I said I didn't understand his question. Tallyman and Cognac smirked.

'*Tu n'aimes pas les nyahs en ville?*' (You don't like the girls in town?)

I was slow to understand the point he was making. Not wanting to waste his own time, he cut the meeting short.

'*Dégage,*' he said dismissively, although the real insult was in his next few words. After two and a half years, my French had progressed enough to make the translation: Take your pay each month, fuck the whores and drink too much, like any other Legionnaire.

I looked at him, then at the other two men, who were almost beside themselves with suppressed laughter. It was humiliating. What I considered a simple request turned into something very different: the belittlement of a Legionnaire's wish to save his pay. I'd assumed that Legion superiors would assist their men in making provisions for the future. How wrong I was. With a whipcrack salute and a '*Je peux disposer. À vos ordres, mon Capitaine!*', I left.

The difficulty was that Legionnaires either had their monthly *solde* paid in cash to them or left part of it in the CNE. We were not allowed bank accounts of our own and, even for a French Legionnaire, to transfer money to family members, one had to go through at least two time-consuming administrative steps. It was as if the Legion wanted us to spend everything we earned so that we'd have no choice but to stay, with no more to look forward to than the next pay packet and the next binge in town.

In a practical sense, this also meant that every payday at least one hapless Legionnaire had his *solde* stolen from him. Usually it was stolen from the pocket of his shirt, left on his bed as he went for a shower; or in the evening, while he was out on the town, when someone would break into his locker and take his money. Much more rarely, he might get robbed by a prostitute or a taxi driver.

Asking around the British mafia, I finally found a system to get my money home to Australia. But to send it home I had to access my money, and to do that I had to wait on the whim of the *capitaine*. Weeks after that first meeting with Rocky, and following a number of conversations with *Lieutenant* Tallyman, who finally empathised with me, I was able to withdraw from the CNE all the money I had. With the Djiboutian equivalent of 100,000 French francs, or 25,000 Australian dollars, I caught a taxi into the city and lay the cash on the table in front of the bank manager. I watched the apple bob in his throat as he asked one of his underlings to come and count the notes.

By December, I had been in Africa over a year and was accustomed to the routines, the heat, the repetition and the hollow claims of excellence. What I never became accustomed to was violence, and the need to inflict it on others. I knew it was necessary on occasion, and I had hit Legionnaires, most often in the context of their disobeying an order. Usually though, it was sufficient to intimate that you were going to thump a Legionnaire to ensure that orders were properly executed. But not always.

On parade at 1600 one afternoon, we in *4ème Section* were told that we were going on terrain for three days from 0600 next day. I ordered everyone in my *chambre* to prepare their *sacs* and equipment straightaway, in readiness for the morning. I began the task myself and everyone followed. Except for Micloski, who just sat on his bed and watched the others.

'Do you have a problem?' I asked the Pole, in French.

'No.'

'Are you sick?'

'No.'

'So why aren't you doing your pack?'

'I don't feel like it.'

Alarm bells. But he was young, I knew that. 'Do it now and you won't be in a hurry tonight or tomorrow,' I told him, patiently. 'Also, that way you won't forget anything and we won't have to help you out.'

'No,' he said again.

Oh dear, he was looking for a problem. I gave him one more chance. 'Do your pack, Micloski, or I will punch your face in.'

'No.'

I got up and so did he. The *chambre* watched.

'Be careful, Corporal, I do karate,' he warned.

Those were his last words. I gave him a straight right and left that toppled him over his bed. The young Pole scrambled away to the far end of the *chambre,* where I thumped and kicked him until he was limp. 'When I say something, there is good cause,' I said finally. 'Just do it.'

I sat down on my steel-framed bed and continued with preparations for the morning. Not long afterwards, Micloski rushed by yelling, 'I'm going to see the captain.' He was gone. Oh well – but it was the right thing to do.

Fifteen minutes later, Micloski returned. Looking at his face, I could see a new black eye, matching the one I'd given him. He didn't say a word.

Before he could get to Rocky with his tale of woe, he'd run into *Sergent-Chef* Amrak. Getting no sense out of the young Legionnaire, the *sergent-chef* took him back to the *section* office where, after hearing Micloski's story, he gave him another thump for good measure. As Amrak told me later, he did so because, first, Micloski ought to have done what I said, and second, because the Pole should've taken his problem directly to him, not *Capitaine* Rocky. Things in *4ème Section* were now very calm.

As I sat back on my bed, looking across the room at the others, I reflected that while I could hit a Legionnaire, I could never hit or hurt a *nyah*. It was easy to understand why. With a Legionnaire, things sometimes got to a point where you had to react; you had to either face up to the problem and deal with it, or face a future with many more problems. I knew this and understood it, from the train ride to Aubagne and from life in both Castelnaudary and Djibouti. Of course, with a *nyah* it was different. Although many men I knew hit them and hurt them, there was nothing in it that I could understand. At least, there was nothing rational that I could see – no need for self-preservation or assertion of dominance. Hitting a Legionnaire on occasion was not really something you had a choice about. With a *nyah*, there was choice, and, in thinking about it, there was absolutely no excuse.

Early one morning in mid December, at 0545, just before a company parade, those who intended to go to the *infirmerie*, and therefore not engage in *footing*, lined up in front of the *bureau de semaine*, close to *Capitaine* Rocky's office. This was part of our company commander's new policy. He wanted to know why the men in *3ème Compagnie* were crying off sick, and so from now on they would only go if they had his consent.

On this particular morning, there were some twenty men lined up – almost a quarter of the company – and Rocky was not pleased. He clenched his fist and raised his voice. '*Vous êtes tous des cons!*' he yelled. Rocky's bedside manner thus established, each Legionnaire had to present himself and explain why he wished to visit the *infirmerie*. If it was for a broken finger, a cut or the like, the man was given permission with a curt 'Okay' or a swish of the wrist. Unfortunately, of the twenty, fifteen were afflicted with some kind of sexually transmitted disease, Micloski among them. Before allowing these men to go and seek medical help, Rocky punched or kicked each one and abused him. '*Tête de noeud*' and so forth.

The direct effect of this abuse was that fewer Legionnaires with sexual infections sought professional advice. Instead, men purchased what they thought were the necessary antibiotics over the counter in town and asked the company medics to inject them. This meant that there was no follow-up treatment, with all the dangers this entailed. I wondered what the regimental medical officer, thought of it all, but he probably had no idea.

As I was to learn later, almost all the men in *3ème Compagnie* were infected with at least one sexually transmitted disease in the course of their two years in Djibouti. The result of this was that, in our ranks, we had Legionnaires who carried all the lesser forms of sexual infection and also hepatitis B and C and HIV. If a man didn't present himself at the *infirmerie*, his HIV-positive status would not be revealed until he returned to France. I knew that this happened on more than one occasion.

Friday, 28 December 1990

Dear Mother,

Christmas was the long-anticipated disaster. One thing about French *officiers*, they certainly are consistent. Everyone was very drunk, though not happy drunk. As usual, very angry people abounded in the *quartier*. They looked like caged animals pacing the short bounds of their prisons. The only highlights were those provided by Legionnaires.

First, there were the sketches. The first from our *section* I had written myself on the subject of Hungarian deserters to Somalia. It went down splendidly. The crowd roared and the Hungarians were very peeved. The second sketch was the one spot of culture of evening. A cast of tarted-up Legionnaires with lipstick and eyeliner, mask, flippers and tutus performing the opening few minutes of *Swan Lake*.

The second major highlight was the English Christmas dinner. As happened last year, this saw the anglophones – Irish, Scots, Welsh, English, Danes, a Finn, Yanks, Canadian and an Aussie – together for a traditional Christmas dinner.

As I had done last year, I gave the Christmas address. This was particularly sensitive, having lost Gungie in the course of this year. The audience was very attentive and at the conclusion of a recitation of the first verse of Rupert Brooke's 'The Soldier', everyone lingered long over the toast, 'Lest We Forget'.

Love,

David

Three days after I wrote this, on New Year's Day 1991, half the company was unconscious on their beds. There were dried, scumbled splotches of vomit about the parade ground being scavenged by birds that swooped down from the surrounding trees. Krapo, a Pole who'd arrived with the December detachment just a few weeks before, was missing. Krapo had a melon-shaped head, golden hair cut to a bristle, and looked like an overweight and vacuous weasel. Keyman dismissed him an 'oxygen thief'.

Speaking of Keyman, I went to visit the one-time REP man, having seen him the night before, screaming and threatening to bash anyone who would take him on. I was reminded of how, when we first met in Aubagne, he'd clubbed a *caporal* in the REP. The moment I arrived in his room, I was assailed by the stink. Keyman lay naked and unconscious on his bed, his red hair and body covered in his own shit and the acid bile of his stomach contents.

On the steel-framed bed a metre or so away, lay a Legionnaire, his eyes open, dead in life, hands across his chest, face purpled from punches and smeared with Keyman's shit. After some gentle questioning, I moved this man to the shower, where he tried to scrub away the excrement and humiliation. I then rolled Keyman into a position where, if he vomited again, he wouldn't choke to death.

I had to get out of the *quartier*, so I headed off to the circus, which had set up next to Djibouti's Olympic Stadium. A chest-high mesh fence surrounded the circus, describing a rectangle some 150 metres square. I supposed the fence was to keep in wayward animals attempting to escape the circus. It certainly didn't prevent the entry of many young Djiboutian boys.

At one end of the rectangle, towards the main road that led into the city, were the big top (the only tent) and the caravans housing the circus troupe and their animals. At the other end was the *tonneau de mort*, a tunnel some 10 metres high and 5 metres wide, its interior lined with wooden planks and supported by scaffolding that would never have satisfied any safety regulations. The car that was to defy gravity was not in working order, although the revving of its engine and the antics of its mechanics provided endless amusement for the many boys grouped around the machine. Set up against the fence on the way to the big top was a stand selling cold drinks and melted chocolates. I got myself a Coke.

Before I'd made it to the ticket office outside the big tent, I felt a small hand in mine. I looked down and gazed into two shining dark-brown eyes. He was eight years old maybe.

'Mr Legionnaire, are you going to watch the circus?'

'But of course.'

'Could you buy me a ticket?'

I looked down into those eyes so bright with hope. I asked him where his friends were and he pointed to the right of the drink stand. Three young dreamers stood watching; all like the one with me now, dressed in dirty shorts and ripped shirts, with bare feet. Waving them over, I asked them if they too wanted to see the circus. There was a musical chorus of 'Oui, oui!' At the ticket office I purchased five of the best tickets, which I then presented at the tent as the four scooted off to find seats. I never saw them again.

I sat near the ring, next to a Chinese man, one of the merchants in this crossroads to Africa, who had brought along his young son. Aged no more than six, the boy was very dark-skinned, with shining almond eyes. He loved the circus. His unabashed joy at the parade of acrobats, clowns and chimpanzees made my evening. This was true *joie de vivre*. At Quartier Monclar there was none. I was the only Legionnaire at the circus.

21

MY GULF WAR

Ça va toi?
(You all right?)

A letter home to Canberra, dated Friday, 25 January 1991:

Dear Mother,

Looks like Operation Desert Shield, the first part of the plan to recapture Kuwait and defeat the Iraqis must soon be over. If the United States waits too long – after all, it seems they are the driving force behind this fight – it will surely become too hot to operate in that environment, maybe too expensive and surely too difficult to keep such an extraordinary coalition together.

In the meantime, please find enclosed a typical piece of Legion mythologising, found in the pages of *Time Magazine* dated 14 January 1991. It focuses on an American with the Legion in the desert of Saudi Arabia, part of the French contribution to the coalition. The piece is nothing more than a reiteration of Legion stereotypes. It begins with the twenty-year-old John Grachi, a 'former Ranger', now a Legionnaire, who says, 'I didn't like the

US Army. I didn't like anything about it. I am not confident in the US troops here. A lot are boys. They don't know what to expect.'

Does John? At least the US guys would be better trained, better motivated and better led. He (Grachi), 'joined a force that fulfilled his idea of a disciplined fighting machine: the French Foreign Legion. "The Legion is tough," he says, "you have to earn your place. These guys don't sign up because they want a college education. They sign up because this is where they want to be."' Well, I doubt that 5 per cent would know what a college degree was. I know they signed up because they wanted to be where they wouldn't have to worry about what to eat or where to sleep. They wanted to be where someone offered a useful passport.

And what about the imagery on page 12: '. . . tents, bought on the local market' (probably because they didn't have enough to bring over from France) 'cluster around a white flagpole that flies a large tricolour and a banner with the traditional green and red of the Legion. "Green is the color of Islam," says a Legion *officier*. "Red is the color of blood."' What a perceptive fellow is this French *officier*! But what does it really mean? More wilful mysteriousness from the French. Is a dream any match for competence? I think not.

Is it?

Love,

David

Well, what happened? By the beginning of March 1991 the cease-fire was signed and the war was over. Following the Iraqi invasion of Kuwait on 2 August 1990, there was Desert Shield, followed by Desert Storm and the air attacks from 17 January and the ground assault from 23 February. After just a hundred hours of the ground attack, the war was done, even though from where I sat on a hill looking into Ethiopia, listening to the BBC on my radio, it did not seem to be altogether neat or final. At least Kuwait was liberated, although Saddam was still in power and appeared likely to stay there.

The French played a significant role in the war. In fact, the second largest European contingent was France, which committed 18,000 troops. The French called their contribution '*Opération Daguet*' and operated on the far western flank of the main force. The main French Army force was the *6ème Brigade Légère Blindée* (6th Light Armoured Division), which included troops from the Legion's Infantry, Engineer and Cavalry regiments.

And closer to home? Some within the combat company were allocated to go, including me as an English speaker and a marksman. I was issued dog tags too, but in the end no one went. There was no need; there were so few French casualties, and certainly no need to supplement any forces or replace anyone.

In fact, it was probably more dangerous at the rifle range at Arta Plage, some 1500 metres to the west of CECAP. We were firing over 25 metres *par rafale* (on automatic). I was behind the men firing weapons and distributed magazines full of rounds. At the conclusion of one shoot, *Lieutenant* Tallyman inspected the rifles of everyone on the mound except his own. As he walked back towards me, I watched him cock the weapon and take the magazine out. Just as he reached where I stood, his index finger moved the *selecteur de tir* from safe to fire. Then he squeezed.

I ducked just as the firing pin struck the base of the round and the bullet passed by my head. Tallyman leaned over me and asked, '*Ça va toi?*'

Was I all right? What an idiot question . . . I got to my feet, brushed off the dust and said nothing. I then walked off some

20 metres on my own. Had I not done so, I'm sure I would have thumped him. There were no apologies.

To offset this stupidity, it was good to receive word that *Caporal* Krapski, the Polish *fut fut*, had been booted out of our *section*. The *lieutenant* called him a lazy wanker, put him in jail for incompetence and palmed him off on another *section*. It meant that other people would have to deal with him now.

For some reason never explained, but presumably for reasons of security, in mid March, we commenced building barbed-wire defences around Quartier Monclar. This activity raised wry smiles, as we knew it was possible to come and go through the wire if one wished to avoid the front gate.

During a short break, a few of the Brits decided to play some cricket. There was Scouse, Jock, Geordie, Paddy and me. We had a shovel, stones and three star pickets. The Frenchmen and the Eastern Bloc-ers were bemused, never having seen anything even close to cricket being played before. This was more fun than stringing wire to the design of a French *officier* who didn't know what he was doing.

This officer, with the three gold bars of *capitaine* across his chest, stopped and watched for a moment. He asked what we were doing.

'*Nous jouons au cricket, mon Capitaine.*' (We're playing cricket, Captain.)

'*Ah. Anglais, non?*' he said – a logical conclusion.

'Commonwealth, *mon Capitaine.*'

'*Je m'en fou . . .*' And with that, he directed us back to work and told us to ensure that all the wire was fixed tight.

I suggested that if we kept it all tight, it would be easy to cross. He told me to *dégage,* and said that the French Army had plenty of experience with wire. After all, had it not won the First World War? He walked off kicking star pickets.

This brought smirks from my friends. One expressed it neatly when he whistled and said that the *capitaine* had 'no fookin' idea'. What was clear was that the Legion had no idea about winning the war against the neglect of safe-sex practices either. In *4ème Section*, it fell to me to give instruction on the subject of sex. Or rather: the subject of how to avoid the ramifications of unprotected sex with the proper use of condoms.

To this end, I secured a porn centrefold, a *Time Magazine* photograph of a woman with full-blown AIDS, a broom handle, and a supply of good French condoms. The need for even a basic form of sex education was essential because, despite the availability of condoms, the very first time these fellows went into town, a quarter of them caught some STD or other.

I sat them down and talked frankly about *nyahs*, AIDS and the gamut of sexually transmitted diseases. Then, an action demonstration with the broom handle and a *capote*. When I squeezed the air out of the end of the condom and left a little to hang over the end of the handle, as required before practical use, the majority of the men appeared genuinely surprised. They never used condoms in Poland or in other parts of Eastern Europe, nor had many of the French.

Perhaps it was fitting that, as the eyes of the world were focused on events in Kuwait and southern Iraq, the Legion talked *capotes*, and a face from my past should appear. Newly arrived in Djibouti was *Sergent-Chef* Westway, the man with the cold blue eyes who interviewed me at Legion security in Aubagne, close to two years ago. Recently promoted, he took one look at me and said, 'I know you.' He smiled. 'That Rolls-Royce is still up on blocks, isn't it?'

I laughed, remembering his metaphor: my life was a luxury car sitting in a driveway; all I had to do was jump in and go – get the hell out of Aubagne.

'The Legion is a load of shit, is it not?' the Englishman added mischievously.

We both laughed now, because while we knew the truth of it, there was nothing we could do. I congratulated him on his promotion, he on mine. Then with a handshake, we parted ways.

In the final week of March, we were up in Oueah again with the *Escadron de Reconnaissance*, a familiarisation trip for the new Legionnaires in *4ème Section*. This familiarisation included a visit to the local bar. Below the quartier, at the bottom of the hill near the wadi crossing, was a bar attached to a service station. Keen to see the sex-education sessions put to practical use, I made sure there were plenty of condoms available and we adjourned there one evening for drinks.

On the left, inside the Bar Toucoul, was a benchtop of shiny metal but no cash register, I noticed, all cash being kept in a drawer under lock and key. This key, along with a number of others, was attached to a bracelet worn on the proprietor's wrist. With a yellow-toothed smile, he said, '*Bienvenu à la maison d'amour*' (Welcome to the house of love).

Drinks for all and the pulsating, if not altogether clear, beat of the Rolling Stones. After five minutes or so, word had got around, and twenty Legionnaires found themselves receiving the attentions of a crowd of local girls. Before long, *nyahs* and Legionnaires went outside for their brief – and, for the *nyahs*, very profitable – coupling. There was no grass out there, no mattress. Instead, depending on the Legionnaire's preference, the girl lay on her back or on her front on top of the large boulders common to the area. I called this 'love on the rocks', and everyone laughed a too-hard laugh.

On 28 April, two days before another Camerone Day, we held a *pot de départ* (farewell drinks) for *Lieutenant* Tallyman and *Sergent-Chef* Amrak. The *lieutenant* was to leave for France and the *sergent-chef* for another *section*. After a few beers, Tallyman took me aside and told me he had recommended me for the Legion's *sergent* course when I got back to France in November. He said I had a *belle carrière*, that I was an excellent member of the team, and just what the Legion needed in order to move into the next century.

I thanked him, but I didn't have the heart to tell him I wouldn't be taking this route. If I were to do the *sergent* course, the prelude would be at least one *section d'instruction* at Castelnaudary, followed by the course itself, and then the combat course. In all, the requirements added up to almost a year. I would also end up being posted to Castelnaudary afterwards, where I'd be doing the kind of things I had already done. Besides, I had decided on the Legion's Parachute Regiment on Corsica.

At least I wouldn't have to endure any more Camerones in Djibouti. This year's was precisely the same as the year before: sport, eating and drinking. And on the subject of drinking, having recently got free of Krapski, we had a new problem Pole on the block.

Saturday, 11 May 1991

Dear Mother,

Let me tell you about the endearing Krapo. Polish, he is fat, ignorant and a drunkard. This is the fellow who was returned from jail to the *section* before having to pass *rapport*. He went from room to room, asking for some aftershave. Having secured a quantity, he locked himself in the toilet and drank the lot. What are they doing at Legion recruitment?

On the day in question, Krapo had been released from jail to work for the good of the *compagnie*. I had just retired to my bed to enjoy the afternoon siesta, when the *caporal de semaine* came to me and asked for Krapo.

After a brief discussion, it was decided that Krapo would be at the *foyer*. I would find and present him at the *semaine*. So, having dressed myself in sports kit, I found him sitting outside the *foyer* with some of his compatriots. Inviting him to come with me, he did something very foolish. He said he'd be on his way when he finished his beer.

It was too much for me and I pulled the chair from beneath him. As he fell to the ground, I began to rain blows on his head, not knowing the injury I was doing to my own hand. The Poles sitting around the table did nothing to assist Krapo. They simply sat and watched impassively, leaning back to tip more beer down their throats. When I looked up from the beating, they reminded me of a flock of sheep; they even seemed to me to have sheep's eyes.

I began to drag Krapo away from the *foyer* on the gravel toward the *compagnie*. He began to cry and he pleaded with me to let him walk. I did (it's hard work dragging a person about), and soon presented him at the *semaine*, to *Caporal-Chef* Lap, who gave Krapo a kick for good measure. Lap then had what he thought was an excellent idea. So, with a noose around Krapo's neck and secured to a tree, his hands secured behind his back with plastic ties, Krapo was left with a bowl of water that he was only able to drink when he lapped at it, like a dog. Lap laughed a mean, narrow laugh and thought himself very creative.

Tomorrow I start the *Stage Infirmier* to become a combat
medic. It is a course of some three months in which we learn
basic skills, like injection giving, blood taking and sewing up.
I'm looking forward to it.

Love,

David

What I did not tell my mother was that when I hit Krapo I
enjoyed it. Even when I felt the bones in my wrist crack as I hit
him; even when I felt the tendon tear off the end of one finger.
I became for a short time, quite mad. I was angry at having to
retrieve him from the foyer and angry at his disregard for me.
Most disturbingly, I was mad because as I bent over his body,
punching him again and again, his Polish friends did nothing
and nor did those *caporal-chef*s and *sergents* who simply turned
away their heads as they walked by. For a short while, I beat
what I loathed: indifference and neglect of responsibility. It
was a shit of a life. At the same time, I could hit someone like
Krapo without sanction, I could find myself hit or humiliated
with little cause and with little redress. There was no law, justice
or certainty. There was rank, power and control. There was no
one to protect you but yourself.

Krapo's compatriot Krapski was back in my world from the
middle of May. And, true to his character, he cheated during
one of the first exams on the *infirmier* course. He transcribed
a record of most parts of the human anatomy onto his wooden
desk top before the exam. *Sergent-Chef* Danner, our instructor,
spotted this little piece of initiative and chose to deal with it by
marking Krapski last. Outside the classroom Krapski swung his
arms around like the robot in *Lost in Space*, extremely pissed

off that he had been so badly treated. I told him to fuck off, and while he was at it, he could clean the ink smear from his arm that marked him for the liar he was.

As for me, I had no problem with exams, taking blood or giving injections. I felt nauseous just once, when I played a leading part in the removal of an ingrown toenail. Just able to swallow the morning coffee that flooded into my mouth, I drove the *sonde cannelée*, a 20-centimetre-long, thin stainless steel tool, under the nail of a big toe to the root and gave a twist. Once the nail was lifted, I gripped it with pliers and extracted it with the root still attached, looking like the soft shell at the tail end of a deep-fried prawn. I learned that in the course of such a procedure, a patient will quickly tell you if they require more nerve-numbing injections.

The daily routine of the stage came to an abrupt stop, however, on 26 May. There was an alert. Orders were shouted to clear everything from our *chambres* for occupation by refugees from Ethiopia. These were not indigenous refugees, but expatriates and diplomatic staff from a number of European countries. We understood, from the BBC World Service, that the Marxist regime of Mengistu Haile Mariam, which had ruled, repressed and murdered many in Ethiopia since the overthrow of Emperor Haile Selassie in 1974, was soon to fall. The liberating rebel forces, the Ethiopian People's Revolutionary Democratic Front, had the Russian-backed army on the run.

On their arrival from the airport, the refugees found a bevy of Legion *officiers,* colourful ribbon bars on their chests and gold-patterned kepis on the heads, to greet them. The officers took the refugees in hand and led them to the foyer, where a banquet was laid out. These refugees didn't cry or suffer; they drank wine and beer and fed themselves full of pastries. One girl, aged maybe seventeen or eighteen, actually brought along her dog – a ball of fluff that appeared to be the object of much attention from the Legionnaires. It wasn't the dog, though. Having been briefed before hand, the girl's parents watched their daughter like hawks, refusing to let her out of their sight.

22

KNIVES, NEEDLES AND GODARIA

Ceci, c'est le sale boulot.
(This is dirty work.)

Another alert. In the early hours of Monday, 27 May, we were woken to the news that all courses had been cancelled and the sounds of orders being shouted and trucks leaving the quartier. From the information I could glean, it seemed that the best part of Mengistu's army was retreating to Djibouti, with many civilians in tow. Military personnel alone numbered around 20,000, their vehicles streaming along the main road, forming an almost continuous convoy.

According to what I could make out from our officers, Djibouti was now coming under attack from the defeated Ethiopian army that sought to either join forces with the neglected Afars or seek refuge from imminent collapse or worse. With most of *3ème Compagnie* having already gone to Yoboki, in the west, *4ème Section* was to stay on permanent guard duty at Quartier Monclar. I was furious. I didn't join the French Foreign Legion to do bloody guard duties!

I need not have worried. The following day, an element of our *section* was called out to Dikhil, due west of Ali Sabieh, in the south of the country. With *Sergent* Mex, I took ten of our Legionnaires and formed up with others in the company to create a *section de marche*, a composite *section*.

Thus we were part of what the French had christened *Opération Godaria*. In the words of a British cavalryman from the escadron, this would be '*le sale boulot*' (dirty work). With the promise of United Nations assistance and the prospect of refugee camps being set up in Djibouti, the Ethiopian military personnel had agreed to surrender themselves over to the authorities our side of the border. Weapons were handed over as a precondition to their receiving food and water, after which military and civilian refugees were led off by convoy to Ali Sabieh.

The soldiers surrendered all their weaponry and other materiel – thousands of rifles and pistols, rocket-propelled grenades, old Soviet tanks, anti-aircraft weapons and heavy mortars. The small arms, in particular, were better than ours and were well maintained, clean and oiled. After all, this Ethiopian army had been at war with Tigre and Eritrea for thirty years. While their clothes were rags, they knew what was important.

While the defeated Ethiopians were co-operative, I had to stamp my authority with the Legionnaires during that first day of the operation. *Adjudant* Marten, a Portuguese veteran of war in Mozambique, had given the order to load magazines on weapons and fix bayonets. In a curious accent that mixed Portuguese and Afrikaans, in English he said to anyone within shouting range: 'I know how to deal with the fekkin' blecks. Shoot 'em if they even luke like playin' up.' Once we'd started to move among the refugees, though, I ordered everyone to remove the bayonets. Some of my Legionnaires pretended they hadn't heard. A while later, I formed them into one rank and thumped each man on the chest, telling them they had no place hurting or humiliating people who had been through much and had surrendered. After this dressing down, I had no problem with these men who, for the most part, looked lost among the heat, misery and pain of a defeated army.

My task as a *chef d'equipe* in the composite *section* was to coordinate and organise the distribution of water and food as the lines of vehicles came through along the N1 – the sole sealed road that, from Dikhil, headed in a generally north-west direction through mountain passes to the border, before making a long arc around and down to the Ethiopian capital. These travellers would have endured a tough ordeal just to earn their allocated half-litre of water, I realised. Ironically, the food consisted entirely of dates donated by Saudi Arabia, the nation reviled by many in this region during the Gulf War, not so much for aiding the Kuwaitis, but for allowing so many unbelievers into their country as a base from which to attack Iraq.

Already at this time of year, the days were hot – up to 50 degrees Celsius. When you got this hot, you'd find the liquid around your brain and in your eyeballs starting to expand, as if was about to erupt and run down your face. A wide-brimmed hat would've been ideal, but the *adjudant* insisted that we had to look the part. So each man wore his beret and got sunburnt, while imagining brain fluid dripping down his face.

Our location was just to the west of Dikhil, on the road to Addis. Forward from the distribution area, we'd set up a roadblock. It was a flimsy affair really, just crossed pieces of wood with a little barbed wire wrapped around them, but then it hardly had much to 'block'. Those arriving here had no food, no water and nowhere to go.

Nevertheless, the first night was near anarchy. There was occasional rifle fire and I remember our *chef de corps* arguing with a high-ranking Ethiopian officer and pushing him in the chest. The man was clearly tired and simply trying to secure more water for his soldiers' families. The response from the *Colonel* was clear: there was no more. That night we camped on the eastern side of a wall that extended for three sides around a cemetery. The western side was open to the winds, dust and the setting sun that swept in from Ethiopia.

The following night, a Wednesday, with *Sergent* Mex we took the *garde* at the roadblock. Marching down the road late in the afternoon, I looked over my shoulder to where I could see the cemetery's earthen mounds thrown into relief, like gently undulating dunes. There were no trees to break the line of the horizon or to provide shade to the living or to the dead. The sight of *Capitaine* Rocky, however, distracted me.

With red and green Legion pennant flying from the aerial, his gold seven-flamed beret insignia reflecting the setting sun, and ribbons on his chest, the *capitaine* was off to Dikhil in his Jeep. As he left, his second-in-command handed him a bottle of whiskey. Soon after, a crowd of cheerful *lieutenants*, each in a jeep, followed Rocky's vehicle. It was a liaison with United Nations authorities.

As the sun sank that evening, the road became a dark river carrying human flotsam to refuge. Its surface was soft from the day's baking sun and it pulled gently at the soles of my boots. Our guard post was reached by crossing a small bridge over a wadi, intersecting the N1. Beyond the wood-and-wire checkpoint stretched a single line of vehicles filled with people, boardered at the roadsides by fractured, brutalised rock.

We made our camp in the wadi, protected from the drying winds, with the sand as our beds. Divided into two shifts, our guard duties required that we station ourselves by the wire and let no one pass or give anyone water until the checkpoint re-opened for business in the morning. We were ready for trouble; we had twenty 5.56 mm rounds in the magazines on our rifles and more magazines in our pouches. Mex led the 1900-to-midnight shift while I took midnight to dawn.

After waking just before midnight, I climbed the bank up to the road, where the Legionnaire on sentry told me all was quiet. It didn't look like anyone would rush the wire, although there was a group of women standing a little too close to it perhaps. Walking up to our makeshift barrier, I noticed two shapes at its base. Stones? Bombs? In the clear, starlit night, I knelt down and saw them now: two tiny, lifeless forms wrapped in rags. The sentry told me that the *sergent* had ordered him to touch nothing, but to leave things until morning.

Later, a figure broke from the group of women and approached the barrier. We watched one another for a time until she squatted on her haunches and held a little bundle to her breast. She rocked slowly back and forth and murmured a few words, the tone of which spoke of deep sadness and regret. She brought the bundle to her cheek and then, gently, carefully, with her palms stretched up to the stars, the woman placed it between the two others. She looked at me for a moment before gliding away into the dark.

Just before dawn I woke Mex and the Legionnaires. In the half-light, we picked up the three rag-wrapped forms and buried them as deep as we could in the wadi sand. I stayed there for a moment, on my own, and considered saying a prayer. Instead, I lowered my gaze to the three small mounds of sand, wishing that heat, water and time would dissolve them into the earth from which they had come. Just then, from the corner of my eye, I caught a glimpse of flowing red silk. Or maybe it was just a scarlet beam of light from the new sun.

Later that morning, I was stationed near the *capitaine's* tent but there was no sign of the man himself. The *tricolore* had been raised and Ethiopian vehicles were again moving through to the east. At about 0900 he summoned me to the tent. His face a mask of white, Rocky said he was unwell. He gave me a shit-eating, sickly smile and asked that I get him some water.

Twenty-four hours after the burial, I was back at the distribution point, a few hundred metres behind the roadblock and the forward station, with the checkpoint having recently opened for the day. Here, beside trestle tables laid out with much-needed water and food, yet another truck full to bursting with human cargo pulled over and disgorged its throng of tired, pitiful refugees.

Perhaps I was tired also on that particular day. Before the people were all properly on board the truck, I ordered the driver to move on. I don't think I even noticed the man making a last-minute leap towards the side of the open-tray vehicle, just gaining a precarious foothold in front of the rear wheels, one hand reaching up to grab the top of the tray. But I did see him lose his foothold, slip and fall onto the road. In the second or so that followed, I looked into his face – alight with surprise, then dread, with the knowledge that his head was about to be trapped under a wheel. He looked at me, his eyes widening, and as they did, I knew two things. He knew death was coming. And, as the windows to his soul opened for that fleeting moment, he stole from me my sense of righteousness. He did so because, in that last second before emptiness, there was fear, anger and hope; and I did nothing. The sound of his head exploding was like a wide and heavy block of wood being dropped on a watermelon: a low-pitched 'pop'.

I ran over to the man's body and saw that his face was still intact. The fear-screaming eyes were dull now, and his visage lay suspended over the cavity that was his skull, like a novelty-shop mask. Brains, resembling lumpy porridge, had settled on the road. I searched his body for identification, but found none.

Having told the driver to move on, I dragged the limp, skinny corpse off the road. Once *Adjudant* Marten had made a brief inspection, a bulldozer arrived to scrape a hole. Into the shallow depression we placed the remains of a man. The bulldozer quickly filled the hole before driving over the slight mound twice, flattening the ground. Then, just like the truck, it too was gone. It was as if the dead man had never existed.

Feeling nothing, I continued directing the checkpoint and wondered how the death of someone could have so little effect on me. Numbness again.

On another day, a man and his family came passing through, driving a newish-looking four-wheel drive vehicle, when a plump *capitaine* of the Djiboutian Gendarmerie directed them to the side of the road. From a short distance away, I could see and hear what transpired. The *capitaine* offered to purchase the vehicle for some FDJ 30000 (about 250 Australian dollars). The driver said no and shook his head. As he did this, the policeman took the pistol from his belt, put the muzzle to the man's temple and said, 'Get yourself and your family from the car. It is mine now.'

Before long, the family and their possessions were sitting among the dust and rocks on the roadside. The *capitaine* gave the man some notes and drove off to Dikhil. He soon returned in a *gendarme's* vehicle and resumed his post just off the road.

This was theft and injustice, and I radioed my report to a Legion *capitaine*. He came to my post and interviewed both the man who had lost his car and the Djiboutian. After a few minutes, the Legion officer threw his hands in the air and declared, '*Trop difficile et compliqué. Je m'en fou.*'

Turning to me he said, in English, 'It's their stinking country. Let them have it and everything else besides.'

By Saturday, 10 June, ten days after being called out to halt the Ethiopian army, our composite *section* had disarmed thousands of men and given them, and the civilians who travelled with them, food and water. We told them they would be going to camps set up by the United Nations, and it certainly looked that way. There were UN flags and uniforms everywhere and plenty of Jeeps and trucks with United Nations insignia and pennants on them. But there were no UN camps.

Most of the Ethiopians were sent back home to whatever fate awaited them. Only the highest ranking refugees were offered sanctuary. But what were such small things when the future of an African state hung in the balance?

So we packed up at Dikhil and headed east, back to the coast and the twin opressives of terrorist threats and stifling heat. At least I knew my time here in Djibouti was drawing to an end, with just five months to go. A change would be good.

Before long, those of us on the *infirmiers* course recommenced our studies. We continued to work on a rostered basis in the *infirmerie* at Quartier Monclar, as well as doing shifts at Bouffard, the military hospital. At the inpatients department, there was always work to be done. There had been a number of cases of meningitis, and a young French Marine had part of his face paralysed from the infection.

Another patient was an AND *sergent*, who, suspected of having meningitis, needed his spine tapped. I'd always thought this sort of procedure was done in an operating theatre, but here, things were different. The doctor, a French Army *capitaine* in her mid thirties with a penchant for chunky gold earrings and necklaces, simply strode into his room and declared, 'Time for a needle.'

A gentle light through the thin cotton curtains filled the room and dust motes seemed to hold up the high ceiling. We turned the chair around that was at his bedside desk and had him sit down facing the backrest. I was the bearer of the kidney-shaped tin containing cotton swabs, plastic gloves, antiseptic solution, test tube, bandaid and the long – very long – needle that was to be inserted just below the fifth vertebrae and into the spinal canal of the patient.

The idea was to tap into the canal and withdraw a sample of spinal fluid. The needle is inserted into the spinal canal and a long, fine metallic pin is withdrawn from the interior of the needle allowing fluid to escape and be caught in a test tube. If the spinal fluid is cloudy, it is a positive indication of meningitis. Even so, if it's clear, it still had to be collected and tested.

The doctor snapped on her gloves. I opened a packet that held a swab and presented it to her, and she took it to clean the patient's lower-back area. He made no move or indication that he was in any way distressed. I wasn't even sure he knew what was about to happen.

The *capitaine médicin* counted the vertebrae and, at the site she wanted, swabbed and stretched taut the skin. She put the sharp end of the needle to the flesh, pushed, and paused. Then she looked at me and said that I should do it. 'It's like pushing through cheese,' she added, 'until it gives a little.' Then I would know I was in the canal. As I pushed, she said '*Souffle*' (Breathe) to our patient. I suppose this was to relax the Djiboutian, but it didn't seem to make any difference to him at all.

Still, this huge needle went in until I was sure it would punch through the unfortunate man's belly. I was willing him not to move when I felt the change in density. At the doctor's instruction, I screwed off the end of the instrument and extracted the pin. We waited, and watched enthralled as the clear liquid dripped, drop by drop, into the test tube I held. When the *capitaine* deemed there was enough liquid, I sealed off the appliance and began to extract the needle. When it was done, I placed a bandaid over the site of the puncture, helped the fellow to his bed, replaced the chair under the desk, and with the kidney dish in hand left the room. The entire procedure had taken less than five minutes.

A more routine part of my tasks was to take blood, which was a 0600 ritual at Bouffard. On one of these mornings, I met Abdou, a baby boy newly arrived at the nursery, aged perhaps four months, although no one could be sure. As well as the children of serving AND personnel here, there were many babies who had been abandoned – in alleys, rubbish bins or at the door of the local Sisters of Mercy. Sometimes dehydrated and near death, these newborns were brought to the hospital to be tested for disease, the most important test being for HIV.

Abdou had not been sent to the hospital sooner because it was expected he would die. When the Djiboutian wet nurses came into the nursery that morning to hold, feed and play with the infants, one laughed and said that Abdou could've been my son – '*un petit Légionnaire*'. Not that he looked like me; she was simply referring to the fact that his skin was more cream-coffee coloured than the typical blue-black.

As a rule, the taking of a baby's blood is no easy thing, and it's made more difficult if the child is malnourished. With Abdou, it was near impossible to find the correct spot to insert the needle, because he wouldn't respond (that is, cry out) when his feet and arms were pinched – the traditional methods of determining the spot. Finally, like something welling up from his soul, he let out a series of wails, so the nurse and I could at last identify the pulse of his carotid artery.

When we were done and had extracted the needle and applied a bandaid, I brought him to my chest and rocked him gently until he slipped back into his torpor. I held him close to my body and felt his small body move and snuggle into my arms.

Days later, I arrived one morning especially enthusiastic and keen to find out what the future held for Abdou. I soon learned that instead of the prospect of adoption by a loving French couple, he had been moved to the end of the nursery. The quiet, dark end. I paced over to where he lay, his breathing barely perceptible. I watched him, and wondered at life, giving and taking at the same time.

The wet nurses advised against bonding with any of the children, but sometimes their advice was too cruel. What harm did it do the little ones to be held and rocked or have gentle words murmured in their ears? So I reached into Abdou's cot and held his tiny body against mine. I spoke warm things in his chocolate ears and he stirred a little, sighed, and wrapped small fingers around mine. After a few minutes of this, I placed him back in the cot, where he stretched a leg and curled his toes. I turned around to face the wet nurses, who were looking at me, thin-lipped, disapproving.

Later in the afternoon, I checked in on the nursery, to see how Abdou was faring. His cot was empty, the paper with his name on it had been removed, the plastic mattress now shiny with disinfectant. Abdou was dead. Worse than dead, it was as if he had never been. I stood next to the cot and felt one of the strings that bound my heart to my soul stretch and snap with a pang.

My time at the military hospital also reminded me that even small wars have their victims. A doctor approached me one morning to ask whether I could convince one of the Djiboutian soldiers to agree to have his leg amputated. Hassan had been wounded in his left leg in an ambush with FRUD fighters and the nerve had been severed. It meant that even though the blood continued to circulate, the muscles in his leg would shrivel and the skin and bone would become infected. In time it would kill him. What had happened to Hassan with his leg could've happened to me on top of that spike at Castelnaudary.

I had seen Hassan moving around the wards. He swung his body between crutches on his way to visit other soldiers who had been wounded. So I sat with him one morning, a white Australian in a foreign army, speaking a foreign language to a man whose religion I did not share. But men who are soldiers, no matter their country, colour, race or religion, are always able to speak together. There are shared experiences and hurts in being a soldier that are always understood.

After talking about my family and his family and children, I asked Hassan about his plans for the future. I watched his face change then, his shining ebony eyes darkened and lost their lustre. I asked him what he intended to do with his leg. The muscles rippled across his jaw and through gritted teeth Hassan said that he would never lose his leg. With it, even as it was, he was wounded. Without it he was less than a man.

He put his right hand over my right wrist and cried, 'Don't let them take it from me!'

•

This year, the usual Bastille Day festivities included the passing of command in *3ème Compagnie*. Our new commander, we learned, was to be a *Capitaine* Fleur de Lys.

The evening before Rocky was to depart, following his two–year stint in Djibouti, we had a gathering that doubled as the 14 July celebration. For some reason, the *capitaine* was feeling open and magnanimous and invited Legionnaires to speak with him frankly, on matters close to their hearts. The evening saw many people very drunk and, as so often happens in armies, offices or even among families, some drank too much and so, perhaps inevitably, said too much. Legionnaire Berko was one. Suitably smashed, the Pole went to the *capitaine*, put his arm around him, and tried to develop a very meaningful conversation. From where I sat, I could just make out the blurred speech relating to how the company was run and how improvements could be made.

Sitting next to me was *Sergent-Chef* Solo, the very same from Castelnaudary and newly affected to the training section here at Quartier Monclar. The Italian was not impressed. He went out of his way to ask, Henry II style, 'Who will rid me of this fool?' No one felt compelled to do anything at all. Not then, anyway.

The following day Berko was found lying in his bed, bashed and barely conscious. Someone had done the job, and that person was never identified. This was curious given that Berko shared a room with seven others. There was a lesson in this: no matter what an *officier* said, never take it as read that you could treat a conversation with him as a one-to-one that had no sanction. As a Legionnaire, you were powerless.

If one Pole in the company was made to suffer unduly, another deserved everything he got, as far as many of us were concerned.

By early August, we had finished up at the hospital and had only to sit to a final exam. This consisted of a written test in the morning and a practical one, to be held in the *infirmerie*, in the afternoon. For all the *stagiers*, the practical test was completed relatively quickly, in just fifteen minutes or so. All bar one of us, that is. *Caporal* Krapski was there for almost an hour, being tested under very close scrutiny. Waiting outside, we were certain he wouldn't pass the course, and nor did we think he should. In the end, Krapski finished the afternoon very distressed. His underarms were dark circles of nervous perspiration and his forehead was greasy with sweat and fear. But he passed.

On Thursday, 5 September, I began my first leave in Djibouti, after twenty-two months without any leave at all other than the irregular Thursday night. During my two years I was entitled to twenty-eight days' leave, though what this meant in practice was hardly exciting. I could not travel outside the country. I did try to get to Ali Sabieh, a town I liked, but the railway was out of bounds to Legionnaires and the clerk at the station in Djibouti city refused to sell me a ticket. He looked at me, pointed to the west and raised his eyes in surprise. 'Don't you know there's a war on out there?' he asked. I returned to Monclar, sat on my bed and began to read, promising myself that one day I would ride the train from Djibouti to Addis Ababa.

We received another batch of newcomers in *4ème Section*. They were almost all Hungarians, Romanians and Bulgarians. If they were anything like the previous bunch, they would get infections easily, get very drunk whenever they could and contract at least one sexual malady within four months of arrival.

The latest news on the HIV front was that at least half of the working girls in town were HIV positive. The *médicin chef* told me that the incidence of AIDS in 13 DBLE would've been similar had we been based at Marseilles. Not a good recommendation for French working girls, or for us.

As for me, I was counting down the weeks and then days to the end of my time in Djibouti. As was customary before a departure from the regiment, I went before the *capitaine compagnie, Capitaine* Fleur de Lys. I liked him. He was more thoughtful than his predecessor, having at least stopped the morning inquisition prior to *infirmerie* visits. Fleur de Lys told me I was an asset to the Legion; apparently, I was a leader, a teacher and someone who could be trusted. This was interesting stuff. Other than from Tallyman, one rarely heard anything approaching positive feedback in the Legion unless it was just before leave, when they wanted to make sure you came back. According to the *capitaine,* I was to do the *sergent* course after taking long leave.

I thanked him for his words, saluted and left. As I walked out the door, the *sergent* in the orderly room muttered that I'd most likely desert. I told him to get fucked and repeated that word of defiance from three years before: *'Jamais!'*

The following day, Thursday, 14 November, those who had done their two years in Djibouti, and survived, caught an Air France flight to Paris.

23

COLD WELCOME

Tu vas voir!
(You'll see!)

The skies above Paris were a soupy grey when we arrived at Charles de Gaulle Airport that Thursday evening, marking the first days of winter in Northern Europe. The first thing that struck me once inside the airport terminal was not the air-conditioning, not the air free of a rotting Africa, but the fragrance of women – their perfume, their scent. I had arrived at a place where women could be independent, carry briefcases, wear high heels and pencil skirts. I loved it. It had to be civilisation at last.

We were bundled into a waiting bus that took us to Fort de Nogent; back to where it all began for me. The Legionnaires we spoke with were careful with us, as if we were hurt or damaged somehow. In a way that even the Legion recognised, we all were. We were also tired and dislocated from the world around us. Next day we repeated the steps I'd taken back on that day in late spring 1988: a bus through Paris's clogged arteries to Gare de Lyon; the overnight train to Marseilles; and a surburban connection from Gare Saint-Charles to Aubagne. Perhaps the only challenges to the sense of déjà vu were the autumn weather and the fact that we weren't locked into the carriage this time around.

We arrived at Aubagne on Saturday to learn we were *consigné au quartier* for the weekend. Indeed, we were not to leave Quartier Viénot until the following Friday, when we would receive our *grande titres de permission,* our permission slips for long leave. So we settled down on the first floor of the CAPLE building, where we were very cold and lived in a permanent fugue of cigarette smoke; courtesy of a *caporal-chef* with fourteen years' service who took great pleasure in sharing the smoke from his putrid Gauloises.

As with every group of returnees from overseas, there was a tension among us regarding the upcoming medical tests and what they might reveal. Every Legionnaire was now being confronted with the results of his behaviour during those two years away. Syphilis and the other infections could be cured; AIDS made death feel too close. Of each detachment that returned, there would usually be at least be one or two who tested HIV positive. Among us, who would it be?

The first test arrived on Monday morning, when we gave blood at the *infirmerie*. We would find out the results late that week, they told us, on Friday afternoon, when the *grande titres* were distributed. Over successive days, we went to the military hospital at Lavéran in Marseilles' north, that place of depression and dust, and had our chests X-rayed for TB.

That week, one thing occurred that well and truly distracted me from the dreary grind of hospital visits. In fact, it took my mind back almost two years, to a New Year's Eve on Rue Éthiopie and a Legionnaire lying on the footpath . . .

It was on Tuesday morning, just minutes before we were due to form up on CAPLE's gravel parade ground, when a French *caporal* sidled up to me. Standing near the coffee machine at the back wall of the CAPLE near the parade ground, I felt more than saw him approaching. When he spoke, it was in a low whisper.

'*Marino dit bonjour.*'

So, a message from Marino – Amir the Turk's accomplice . . .

'*Marino t'attend au Vieux Port,*' he said. '*Il veut te voir.*' (Marino is waiting for you at the Old Port. He wants to see you.) Then, with a thin-lipped grin, he drew a finger across his throat.

After watching this *caporal's* face for a moment, and aware of others around who were becoming interested in our little exchange, I grabbed his throat with my right hand and pushed him up against the wall of the building. Then I squeezed. It was fortunate that I'd pinched my fingers around his oesophagus, because almost immediately he began to gurgle and gag.

I raised my left hand and, while I was inclined to splatter his nose across his face, I knew there was more to this encounter. I said, '*Je m'en fou*' to this green slime, and to anyone else here who was interested. I didn't care what Marino wanted, thought or did, I told the *caporal*. Any Legionnaire who stabbed another in the back was a *chien,* a dog, and nothing to me.

And then I looked right in his face, wanting to make sure he understood, and demanded, '*Tu comprends?!*'

Then a second time, my voice bellowing now: '*TU COMPRENDS?!*'

He tried to nod, his eyes began to bulge and his gagging became higher-pitched. The French Legionnaires standing around made a lot of noises but they did nothing. A Brit was more helpful, and said in my ear, 'Think about what you're doing, mate.' I did and relaxed my grip on the green thing with the red face.

As he slunk away clutching at his throat, all he could say was, '*Tu vas voir!*' I never saw him again.

Among the tests and debriefs at Aubagne was an interview, on the Thursday, with the *colonel* in charge of the *Bureau Personnel de la Légion Étrangère*. He told me that I had done very well during my time in Djibouti and that I was marked for rapid promotion. I had a '*belle carrière*'. I would pass *sergent* and in two to three years could think about beginning the course for *sergent-chef*.

I thanked him for his confidence in me – and then politely declined his offer. I did say that I would sign on after five years (after all, if I didn't I would be allocated some dreadful task like being stuck in Aubagne carrying people's mail). And I told the colonel that I wished to experience more of what the Legion had to offer. In short, I wanted to go to Calvi and the Parachute Regiment. He nodded, shuffled some papers in front of him, closed a file and with a sigh of resignation said, 'There are very few like you and we need you.'

We looked at each other for some moments without saying a word. We both knew what was at play. On returning to France from overseas, if you were sent straight to Castelnaudary, you would be there for years, doing repetitive work in a *section d'instruction*, with low pay. I joined the Legion for adventure, for combat. And importantly, I refused promotion in an environment that merely assisted in maintaining the illusion that the French Foreign Legion was something that it wasn't.

I came to attention and declared, '*Je peux disposer à vos ordres, mon Colonel,*' saluted and left the room.

On Friday afternoon, on the gravel behind CAPLE where thousands of men from around the world had paraded, the thirteen of us formed up for the distribution of the *grands titres de permission*. The newly returned detachment watched and waited to see where the hammer would fall. Only 10 metres from us stood the rest of the CAPLE personnel, awaiting the allocation of duties for the afternoon. The *adjudant-chef* cleared his throat and looked down at his clipboard.

To not a little relief, my name was called early. As each man's name was read out, he moved and formed up into another small group. So, there was no escaping from the fact that two men had not received their long leave passes.

The pair looked disbelievingly at the *adjudant-chef* and across at us in desperation. But there was nothing anyone could do. Kemal, a Turk, and my old friend from the drivers' course, De Olimop, the Portuguese *caporal*, remained where they were. They had to present themselves before the *médicin chef* the following day – if they were fortunate, otherwise they would have to wait until Monday. They could be HIV positive, or have something relatively benign like TB; no one told them. They'd just have to go through the torture, running through the possible scenarios in their minds, for yet another night at least.

I arrived in Paris, at the Gare de Lyon, at 0550 on Saturday, 23 November. After a shower, a shave and some coffee, I took the Métro to the Australian Embassy, a few blocks from the Eiffel Tower, where I picked up a passport. I purchased a plane ticket with my hard-earned French francs and took almost three months' leave in Australia. It was a time of eating fresh food and sleeping without the fear of being rudely woken, bashed or having to bash someone.

In many ways I felt fragile and vulnerable; isolated in a bubble of emotion. I was delighted to be out for a while, but how could I relate to the people around me, on the QANTAS flight or at a dinner table, who did not and could not know the life I had led? I did know that my brain had turned to jelly. It was as if the intellectual parts, the parts that favoured poetry and political discussion had ceased to function. Without being tested and tried, the thinking parts of me had become fragmented and uncoordinated, something I had noticed years ago during basic training. It was not until I was with educated, thinking people again that I fully recognised another toll of being a Legionnaire.

At Christmas with familiy and friends there were long silences after I had spoken. It was not that I sounded different, or that it was odd having me home after nearly four years, or that my knowledge of recent world events was so poor; it was because my family had thought I had become stupid.

All this was tempererd by the knowledge that I was returning to the Legion. I knew I had to go back, to be true to myself and what I had undertaken. One night I returned home not long before dawn and collapsed into bed. I heard the door handle turn and the door to my room was opened a little, so I could just make out my mother's face. I didn't move, and held my breath. She paused for a moment and sighed deeply, with resignation and loss. I was another person, a stranger to her, and although I slept in her house I was a long, long way away.

While I was at home in Canberra, my family were gentle and tolerant with me. I spent as much time as possible having sex with any consenting woman I could find, drinking until I fell over, and generally sleeping without dreams – or at least not remembering many. There was one I recall; it was Jesus Christ looking up from his tatooed place on a broad back. With narrow eyes and gritted teeth he took his right hand from the Cross and drew his index finger across his throat.

It was mid February 1992 and very cold when I made my way back to Paris. Having returned to the Australian Embassy to deposit my passport and other personal items, I arrived at the CPLEM – Malmousque – the following day. With a sinking feeling, I reminded myself what a bloody dreadful place it was. It stank of old cigarettes, spilt beer, stale urine, old men and hopes long dead. Fortunately for those sitting about nursing their hangovers, there was a new beer machine, it was cheap and it operated all hours of the day.

Sitting at a window, overlooking the Mediterranean towards the Château d'If, were men I had known for years. Keyman and Bunt, one of the Brits who'd been such a great support during my *caporal* course. The two of them were plotting what to do that night. Keyman told me he was all right; he was having sex with a woman from a bar just up the road from here. Indeed, I told him, and no doubt fresh and willing. I remembered what the *médicin chef* told me in Djibouti about Marseilles and its working girls.

Two days later I was back at the CAPLE in Quartier Viénot, and just as I'd finished with regulation, the process of signing in after a period of leave, someone I knew told me that Krisson had deserted. While not surprising, this was depressing. I first met Krisson in Castelnaudary and we were in the same detachment for Djibouti; another good man gone.

In between guard duties of various types, I did physical tests for entry to 2 REP and fell prey to indiscriminate *corvées*. One afternoon I was selected to assist with filing and shelving personnel records. Among the dusty paperwork, I was able to read Gungie Whyte's file. The final document was a so-called record of an *accident de circulation* (traffic accident) in Djibouti in which Gungie had been killed. This was very different from the reality that his life had been blown apart by a 120 mm mortar round. In this closed environment, where there was no external scrutiny, the Legion could write its own past and present as it wished. The Legion couldn't even be honest with itself about the way it killed its own men.

The Legion killed its men in many ways. To numb my anger, I had a few beers in the foyer with some of the Brits. One, just back from Djibouti, told me that Legionnaire Meng had shot himself. Not long after midnight on the guard up at the *Escadron de Reconnaissance*, Meng sat himself down, leaned his back up against the wall of the disused open-air cinema, put the barrel of the rifle in his mouth, and with his thumb pressed down on the trigger. The resulting burst of three rounds blew off the back of his head and smeared the whitewashed wall with blood and brains.

I remembered Meng very well. He was Burmese and new to the *4ème Section* at Djibouti. He was young, warm-hearted, intelligent, helpful and friendly. Physically he was short and slight. These very attributes were probably seen as weaknesses and vulnerabilities by those who'd been taking advantage of him. Although he was surrounded by men who were, according to the Legion Code, his brothers, he didn't feel as though he could talk to anyone about what was weighing on his mind. In the end, he must have been very lonely.

While everyone in the Legion knows homosexual activity takes place, the Legion is outwardly very homophobic. Some men I knew in the *escadron*, who were unwilling or unable at any price to secure female companionship in Europe or Africa, preyed on young Legionnaires like Meng. They took what they wanted by force. Even though the rest of us knew what was going on, none of us did anything about it. Predatory homosexuality, alcoholism and endemic sexual infections were commonplace. Because everyone, including *caporals*, felt isolated, exposed and vulnerable, they said and did nothing.

24

TO CALVI

Nous, on n'a pas besoin de ça. On est la Légion,
n'est-ce pas?
(Us, we don't need it. We're the Legion, aren't we?)

I was at last going to the Legion's best, its elite regiment. This was where I'd planned to go at the end of instruction, back in September '88, but the prospect of rapid promotion had appeared and changed my direction. I had seen the Training Regiment, I had spent two years in Africa with the *13ème Demi-Brigade* on operations, and in both cases I'd been disappointed. Despite what others might have told me about the REP, I intended to find what I had been looking for.

On 7 March 1992, a Saturday, I caught the overnight ferry *Maria Casanova* from Marseilles to the north-east of Corsica and the port of Bastia, which, like the whole isle, is significantly closer to the Italian coastline than it is to France's Côte d'Azur. Once on the vessel, I got a cabin with some REP men who had just completed the *caporal* course at Castelnaudary. Three years after my own course, *Adjudant* Raype was still there, instructing the Legion's junior ranks in French Foreign Legion minor tactics.

On a bus from Bastia to Calvi, on the northeast coast, I looked out the window and got my first taste of local politics. Near Lumio, on a rock face beside the road, in giant white letters, some disaffected Corsican had inscribed: *Légion dehors!* (Legion out!) You couldn't miss it. As in Djibouti, it appeared that the Legion was not universally loved here. Judging by the acronym that appeared under these words, an organisation called the FLNC were taking the credit for this particular comment.

The modern history of Corsica began in the 1750s, when a republic was declared after three decades of power struggles with the notoriously ruthless Genoese. Any gains were short-lived, however, as the French then purchased the island from the Genoese and invaded in 1769. While France imposed its rule and its language, some native Corsicans continued to reject the French claim. The early 1970s gave rise to the Front de Libération Nationale de la Corse (FLNC), the largest and oldest terrorist organisation in Corsica. It still operated in the '90s, occasionally destroying the empty summer homes of French mainlanders.

At Lumio the bus came to a rise from which we could clearly see, across a valley to the south-west, the citadel of Calvi on its tall promontory, with the Mediterranean to the west. The Legion's Corsican base, Camp Raffalli, was sited on the road across this valley, some 4 kilometres from the citadel. To the east, the hinterland mountains rose up steeply to the sky. On this day in March, they were covered in snow.

We turned left and passed through the gates of Camp Raffalli, after which the regimental museum came into view, on our left. The bus soon stopped outside the office of the *officier de permanence*, the duty officer, just 50 metres from the front gate. After plenty of unprovoked yells from NCOs, we formed up in a rank across the avenue that led up to the regimental headquarters. We were met by our *moniteur* (instructor), *Sergent* Graba, who directed us to load our luggage onto our backs and follow him on a tour of the camp. The tour was mercifully short. I found it pretty difficult carrying a 30-kilogram *sac* on the end of each arm. The reason they were so heavy was because I'd recently bought a lot of new kit in the hope of making life better for myself while out in the field. Instead of having to rely on the rubbish we were issued, I brought along a goretex jacket, a goretex bivvy bag, a down sleeping bag and an Australian Army lean-to.

Piled up with all this gear, I just made it over to our temporary home, the *bâtiment des stagiers*. At this point, *Sergent* Graba introduced us to our *caporal*, Seric, all parachute courses here being looked after by a *moniteur–caporal* team. Under his dark, tightly cropped hair, *Caporal* Seric didn't appear altogether enthusiastic or very bright. He had the air of someone with a heavy burden on his shoulders, the weight constantly bearing him down.

Our stage was made up almost entirely of recruits fresh from Castelnaudary. The 23 of us installed ourselves in a room, the walls of which were filled with REP memorabilia, pictures of paratroopers and aircraft, and other images of a similar theme. The caption on each picture listed the names of the *stagiers*, *moniteur* and *caporal* and the number of their promotion, or promo. We were the *621ème Promotion*.

So on 8 March 1992 – Calvi, Corsica, the *2ème Régiment Étranger de Parachutistes*. I had arrived.

•

First thing next morning we had a run. Up to the water tower on the ridge to the south of the camp, then down to the beach, just west of camp, and along much of its length to the *Centre Amphibie*. The latter was the training base for *3ème Compagnie*, 2 REP's amphibious company.

Later, after a shower, we visited the *infirmerie*. During my visit, the *médicin chef* leaned back in his chair, brought his fingers together into a tent shape, and said he was surprised that throughout my time in Djibouti I hadn't caught a single STD. He had never seen anyone return from Djibouti after a two-year posting without having contracted something. What was my secret? Thinking back to Fatima, I replied, '*Capotes.*' He smiled.

My second day there began with another run, this time to the back of the camp, across the stream that flowed through the eastern end of the *zone de saut*, our parachuting drop zone, and then north up to Lumio. Graba detailed me to take up the rear of the promo with Meare, an officer cadet – or *aspirant* – who was having a lot of difficulty keeping up with the rest. *Aspirant* Meare was a doctor fresh from medical school. He had elected to do his National Service in the Legion, but this was a poor decision. He wasn't up to it; he couldn't even manage a single chin-up, when a minimum of ten was required, and he lagged far behind the others on the runs. Meare did have one redeeming feature, though: a wonderful sense of humour. In any event, although he would go to the *infirmerie* to work, he had to do the promo before he could wear his 'wings' and the regimental badge of the winged dagger on his green beret.

Also on that Tuesday, we had lessons on how to leave an aircraft, in the square steel mock-ups located in front of the *Section d'Entretien de Pliage Parachutes* (SEPP), the parachute packers beyond the *ordinaire*, where specifically trained

Legionnaires spent their days folding 2 REP's parachutes. As in other Legion regiments, the Legionnaires did everything here too. They had no need of others, least of all civilians.

That evening, as on most as it turned out, under the direction of *Caporal* Seric, we did many sit-ups and pushups. At 2200, after *appel*, Seric locked us in our room, gave me the key, and went into town to visit his *femme*. She was the weight on his shoulders. He favoured me with a look at two photographs, of his wife and daughter. Of course, I said the usual: 'Isn't she attractive' and 'What a cute smile!' The facts were rather different. His wife, even in her photo, had the hard-bitten look of a Marseilles prostitute. She looked out from the photo with eyes like stones. She had long black hair and a pinched face; intolerant and hard. Maybe she realised she was losing her charms and set her sights on a regular pay packet. To Seric, I wished his family well.

Wednesday brought more physical tests – sit-ups, 90-metre run with sandbag, chin-ups and climbing a rope without the use of feet – followed the next day by runs of 1500 metres and 8000 metres. I came in second behind a new Legionnaire, a former *sergent* from the *Chasseurs Alpins*, a very well known unit in the French Army, with a nineteen-year-old Legionnaire finishing third. 'Not bad,' said *Sergent* Graba, nodding his head at me, 'for a 31-year-old.'

On Friday, we had another seven Legionnaires arrive to do the promo with us. I knew two of them. The first was *Caporal* De Olimop, like a couple of the others, back to do a refresher course. He was in my detachment from Djibouti and the very same fellow who last November had been kept waiting at Aubagne by the *médicine chef*. He refused to answer me directly when I asked why he'd been kept behind; it was not unheard of for HIV-positive men to be sent to the REP. He did tell me that one of our detachment committed suicide before returning from leave. No one knew why, but the speculation was that he was HIV positive and preferred not to face the future. The second familiar face was that of Legionnaire *1ère Classe* John, a Brit. I'd first met him just after he had done time in Aubagne's jail for returning late from long leave after two years in French Guyane.

After the morning's *footing,* we were driven out to the quartier's airfield in open trucks. Our afternoon was spent weeding with our fingers, the staging point for the donning of parachutes. It reminded me of my time as a recruit at Bel Air. And unfortunately, it was another appalling waste of time. If you were passionate and motivated to do and create things in life, the time wasting in the Legion was a sin. You had to slow to its rhythms and priorities; be flexible and adaptable. Time was not your own and whether you liked it or not, time could be frittered away on useless things – such as scrubbing already clean bed frames for a week or weeding with your hands.

As for John, he was not having a good time at all. Were it not for the *aspirant,* John would have been last in almost every activity, including the most important of all: *footing.* And no matter the activity in the Legion, last was no place to be. John began to look worried.

Before long, and even though I felt and looked in excellent health, I developed a boil on my upper right butt cheek. Exquisitely painful, it meant that I found it very difficult to lie down. I took myself off to the *infirmerie* to have someone look at it. As soon as I lay down and exposed myself to the doctor and his medics, there was an exclamation bordering on glee. I asked *Aspirant* Meare if he could get me some antibiotics and the *médicin capitaine* later prescribed an injection. As was so often the case, however, there was no appropriate antibiotic, so I was sent back to the stage with no injection.

The thing on my backside made simulated parachuting landings a very painful activity. For days I was unable to sit down properly. On a later visit to the *infirmerie,* two medics, one Japanese, the other Canadian, did plenty of squeezing and cutting around the site with a scalpel. The infection sat on a nerve, I realised, so whenever they squeezed it, I'd feel pain shoot down to my right foot. The Canadian told me that there was now a splendid hole in my right cheek, which he duly filled with gauze to help it heal properly.

But still the course went on, and we needed six parachute jumps under our belts to qualify for our wings, the *brevet parachutiste*. Around this time, heavy cloud and rain forced us to sit out a whole week – we just waited for hours on end in the back of trucks beside the zone de saut, with our kit around us. Sometimes we didn't even leave the camp; we just looked out the windows at the pine trees and the snow-covered mountains in the east.

Standing up with all the gear on was certainly not easy. You had a helmet, the parachute on your back, the reserve on your chest, and the *gaine*, which was a velcroed pack that held your *sac à dos* and personal weapons container. The *gaine* was attached at the chest and you released this heavy pack by pulling its handle, which would result in the *gaine* falling some 6 metres below your body – while still attached by a cord to your harness.

On 10 April, we left the airport at Calvi for Borgo, a drop zone inland and south of Bastia. I volunteered for the door, so as to be first out, but Graba gave the port door to *Aspirant*

Meare and the starboard to the youngest of the *stagiers*. I lined up as number two on the starboard side.

Jumping out of an aircraft is the closest you can come to death while being joyously alive. You must surrender yourself to the air and, for a moment, just as you step out and are sucked from the door, you fall. The sensations are so intense that you lose a moment in time; the closest thing on earth to an orgasm without having one.

Aspirant Meare, however, was a long way from orgasm. He shattered an ankle on his very first jump. An ambulance with flashing lights arrived to alarm the other jumpers and carry Meare away. My worries were few in comparison; I had much of my canopy drape itself over a large prickly bush of maquis, and was kept very busy trying to extricate my gear from the local flora.

Before jumping a second time that day, we were instructed to open the ventral, or reserve, 'chute. In so doing, rather than losing the main 'chute, as in some systems, we descended with both open overhead – a little like the re-entry of a space capsule.

Shortly after these jumps, we managed another three, all in the one day; twice at Borgo and then once over Calvi, to conclude the day. We were still short of the magic six though – and that was when the weather turned bad again. It was mid April, and during this time I was back in the *infirmerie*, having picked up another infection in my right thigh, just above my right knee. I also had a rapidly rising temperature. A medic put zinc cream on the site in an effort to bring the thing to a head.

A few days later, relief came on two fronts: conditions were good and we completed the required jumps, and at last the furuncle burst. I still had trouble bending my knee as the entire leg was hot and swollen. But we had now earned our brevets and were part of the *grandes famille de parachutistes* . . . whatever that meant.

Being part of the family also meant learning another song. It was the REP's '*La Légion Marche*', the words in English being as follows:

> The Legion marches to the front
> Singing we follow,
> Inheritors of its traditions,
> We are with her.
>
> Refrain:
> We are the men of thè assault troops,
> Soldiers of the old Legion,
> Tomorrow brandishing our flags,
> In victory we will march,
> We have not only weapons,
> But the devil marches with us,
> Ha, ha, ha, ha, ha, ha, for our oldest of the Legion,
> Fighting there, we keep in step.
>
> For this knight's detiny
> Honour, Fidelity,
> We are proud to belong
> To 2 REP.

I liked this song because it included a devil, and while the song said the devil marched with us, I knew one was inside me. I knew too that as I grew older and more experienced, I no longer had to respond to each whispered promise or hissed curse. If I wasn't becoming wiser, I was certainly becoming more thoughtful. When we laughed in the song I wondered if we were laughing at the Legion, the world, or at ourselves.

On Friday, 17 April, on a spring afternoon, the 27 of us were paraded in front of the REP's regimental headquarters and presented with our wings. As the sun caught it for a moment I admired mine, a metal brevet of wings to the sides of a parachute, a golden wreath underneath and a five pointed star under all. The number inscribed on my *brevet parachutiste* was 567681, so it seemed that at least half a million men had jumped and succeeded before me. Perhaps it really was a *grande famille*.

Lined up before the main administration building, we were expecting to be given a rousing speech by the second-in-command of the regiment. Instead, the *lieutenant-colonel* gave us something completely devoid of passion and true meaning. It was galling. He reminded us of the *grande famille des Légionnaires* and the *grande famille des parachutistes*, of course. All I heard was shuffling and yawns around me – yet every man here should've been encouraged to feel truly proud at winning his REP brevet, the finest achievement of his Legion career thus far. Not for the first time, I was embarrassed and very disappointed.

At the conclusion of this little ceremony we were marched off to the foyer. Here the commanders of the regiment's companies, or their representatives, put in an appearance. But not one senior officer spoke to a Legionnaire. The two groups stood apart, separated by the table that bore the drinks, arranged as usual to form the Legion flame. As *pots* went, it was depressing, but thankfully brief.

Our *moniteur*, though, seemed more than happy to associate with us. Straight after the non-event in the foyer, Graba took everyone in *621ème Promotion* for a night out in Calvi. A bus was laid on and we dined at the restaurant above Les Palmiers, a bar right on the water in town. We were met by Emile, the urbane, middle aged, multilingual *habitué* of Calvi's nightlife. He owned the restaurant and Les Palmiers. He wore a cravat and a welcoming smile.

We finished dinner quickly and were escorted downstairs to the bar, where at around 2300, Graba had an altercation with another *sous-officier*. Words were traded, fists were thrown and blows exchanged. All the while I had been talking to Lorena, Calvi's sole resident prostitute. No doubt thinking of my wellbeing, Emile and Graba had sung my praises to her. She was in her early thirties, well spoken and well groomed with shoulder-length black hair, and an attitude that said she could pick and choose her clients. She was an attractive, intelligent woman. As graciously as I could (and to her surprise, I think), I declined her offer. Among other things, I didn't want to be sharing my actions with the rest of the regiment. I was more discreet than that.

Not long after the fracas involving *Sergent* Graba, the promo left Emile's and we were driven back east to Camp Raffalli. Few of us had drunk much, for the next day would see us posted to our respective companies. Some, mainly the more recent arrivals to the promo, were going to *3ème Compagnie*, the amphibious company; the rest were allotted to *2ème Compagnie*, known as the mountain company.

So, next day, I stood in front of *Capitaine* Moulin, *2ème Compagnie's* commanding officer. Perhaps I was wrong to expect more, but his welcome was hardly a warm one.

'Everything you have done in the Legion up to now is of no account to me,' he announced. 'All the things written about you in your file are but scratches on paper.' Here he gave a languid swish of his wrist towards the file on his desk.

He paused before adding, 'You must start at zero, for I do not know you.'

Given that he had almost completed his two years as a company commander in Calvi, there wasn't much time in which to impress *Capitaine* Moulin. I supposed he meant that if I did wish to rise to the rank of *sergent* in the Legion's Parachute Regiment, I would have to wait my turn. Moulin was to be replaced by *Capitaine* Grinch from *4ème Compagnie*, I gathered.

Within our company, I had been affected to *2ème Section* under *Lieutenant* Big Bird. There was no English *caporal* or *sergent* in the *section*, so I would be alone again and exposed. Such were the breaks in life. I was the *chef de chambre* in a room with a view across the parade ground to Lumio, 5 kilometres to the north.

In my room were Legionnaires Gimlet, Ponski and Louvier. It seemed there was something of a flap on, thanks not only to the imminence of Camerone Day and the opportunity it provided for making money, but because everyone had to have a new and improved name and matricule sign stuck onto their lockers.

Other *caporals* in *2ème Section* included Fillip, who weighed in at 100 kilograms and hailed from the Wallis Islands; and Poobelle, the wine-stained Frenchmen who didn't trouble me for his facial birthmark, but because he was the sycophantic, whining rat I'd known in Djibouti. Fillip was kicked out of the regiment's reconnaissance and support company because when drunk, he became completely unmanageable. From what I'd already seen, he would go into town for the night and arrive back in camp around 0530, just in time for *appel*, looking heavy-jowled, with a greasy yellow-brown complexion and dark, bloodshot eyes. Soon after appel, he'd start slapping around the Legionnaires in his room; usually O'Paddy, from Galway in Ireland, and Snaggle, a Frenchman with disgusting teeth. Then, at the conclusion of *rassemblement,* he would beg off running, saying that he had to go to the *infirmerie* because of a supposed bad knee. According to a Californian named Holden, Fillip had been like this ever since coming to the *section* six months before.

Big Bird was named after the Sesame Street character of the same name. This was not only a reference to his size – he was almost 2 metres tall – but also because, while patronisingly talking down to his men, he made a big song and dance about everything.

Other *section* staff included a *caporal-chef* veteran of Kolwezi in 1978, and *Sergent-Chef* Chiffon, thought generally to be a rotten bullying bastard, but who considered himself something of a 'muscle-man'. Everyone went out of their way to avoid Chiffon, with the exception of a few brown-noses. These included Poobelle, true to past form, and a too-close friend of his, Legionnaire *1ère Classe* Despute.

Thursday, 30 April – Camerone Day – duly arrived and I, being the new man on the block, was made *caporal du jour* for the week. We marched in the camp, rather than in Calvi, with its FLNC sympathies; the regimental band played, while families and well-wishers whistled and cheered.

Next day was an open day in Camp Raffalli. Chiffon's 'baby', a Chinese takeaway, was set up inside the quartier and sat alongside other stalls where one could eat, gamble with dice or play cards. The entire effect made for a side-show alley atmosphere. These stands were set up to show visiting civilians that there was more to the Legionnaire than soldiering. In reality, there was little more to this activity than making money.

A highlight of that Friday was the appearance of Lorena in a very short white leather skirt and lace-up boots. She flounced through the crowd and around the various stalls, waving, smiling and kissing her many paramours. Kisses and cries of '*Bonjour chérie!*' were delivered whether the recipient was a young Legionnaire or an *adjudant-chef* with wife and kids in tow.

As *caporal du jour*, I took station near the takeaway stands, in case I had to round up Legionnaires for work. A rush on the food came just after 1300, the demand being such that there was not enough being produced to satisfy the hungry hordes around the makeshift Chinese takeaway. Chiffon began to shout. Despite his labours with the frying pan, one Legionnaire failed to meet these yelled demands, so Chiffon turned and punched him, full in the face. The man fell on his back, bringing down on himself the clatter of cooking utensils.

An unprovoked blow like this, in front of so many people, both military and civilian, would be unbelievable in almost any other context. Not so here. The *sergent-chef* was clearly feeling frustrated; so a Legionnaire got bashed, and then Chiffon felt better. I hated myself for watching it, and more so for doing nothing. This was life in the Legion. As a passing *sous-officier* said with a smirk, '*Plus ça change plus c'est la même chose*' (The more things change, the more they stay the same).

Once Camerone was over and, soon enough, my tour as *caporal du jour* also, Chiffon allocated me to the *bureau de semaine* for the following week. Because the building that ordinarily housed *2ème Compagnie* was being renovated, the *sections* were now spread out around the parade ground. This meant that when I had to find people who were about to pass rapport, I could get out into the fresh air.

Regardless of the temporary relocation, this first stint on semaine duties also allowed me to present myself to those officers and NCOs in the company whom I'd not yet met. For, rather than being presented at a morning parade, a new Legionnaire or *caporal* had to seek out all company rankers. Once buttonholed, one commenced a variation on the tried-and-true formula:

> 'Caporal Mason.
> *Trois ans onze mois de service. Trois ans quatre mois de grade.*
> *Nouvellement affecté à la 2ème Compagnie. À vos ordres.*'

It was often tedious and could be humiliating. But at least it meant you had a working knowledge of who was in the *compagnie* and where their offices were to be found.

Thankfully, from the point of getting out of Camp Raffalli for a while, we were to take part in Operation Dragonhammer, a two-week NATO exercise involving ten member nations and held across the Mediterranean. Participation for us in *2ème Compagnie*, 2 REP, would consist of manouevres on the Italian island of Sardinia, south of Corsica. After feeling deflated at how events were handled during the brevet presentation, I was keen to see what the REP did in the field.

We left Calvi in a Transall aircraft on Monday, 11 May and parachuted onto the remote southern tip of Sardinia, just before dark. A few days before this, some members of the company had been sent off in trucks with our *sacs* marine, to make their way to the site of the exercise. Here they set up camp prior to the arrival of the main body. It was a rare piece of foresight on the part of our leaders.

The landing zone was rocky and the reorganisation of our *section* after the jump took almost an hour. It was hard to tell in the growing dark, but the cries and urgent calls told me there were quite a few men injured. People were always getting hurt on difficult jumps like this and we grew used to losing friends. Sometimes they came back to the regiment; sometimes we never saw them again. It was another reason not to get too close to anyone; a friend could be gone, hurt or posted away at almost any time without notice.

After loading Legionnaires with broken bodies into ambulances and handing over all the parachutes and *gaines*, we marched until 2200. Up until this point we had been told nothing, but then word came that we would be attacking a hill. This meant leaving our *sacs* 2 kilometres behind, in the dark. At 0200 we fanned out in an extended line at the bottom of a hill and sought the summit.

Unfortunately for *Capitaine* Grinch, we attacked the wrong part of the hill. Perhaps it didn't really matter. We waited until just before dawn and were then redeployed in pairs along the high ground. This way the 'enemy' on the plain below would know where we were. At least we could see them too, and the fighter aircraft that passed low overhead.

On the summit of the hill we waited for some orders, from dawn until 1600, but there were none. On a day that saw temperatures exceed 35 degrees Celsius, we had no water or food resupply, although the *capitaine* and his *lieutenant*s certainly did, via a liaison helicopter that flew in a couple of British observers. Having dropped our packs a couple of kilometres away, there was place on the webbing for only one water bottle, to be worn over the right buttock, two ammunition pouches, to the front, and a ludicrous tool worn over the left buttock. I carried a saw in a sheath; others carried an entrenching tool or a small machete-type knife. There was no shade up here, nor, I could see from looking across the rocky landscape towards the coast, were there many trees anywhere in this area. I could tell this was hard country, but, sitting on the crest of a ridge, we didn't know where in Sardinia we were, being without maps, nor did we know what we were supposed to be doing there. In the late afternoon, we marched down the hill to be reunited with our backpacks. And that was the end of the attack on the hill.

With *sacs* on backs we marched off in the gathering dusk. We hadn't gone far when *2ème Section* had to deploy on the lee side of another hill, away from the enemy. Once in position, *Lieutenant* Big Bird had the *section* wait until the situation clarified itself. The clarification came with the arrival of a platoon from 4/5 Commando, Royal Marines. In their camouflage uniforms, helmets with microphones, heavy-looking packs, some carrying Milan launchers and missiles, they filed past our *section*. They looked competent and professional. This was soon made evident when, at a signal, they formed themselves into a platoon defensive position, with sentries out and men behind their weapons. It was a drill borne of training and rigour, the like of which I never received or saw in the French Foreign Legion.

While this noiseless routine was being executed, Big Bird called me over. He told me to find the British officer in charge and tell him that he wished to discuss issues of mutual concern. While crossing the 50 or so metres to the Marines' position, I was struck by their efficiency. Each man was digging out a shallow position for himself, known as a shell scrape, which was also something I had yet to do in the Legion; and there was no yelling, just the dull metallic scrape of entrenching tool on Sardinian stone. They were formed up in an elongated circle. I headed for the radio aerial.

Here I found the company commander, a major, who had attached himself to the platoon. He was a 190-centimetre Scot with a red-brown moustache and the kind of twinkle in his eye I had not seen for some time. He was digging in with the platoon sergeant, while a signaller was getting a brew going.

'Good evening, sir,' I said. 'My *lieutenant* would very much like to have a word with you.'

'Would he, now?' the voice accompanying the twinkling eyes retorted.

Big Bird walked up at that point, stopped a short distance away and looked towards us hopefully. The major looked at me, then at his sergeant and finally to the Bird, before making a noise that resembled a snort but may well have been a suppressed laugh. He stepped up from his shell scrape, picked up his rifle and strode over to meet the Frenchman.

Lieutenant Big Bird drew himself to attention and saluted – so it was too late for me to tell him that Commonwealth nations do not salute while in the field. (Was there an easier way to indicate rank to a sniper?) The major responded with a wave about his head. Between them, the two officers settled on a location for our *section* and how the guard for the night would be run.

As we left the Marines to their digging, Big Bird quizzed me on these British troops. Why did they go into all-round defensive position? Why did they dig? Most importantly, why was a major digging with his soldiers? I outlined some of the principles by which, like Australia's army, they operated. Things like all-round defence, protection against mortars and artillery, camouflage and elements of leadership. Army stuff, not the Boy Scouts.

Big Bird shook his head, extended his lower lip and blew a near whistle, '*Nous, on n'a pas besoin de ça. On est la Légion, n'est-ce pas?*' (Us, we do not need it. We're the Legion, aren't we?)

•

We arrived back at Calvi on a landing craft just over a week later. Back on *garde* again for me, and with it some entertainment. Legionnaire Mirk, from *1ère Section*, came in from town very late and very drunk. At the issuing of the weapons, the *sergent* gave him a verbal drubbing – the usual *connard*, *clochard* and the rest. No doubt because he'd had far too much to drink and not enough sleep, Mirk very foolishly responded physically, lashing out with a short, sharp right-hand jab. The other Legionnaires on the guard stood about like lean green gazelles in a herd, and watched the early morning entertainment with interest. Poobelle and I dealt with Mirk, and he came off a very second best, with a blackened eye to go with his sore head. He found himself in the isolation cell behind the guardhouse for a number of days, before going before *Colonel* Gausseres, 2 REP's *chef de corps*, and a sure sentence of many more.

On the way to solitary with Mirk, I witnessed a typically low act. Despute, the sly brown-noser, appeared from behind a door, thumped Mirk in the face with a right hook and made a quick getaway. I threatened to punch the Frenchman's face out the back of his head, but he'd already scuttled away like the coward he was. Despute was a well-known rat, full of purple praise to Big Bird's face, but ready with a range of disparaging remarks when the *lieutenant's* back was turned. I had few views on the Bird's character, just that he was an incompetent leader, but then this was something he shared with pretty much all the French officers I'd come across.

The Legion's *officiers* thought they understood the mentality of Legionnaires. I knew this because they would arrogantly say as much directly to me, and too often within hearing of the men. Officers had imbued in them a perception of what a Legionnaire was, an archetypal image, decades old, of perpetually drunk, irrational and incapable men, lost and without direction.

On the other hand, the *soldats du rang* cared little about what officers thought of them. Whether or not they understood military competence, Legionnaires, *caporals* and *sous-officiers* did know that their officers were very poor, often incapable of calling in mortar fire, properly reading a map, showing leadership or giving orders, for instance. Legionnaires demonstrated their knowledge and disapproval through perpetual complaint and unchecked undermining of command. This never led to a usurpation of command or even an overt challenge to authority, for they knew and understood that they were powerless. What it did lead to was Legionnaires characterising themselves as martyrs to the Legion ideal of self-sacrifice; abused, misunderstood and under-appreciated by barely competent fools. This self-characterisation worked because, either consciously or otherwise, they simply had to make sense of the world in which they lived and make their pain and humiliation mean something worthwhile.

So it was that Legionnaires embraced and wrapped themselves in Legion ideals and wore them with pride. In so doing, they could excuse or justify their poor training, poor treatment and poor leadership by saying, '*C'est la Légion*' and '*Je m'en fou.*' So while they knew they were poorly treated, it meant they could, in their own world view, rationally and with honour, submit and sacrifice their lives because they were doing it for a purpose larger than themselves. In other words, it was a self-perpetuating cycle based on themselves as martyrs to the cause of the Legion. The practical effect was that they could and would endure almost any humiliation and neglect because they were Legionnaires. Of course, they were fooling themselves. Some of them knew it, many did not, and others preferred not to see.

25

DJIBOUTI PART II

Chérie, tu veux faire l'amour avec moi?
(Darling, do you want to make love with me?)

Along with deployments to a range of other places in Africa, including Chad and the Comores, 2 REP supplied a company to Arta in Djibouti to supplement the French forces there. This was known as the *compagnie tournante* – 'revolving' because each company served just four months or so there before being replaced by the next one. It just so happened that *2ème Compagnie's* turn came around not long after my arrival at Calvi.

Before leaving for Africa, I found myself with a number of roles, including medic, marksman and driver. So many of the Legionnaires came straight from instruction that they hadn't had time to do specialist courses. I made up a list of everyone in *2ème Section* in a small notebook, together with their matricules, dates of birth, nationality, next of kin, blood types, allergies, dates of injections, last blood test, and the serial numbers of their weapons. This notebook proved so useful that Big Bird asked me to make him a copy. As I handed him the pages, I couldn't help wondering how he'd intended to keep track of his men without such a list. Then again, other than when it came to deserters, the Legion was hardly known for making efficient or honest administration a priority.

We flew to Djibouti with a slight change in personnel. Firstly, to no one's great disappointment, there was no Chiffon. Instead he was to do a bridging course to become an *officier*. From what I had seen of Legion officers, I was sure he would do very well. Gimlet and Despute also remained behind; they were starting the *caporal* course at Castelnaudary under the direction of *Adjudant* Raype. And at the last moment, we were joined by one *Sergent-Chef* Jasper, a new face to us all. Jasper was from the Parachute Regiment's elite formation, the Recon Commandos, which despite its respected standing, had to live with the unfortunate acronym of CRAP.

We arrived at Djibouti-Ambouli International Airport on Saturday, 18 July and soon headed up to Arta. Within a matter of days of our arrival at Quartier Amilakvari, most of the Legionnaires not doing service were drunk at night and indulging themselves in the delights of Arta's two brothels.

As a *chef de chambre*, I was very fortunate to have an excellent team. In my room were Louvier, O'Paddy, Spanker, Manny, Holden, Ovid and Langle. Apart from Spanker, who would try to get out of any work he could, these were among the best men in *2ème Section*.

Ovid was a Canadian who found his way to the Legion via the United States and Mexico. By his own admission, while working in the Canadian Army, his scam was to access the Social Security numbers of people in uniform and open credit card accounts in their name. He amassed a not-inconsiderable sum of money before thinking it wise to leave the country and join the French Foreign Legion.

Manny was from Dundalk in the Republic of Ireland, just over the border from the north. He was thoughtful and quick – another good lad. Langle had been a *sous-officier* in the French Army before joining the Legion. He was bright, with an interest in and knowledge of the world that clearly exceeded other Frenchmen in the *section*, if not the whole company.

Another recent addition to *2ème Section* was *Caporal* Grenoble, who had spent two years in French Guyane. Hailing from the French Alps, he was good too; a Frenchman on whom I could rely.

When time allowed, we'd often sit near the wire outside the foyer in camp. Manny, Holden, O'Paddy, Ovid and myself – we were quite a little mafia. From there, we could look north, across the Gulf, to where the FRUD forces were based in the hills above the port of Tadjoura, which was occupied by the AND. It was an excellent view thanks to Quartier Amilakvari being sited on the area's highest ridge, which extended west, dominating the terrain south of the Gulf of Tadjoura. Given its dominance and the siting of French Commandos close by, it was not surprising that the Djiboutian President had his summer residence, complete with helipad, not a kilometre away.

As part of my role as medic of our *section*, I visited the *infirmerie* to see *Sergent* Ranes, the company medic. I wanted condoms, having run low after the *section* went out on the town, and two intravenous sets, as men had already collapsed due to the effects of the heat.

So many people in *2ème Compagnie* were sick over such a short period of time that as well as finding myself allocated to the *bureau de semaine,* I took over from *Sergent* Ranes in the *infirmerie*. Ranes was bedridden, and the previous night

Grenoble collapsed with a temperature of over 40 degrees Celsius and had to be evacuated to Quartier Monclar.

On top of that, we were making our first jump down at Djibouti the next morning. I was up at 0300 to wake the company at 0315. We left Arta an hour later and drove along the single-lane road in the dark, descending from the relative cool of the high ground to the heat and humidity of Djibouti city, finally arriving at the airport before sunrise. We marched onto the Transall with all our gear just as the colours of dawn began to paint the horizon. As we exited the aircraft, the sun was cresting the horizon of the sea.

As wondrous as nature was that morning, once we'd landed and grouped around Big Bird, it was clear we'd lost a number of *section* members on the way down – they must've missed the drop zone altogether. After a search of fifteen minutes, all the jumpers had been located, but not Legionnaire Snaggle.

We spread out and moved across the sand between the camel thorn trees that dominated the edge of the zone. A short while later, someone cried out that the Frenchman had been found, and he needed a medic. Once I got to the scene, however, I realised that Snaggle needed a lot more than that.

He was lying on his back, arms and legs akimbo, in a camel thorn tree, the lines of his parachute tangled around his body and the thorns and branches of the tree. The 'chute canopy was draped across the crown of another thorn tree just two paces away, the fabric billowing in a hint of breeze. Camel thorns, some 5 or more centimetres long, had pierced the skin of his cheek, neck and wrist; they'd penetrated his back and his legs too, leaving small bloody spots over his green combats. Snaggle could barely speak, the sound from his lips like that of a kicked dog. His eyes rolled in the back of his head.

'Shit, poor bastard,' muttered Holden.

Moments later, Big Bird arrived, put his hands on his hips and said to those standing by, and to Snaggle, *'Putain, quel con. Dégagez lui de l'arbe tout de suite.'* (Shit, what an idiot. Get him out of the tree right now.) Before he turned away to go, he told us loudly to be sure to take care with the parachute.

Snaggle was sent to the hospital at Bouffard and treated for the various punctures to his body. He was released too early, however, before he could properly recover – but then he was the *section popottier*. It would never do for the staff to be without appropriate service while on terrain.

Along with parachuting, we did the usual duties at Arta, including *garde* of course. The guard at night was run the same way as in Calvi: the *sergent* sat at the post till 2300, one *caporal* did 2300 to 0200 and another took over from 0200 to 0530, at which point the *sergent* made preparations to raise the flag. For twenty-four hours each day, Legionnaires did patrols, two hours on and four hours off.

It was during the first and second shifts that the women, wrapped in their diaphanous coloured cloth, came to the post. Soon their sibilant tones would be tempting the sleep-deprived guards.

They'd start with the obvious: *'Chérie, tu veux faire l'amour avec moi?'* (Darling, do you want to make love with me?)

Perhaps veering towards the romantic: *'Chérie, l'amour c'est un grand sentiment'* (Darling, love is a wonderful sentiment).

Before settling on the practical: *'Chérie, glou glou, pas cher'* (Darling, I suck you off, cheap).

If a guard succumbed, he and the *nyah* of his choice agreed terms before using the volcanic basalt as a bed, behind the guardhouse and beyond the wire. I told these men they were fools. Could they not discipline themselves for a trifling four months? Apparently not, so I left a boxful of condoms on the guardroom table. The next day, with cotton swabs and disinfectant, I'd be cleaning scraped knees and palms where dirt had lodged, trying to prevent them from becoming infected.

At 0230 one night there was a *contre appel* (spot check). The result was fourteen Legionnaires and *caporals* missing, although most were present at the morning rollcall. Later, at the parade, *Capitaine* Grinch was very unhappy. The country was caught in the throes of civil war. We were on an operational footing, and constant emphasis was placed on having weapons close to hand. If there had been an alert during the night, more than 10 per cent of the company would have been absent.

Like the rest of us, Grinch knew that the state of the *quartier* did little to keep people in. Surrounding the camp there was plenty of barbed wire but, as at Quartier Monclar when I first arrived, it was quite simple to get in and out. Indeed, it was a poorly kept secret that the *caporal-chef*s, who had separate quarters some 50 metres from the foyer, down the ridge, waited at a gap in the wire, negotiated terms with *nyahs* and escorted them to their rooms for an evening's entertainment.

Those who were missing at the *contre appel* received seven nights in a jail cell measuring 4 metres long, 2 metres wide and 1.5 metres high. It had a concrete floor, thick brick walls, corrugated-iron roof, barred doorway and a small window at the other end. Fourteen occupants in there meant that things were very cramped. Before breakfast, lunch and dinner, the prisoners ran around the *place d'armes* with musettes filled with gravel. All of this done was under the direction of *Caporal-Chef* Omlet, specifically detached from the *Police Militaire* in Calvi to join *2ème Compagnie* as a prison guard. Apparently, it was more important that a jailer join the company on its *tournante* than, say, another medic, sniper, cook or radioman. The Legion had different priorities from other armies.

By 10 August, we were on *Operation Iskoutir*, as interdisposition, or a monitoring force, between the AND and FRUD fighters. Our position was about 80 kilometres west of Arta, just off the sealed road to Tadjoura and Obock, on the southern side of the Ghoubet; Devil's Island was directly north of us. Our post had a lookout above the road, towards the AND position some 500 metres to the west. About 2 kilometres or so from this 100-man AND camp were the FRUD positions, which sat astride the Tadjoura road to the north and around Lac Assal in the west.

The radio and guard post – for there was always someone on guard listening to the radio, usually a *caporal* – was sited in a green canvas tent facing the east, along the road. Another tent accommodated *2ème Section*, and the kitchen was housed in a similar structure nearby. Our function was to report all road movement to company HQ, located at Iskoutir, formerly a collection of huts, at the southern end of the Grand Barra. The AND camp, so close to ours, used United Nations-issue tents as accommodation for troops and at night we heard rounds, probably .50 calibre, being exchanged between the two warring sides.

If there was trouble along the road, I had plenty closer to home, on two fronts. First, and not before time, I had a run-in with Poobelle. The *section* had six vehicles for the purpose of this observation post, three of which were old Marmons, used as troop carriers. These relics were built in the '50s and were only kept running through the judicious application of rubber bands, chewing gum and wire.

In any event, my Marmon was the worst of the lot. It had little power, so climbing any sort of slope was slow. Poobelle was of the view that it was my driving that had caused our *section* convoy to become separated on the way here. In fact, as the *caporal* responsible for vehicles, it was his job to keep them running, thus any problem with one of the trucks was a reflection on him.

On arriving at our position a while later, the vehicles were formed up in one rank while we waited for *Lieutenant* Big Bird to return from a briefing. From the safety of a truck cabin, Poobelle decided to make some comment about my driving. It was enough. I stepped down from the Marmon and strode over to where he sat, stood on the running board and invited him to get out so I could thump him.

His mouth hung open and I let fly with a blow to indicate my enthusiasm. He had no choice but to climb down. I invited him to back up his words with his fists. He didn't, of course. From my experience, the French generally disliked man-to-man conflict. Even so, I reminded Poobelle – and therefore all the Legionnaires present – that I refused to be fucked about by monkeys like him. *Sergent-Chef* Jasper and the other NCOs sat in their vehicles, watching with interest, but made no move to intervene.

Compared with my and Poobelle's contretemps, the other problem was hard to pinpoint. Once we had occupied the position and settled into a routine, it became clear that either there was something amiss with the preparation of the food, or perhaps the younger newcomers were more vulnerable to the rigours of the environment. In one day alone, three Legionnaires collapsed.

The first was Ovid. We were at the rifle range one morning, close to our camp, when he just fell to the ground and began to dry retch. He started to babble incoherently as we moved him into the shade. His temperature was up at 41 degrees Celsius. I put a line into his veins, gave him an intramuscular injection of aspirin, then wet his *cheche* and lay it on his chest.

I recommended to the Bird that we check the kitchen for anything that might be rotten, and evacuate Ovid to the *infirmerie* at Quartier Monclar as soon as possible. Big Bird had no objection to that. Once at Monclar, I headed to the store room and stocked up on my supplies of bottled ringer lactate and glucose, aspergic and associated injecting material, and imodium and ercefuryl tablets for diarrhoea. I returned to the post later to find another two Legionnaires immobilised by fever and diarrhoea. They were squirting a foul bright green mess. These too we evacuated to Monclar, where I learned that Ovid had been transferred to the military hospital in town.

That evening, another six Legionnaires came down with fever and bad diarrhoea. Another latrine had to be dug – a stressful job, since mines had been haphazardly strewn about this area by the AND not long before. The dangers were brought home when wandering goats tripped some mines not 20 metres from our new *chiottes*.

Meanwhile, *Sergent* Embisill was doing his best to lower morale. Embisill was the Légionnaire *1ère Classe* and then *caporal* I knew when we were both with 13 DBLE. I didn't like him much then either. From the comfort of his canvas cot, where he lay reading pornographic comic books, he berated the sick for being weak. Big Bird kept asking me for more imodium and aspirin. He was not well either.

I spent two days and two nights on my feet, washing the foul green shit off the men, reassuring them, taking temperatures and dispensing injections every four hours to bring temperatures down. Three more Legionnaires were bedridden. Embisill shat his trousers, collapsed and groaned, '*J'ai la chiasse!*' (I've got the shits!) I injected him too.

We had just enough personnel to prepare the food and maintain a guard during this time. But there was no relief for the guard. If there had been an assault on our position, I doubt if we could've mustered more than ten effective rifles – just a third of the *section*.

Whatever the cause was, after three more days the sickness passed. And now I could sleep.

Once the *section* was back to strength, the Bird took us shooting and later took a few of us out for a lesson in topography. When he asked me where we were on the map I quickly located the position. He was not at all happy about this and tore the map from my grasp. Louvier, Ponski and Snaggle had no idea how to approach map reading – and they'd all had more than two years service with 2 REP. Big Bird yelled at them and called them *mongols.* There was no point in yelling; no one had ever taught them.

After two weeks there in front of Devil's Island we returned to Quartier Amilakvari. Grenoble, our new *caporal*, was waiting for us, having been released from hospital a few days before. We hadn't been back a day, though, when told that one of the company's *section*s had to go down to Monclar for various guard duties, including the setting up of ambush posts at the *quartier*'s perimeter. That *section* was ours.

Before going out to set the ambush that evening, I asked what our orders were for opening fire. The *chef de poste* laughed at me and said, 'If you see any nigger get too close, shoot him.' This guidance was of little help to me a few hours later.

I had set up an ambush position with Holden and two others, Foolski and Langle. The post was set up next to the *centre de repos*, the newly built quarters for those wishing to remain in the *quartier* during their leave, not far from the AMX13 light tank graveyard. At 0130 I saw a figure move through a gap in the fence from the outside, where refugees from the fighting in Ethiopia and Somalia had set up camp; he had just entered the AMX park. Some 30 metres away, the figure stood silent and motionless for a moment; I could make out a pair of shorts and a strap over his left shoulder leading down to a satchel on his right hip. He remained immobile for perhaps ten seconds and then, like Golem in *Lord of the Rings*, he glided towards the mesh fence, to the left of us, which divided the AMX park from the rest of the *quartier*. What was he doing?

He knelt at the base of the fence and began fumbling inside his satchel.

I ordered Holden off to my left, to place himself parallel to the mesh fence and stop the fellow if he got through it; if it looked as though he would retaliate with force . . . shoot him. At my side was Langle, and further off to my right, Foolski, who was to warn us if anyone else tried to infiltrate the camp. I pulled off the wire that inhibited cocking the FAMAS (a stupid idea for an ambush, but compulsorily attached as part of taking up the guard), silently cocked it and then set the safety catch to fire. Just 1.3 kilograms of pressure on the trigger was all it would take. I shouted '*Halte!*', then again: '*Halte!!*' The figure was gone, leaping over the outer fence. I didn't shoot.

Next day I went to the fence line, to the place where the fellow had been kneeling. He had risked his life to pick some wild peas that had been growing against the wire.

Shortly after this incident, and because we had been doing so much guard, *2ème Section* was allocated a day of *repos* at

CECAP, the commando base at Arta Plage. Even here, on a day of rest, as we swam and rested in the shade, Big Bird, *Sergent-Chef* Jasper and the three *sergents*, Pimenti, Pratt and Embisill, felt the need to complain about the inadequate service they were receiving from their *popottier*. Snaggle apologised, rubbed his camel thorn-pierced hands together, and promised to do a better job next time.

Back at Arta, at a company parade, *Capitaine* Grinch informed us that *2ème Compagnie* was destined for service in Yugoslavia with the United Nations next year. Following dismissal from the parade, all that could be heard from the *sous-officiers* was talk of money. According to *Sergent* Pratt, the *solde* in Yugoslavia was less than that for Djibouti – it was hardly worthwhile going, he insisted.

26

ST MICHAEL, PATRON SAINT

Ne cherche pas à comprendre.
(Do not try to understand.)

Tuesday, 29 September was St Michael's Day and that night, at Arta, in keeping with REP tradition we celebrated. St Michael is the patron saint for a number of fighting units around the world, particularly for aviators and paratroopers. In the Old Testament and, later, in John Milton's epic *Paradise Lost*, it is Michael who leads the Army of God against the rebel forces of Satan.

All the paras from the French forces in Djibouti thus gathered at Quartier Amilakvari's place d'armes and were regaled with food, wine and song. We sang '*Petite Piste*' and '*En Algerie*', the latter a maudlin favourite of mine because it reminded me that in the Legion, no matter what you did, you were fucked. You lost love, lost a friend or were soon to die. Perhaps one person would remember you, and if you were lucky, maybe they got you a wooden cross.

The evening turned out to be a dreadful experience. Not only because no one wanted to sing, but as was so often the case during formal 'celebrations', there was a very angry atmosphere there around the parade ground. People became very drunk very quickly, and in quiet dark places small, isolated scuffles broke out. Michael's winged army of angels, we were not.

A few days after St Michael's Day – an alert. Apparently, there was a demonstration of FRUD supporters outside the French Embassy down in Djibouti city, forty-five minutes away. And rather than someone down in Djibouti reacting, the response fell to us.

We soon had a truck loaded with ammunition, rockets, 5.56 mm rounds and grenades, and each man kitted out in riot gear – including helmets, shields and bullet-proof vests. The problem was we'd had no instruction on how to use any of the equipment.

It was just as well that the entire activity turned out to be an exercise, designed to demonstrate our reaction time. The alert was instructive on one point, though. That was the day Big Bird lost the plot. He stood there, yelling, screaming and visibly trembling. Everyone ignored him and wondered what would happen if things ever got really tough. Legionnaires and *sous-officiers* shook their heads.

The next morning, after an evening in Arta town on gin and among the dust, rocks and diseased women, Legionnaire Spanker was unable to lift himself from his bed. I punched and kicked him to no avail, and instead resorted to a technique I'd used to great effect during my two years at Monclar: I simply put my hand over his mouth and poured some water down one nostril. His body probably thought it was drowning, and the most fundamental of its mechanisms kicked in to preserve life. Anyway, it woke up Spanker.

Among other nasty little habits, Spanker was a chronic masturbator. When *nyahs* were unavailable, he would take himself off to *les chiottes* to relieve and relax himself before lights out at 2200. Most often, though, he would have to masturbate two or three more times in a night. On one occasion, rather than take himself outside – which was the appropriate and generally accepted way to relieve oneself – the Frenchman lay in his bed.

At around 2300 that night, I was going outside to relieve myself of a full bladder, the product of a couple of beers too close to lights out. Out the corner of one eye, as I made my way past the other beds in our *chambre*, I saw a movement, more a blur, from behind the sheer cover of Spanker's mosquito net. Half asleep and puzzled, I took a closer look, and realised too quickly that it was Spanker masturbating into a white sport sock.

Keen not to wake up the rest of the room, I told him to stop and carry on elsewhere. He grunted and complained but didn't move, so I hit him. Now everyone was awake. I asked Spanker what he'd planned to do with the sock once he was done. He would be adding it to the bucket of washing for the *garçons*, he replied, referring to the Djiboutians who hand-washed our clothing.

Everyone in the room was disgusted and committed to bash Spanker if he ever masturbated in bed again – or if we ever discovered that an other-than-sweat-soggy sock had been handed in to be washed. As unashamed as ever, Spanker rose from his bed, wrapped a towel around his waist and said he'd be back in a few minutes.

•

We were back in the field when, without any warning, *Capitaine* Grinch came to our *section* position seeking to interview all the *caporals* and Legionnaires. After the formal preliminaries, he asked me what I wanted to do: was I going to sign on to continue my *belle carrière* in the Legion?

After telling him that there were many other things I wanted to do, I put a question of my own to him: what was he going to offer?

The company clerk smiled. *Lieutenant* Big Bird looked to the roof of the tent and then at a point beyond my head. The *capitaine* never took his eyes off me, however. Here's the English version of how things went from there . . .

'Frankly, I do not give a toss what you do,' he said. 'Whether you sign on again is of no concern to me.' Then he waited.

'So, if I sign on for a year,' I ventured, 'what can I expect?'

I had struck the right chord, it seemed, for he replied very quickly, 'I give you my word of honour that you will either go to Yugoslavia or do the sergeant's course.'

We knew that there was a chance to go to Yugoslavia – or more correctly, Bosnia – as part of the UN mission there. A few of us even knew there was a war going on in the country, between Serbs, Croats and Bosnians. While some in the company said the conflict was inevitable, I thought this was rubbish. I never agreed that history or ancient animosity was a vaild reason for war. Human beings make their own choices.

And I knew that our officers were very quick to give their word when it came to the promise of us seeing some action out there in the Balkans. Generally, if an *officier* gave you his *parole d'honneur*, it just meant he wanted you to do something. And experience had long proved that it was best not to rely on him keeping his end of the bargain. I could only think that these officers were keener on keeping experienced Legionnaires than ever winning their respect.

So, not being taken in by Grinch's little ploy, I told him I'd best think about it. No doubt, this was the very thing the *capitaine* did not want – why else would he have made an impromptu visit to carry out an important interview? Besides, if *2ème Compagnie* failed to go to Yugoslavia, there were at least four men ahead of me waiting to start the *sergent* course.

As I stood in that tent, looking into his face, I knew I couldn't rely on what *Capitaine* Grinch said to me. As much as I sought more operational experience, who knew what would happen next year? Right now, I didn't have to do anything just yet. I would wait before giving them a decision.

As things played out, *2ème Compagnie*, 2 REP did not go to the Balkans the following year. And only two of its *caporals* went on to do the course to become a *sergent*.

Next up was Exercise Bidley, which took place on 8 November. After running about for most of the day to gather supplies, Big Bird had us group around a map described in chalk on the concrete floor of one of the *chambres*. This looked promising – my first ever Legion briefing before an exercise. But, as always, it paid to not get your hopes up.

On this training exercise, I learned, we would be carrying out an air assault to 'secure' an airstrip close to the border with Somalia. After that, though, the Bird's instructions became somewhat disjointed, littered with interjections and irrelevancies. And that was the briefing. Little wonder then that Legionnaires kept coming up to me later, asking what the hell was going on. I just reminded them to carry plenty of water.

We jumped in the morning. The sun was already full, the red African horizon drawing a line under the bleached blue sky. Unusually, there was a French Army loadmaster by the starboard exit door, where I was. Just as I made to run out after O'Paddy, this man grabbed my left arm to slow me. Sure, I was close to O'Paddy, but that was normal in the Legion; that was how we jumped. In slowing and turning my body, the loadmaster's action meant I left the aircraft like a sack of shit. Instead of exiting in a more or less vertical manner – hands over the ventral, feet together and chin tucked in to my chest – I left the door with legs almost horizontal, arms outstretched and head back. As my body was caught and twisted in the slipstream along the plane's fuselage, my helmeted head hit the exit door frame hard. Very hard.

When my 'chute was ripped open by the static line, I had the helmet torn from my head and, worse, there was a twist in the lines of the 'chute almost to the border of the canopy. It meant I couldn't lift my head to check it. I knew the canopy was only partially open; that much was obvious, because I was descending far more quickly than the others around me. Even with my limited field of vision, their 'chutes and boots seemed to be climbing up into the sky relative to my rapid descent. I was dizzy and choking too, my head pinned to my chest. Unless I got that canopy to open further, I knew I could well be dead.

In a combat jump from 900 feet, as this was, there were only seconds in which to react. I kicked and scissored my legs for all I was worth. Soon I was spinning as the lines to the canopy unwound – and just as the ground seemed to be looming large, charging towards me. From between my legs, I released the *gaine* that carried my pack and rifle. Now the ground rushed up to me, claiming me, and I hit . . .

I lay there still for a moment, winded, dizzy, and angry. But I was alive, and after a tentative check, to my considerable relief I discovered no bones were broken. Landing in the sand as I had, my fall had created quite an impression, I noticed. Maybe Michael was looking out for this winged angel that day. It was a close call.

I got to my feet, picked up my *sac à dos* and rifle, and reintegrated the parachute. The helmet, with a large dent in it, was returned to me later. We then formed up into our *sections* and carried out a couple of infantry assaults. Over open ground, with no cover, we stood up from our prone positions, almost shoulder to shoulder, and slow-marched the 400 metres to the 'enemy'. *Vive Napoléon!* I thought, amused at the Waterloo-era tactics.

During another attack, Big Bird was on the radio to the *capitaine*. At the conclusion of the exchange, he turned to *Sergent* Pimenti, laughed, and said, 'But I don't know how to call in mortar fire. Anyway, we're Legionnaires. We don't need it.'

In his easy Californian accent, Holden leaned my way and joked, 'Hey Dave – follow these idiots into combat and you'll be in hell before you know it.'

Soon enough, it would be different attributes and skills that found our *section* leader wanting. Our *section* was on a foot patrol that evening when, as we halted for the night, *Sergent-Chef* Jasper asked if I had the medical kit with me. I had some parts of it, I replied, and the rest was with *Sergent* Ranes, the company medic, who was accompanying *2ème Section*, as was *Capitaine* Grinch.

Just on dawn, Big Bird asked the Legionnaires in my group for a canteen of water. He wanted it for the *capitaine's* shave and a brew of coffee. Outraged, I told my men not to give up a drop of the precious liquid. If the *capitaine* had asked discreetly,

I would've done something for him, but not this way. Among other things it taught new Legionnaires bad lessons, particularly if I was seen to be too weak to stand up to an unreasonable request from an officer. Big Bird went elsewhere.

At around 0800, the *section* halted for a quick brew of coffee and the Bird, with Grinch sitting behind, decided that he would test the map-reading skills of his *caporals*. In reply to his questions, and seeing as no one at our rank had been trusted with a map, none of my colleagues had any idea where we were, where water could be found, nor where the nearest road was for evacuation. I knew, but only because I'd led a patrol through the area two years before.

Then it was my turn with the Bird. I asked the *lieutenant* if he had seen the movie *Crocodile Dundee*. He said he had. All Australians were like Dundee when out in the field, I told him. After just a cursory glance at the map, I hunkered on my haunches, took some sand in my fist and let it trickle to the ground. After a suitably dramatic pause, I began: 'There is an airstrip at Digri, some 8 kilometres north. The closest permanent water is south-south-east, 5 kilometres away. Ali Sabieh is some 18 kilometres east and the railway, north-west, at 7 kilometres.'

Big Bird and the *capitaine* were amazed. Their jaws hung slack and they looked at each other, eyes alive with questions. How did I know? The Bird shook his head, refolded the map and, with just one small part of the map showing, demanded to know our current position. After indentifying some unusual landforms, I was able to tell the *lieutenant* where we were.

The usual, imperious wave of the hand followed, together with a disdainful '*Tu peux disposer.*' Nothing approaching a 'well done', of course.

•

A day later, Big Bird told me that I was to pass *rapport*. He didn't say why. After some days spent wondering, I stood before *Capitaine* Grinch to find that the charge related to my not carrying all the necessary medical gear during the foot patrol. Like everyone who appeared on a charge, I said nothing. It was obvious that Big Bird wanted me in jail, preferably during the period when we returned to Calvi, so I would miss out on leave. This was a way of breaking a man's spirit. On this day, though, Grinch merely smiled and gave me seven days, suspended for three months. Big Bird was furious, and as I left I heard him arguing with the *capitaine*.

It was a minor victory over petty-mindedness, but I had little defence when it came to sharing guard duties with Embisill. Our *section* took the *garde* for the last week of our time in Djibouti. This was a pain in the arse, as we also had to pack up, clean and clean again. Late in the afternoon of 14 November, I found myself the subject of discussion for *Sergent* Embisill, which was more of a lecture. He began, 'Yes indeed, I notice that someone is trying to break your balls. It happens.' A reference to Big Bird, naturally.

He went on to talk about his life before the Legion. How he spent five years as a lab assistant in a photo-developing business and hardly ever saw the sun. Furthermore, how he had to join the Legion or the Corsicans would've cut his balls off. But how it was that he had then found himself in a regiment based in Corsica, he did not say.

Then he got to the nub of his little homily. Responsibility. If possible, he advised, avoid it and pass it down the chain of command; how one got rid of it did not matter. In life, as in the Legion, we must accept that bullshit follows us, and we must avoid it, preferably by heaping it on to those below us. Never take ownership of a problem if it can be shared, he urged. And never ever take responsibility for failure or mistakes.

'*Ne cherche pas à comprendre,*' the Frenchman said. (Do not try to understand.) Because there were things in life that we could never understand. We must react to avoid imminent problems by simply deflecting them, for we can do nothing to change the way things are.

I watched his wet lips purse and widen, the jaw that moved up and down to his teeth, all the while feeling the knot of anger and hate glow hot inside me. Of course he was happy in the Legion: he was paid for being an automaton, and he liked life that way. Now that he was a *sergent,* all he had to do to survive and collect his pension was avoid responsibility, something I knew he had done ever since that descent on Mount Garbi, nearly three years before.

I was furious. Were we not men – passionate, thinking beings? If we didn't think about the world in which we lived, weren't we mere slaves to circumstance and the direction of others? Embisill advocated something beyond discipline; it was more elemental and disturbing. As the necessary means to survival in the Legion, he proposed a relinquishment of challenge, the abandonment of excellence and achievement. But without the willingness to risk and perhaps fail, what was a man? I loathed his ignorant, smug certainties, but said nothing. What would I have achieved?

Next day we were pulled off guard to find ourselves involved in a review of vehicles. It seemed to me that everyone wearing green or gold stripes was running about yelling and gesticulating: 'I'm not responsible', 'It wasn't me' or 'Hey, no one told me.'

Embisill described how the Legion really was. And I hated it.

27

CALVI, ONE MORE TIME

Un bon petit boulot, tranquille.
(A nice, quiet little job.)

We flew back to Corsica on Monday, 16 November. Having had our luggage searched by the *Police Militaire* in Djibouti, their counterparts in Calvi now repeated the procedure on the *place d'armes* at Camp Raffalli. We stood on the burnt red gravel, felt the cold wind of the snow-covered mountains cut through our summer uniforms and shivered.

The upside was we had two weeks' leave. I flew to the UK and walked the West Highland Way in Scotland, through snow and short winter days to pubs and hotels with deep beds and hot showers. On my return to the regiment, I knew it was time for me to move away from *2ème Compagnie*. As is so often the case with 'short-timers', I spent the last few months of my contract with the *Police Militaire*.

I had discussed this option with a couple of the MPs up at Fort Charlet in town. They were after volunteers. Then I asked to see *Lieutenant* Big Bird and expressed three things.

First, given that we had been told our company would not be going to Yugoslavia, yet others in 2 REP were, I would not be signing on to stay in the Legion. Second, I wanted to take all my permission at the end of my contract so as to leave earlier, perhaps in late March or early April. Third, I requested an attachment to the *Police Militaire*.

I then went before *Capitaine* Grinch, who nodded his consent before waving me away as someone lost to him. Next day, 12 December, I packed my things, loaded them into a Jeep and transferred to the *Police Militaire*.

Fort Charlet was the town's citadel and it felt like I'd stepped back into another century; it had old stone walls, a moat (drained and full of weeds), a gunpowder room and cells. The cells were similar to those in the movie *Papillon*. Only a few years before, transgressing Legionnaires used to be locked in cages alone, with bars over the roof, where they could be spied on by the guards. According to *Caporal-Chef* Graves, the prisoners would have water thrown over their naked bodies. In winter. What a place.

My *chef de section* was *Adjudant* Manier. He was soon to retire. An *ancien* with the Kolwezi ribbon, he appeared to be one of the brightest French *sous-officiers* I had met. Other personnel included *Caporal* Gretin, also from *2ème Compagnie*, and Légionnaire *1ère Classe* John, one of the men on my promo. Never the athlete, John took every opportunity to get away from his company and its routines of running, marching and swimming.

Christmas Eve 1992, my last in the Legion. We MPs patrolled all night, until 0600. There were no problems, just the usual activities, with plenty of drunken Legionnaires staggering along Calvi's otherwise silent cobbled streets. Also predictable were the *officiers* and *sous-officiers* all very keen to be seen shaking hands with Legionnaires, and wishing them a *joyeux Noël*. It was the same thing year after year, and I wondered why there seemed to be a correlation between those who seemed most eager to shake hands at this time of year and those who most humiliated people during the rest of the year.

On New Year's Eve it was cold, and my breath blew clouds that preceded my walk around the town. That night I walked the cobbles and paths of Calvi's waterfront and bar area without picking up anyone, hitting anyone or even raising my voice. I simply directed the men to waiting taxis for the ride back to camp.

Later in January '93, we began to receive news of Legion casualties in Sarajevo. At first it was a shrapnel injury, a week later the Legion's first death in the conflict. During this time, there were some among us who were willing to fight the Serbs any way they could. Along with many others from *2ème Compagnie*, Holden and Ovid did not return from their post-Djibouti leave. Holden told me before he left that he and Ovid were off to join Croat forces and kill Serbs. The Californian was unable to get to the front, but Ovid did.

Holden was back in Calvi now and serving forty days in jail, so I was able to learn first-hand what had happened. The two of them went to London and enquired about whether Holden could get into Austria with just his Legion identity card; not a problem, said the airline. So they fronted up at Salzburg's airport. They were told that while Ovid could stay – the Canadian, having acquired a passport under a false name – Holden would be sent back to Britain. His ID card was not sufficient. All this when they only wanted to transit through to Croatia.

Still, the immigration officers in Salzburg were very helpful. They gave the Legionnaires the addresses of people and organisations to contact in Croatia. No one liked the Serbs and what they were doing. Months later I heard Ovid had been killed, targeted by one of the Serbian death squads that specifically sought out foreigners who had joined with the Croats.

One Friday in mid-February saw Spanker, that troubled former room-mate of mine from *2ème Section*, lose control of himself and surrender to despair. He helped himself to bottles of Pastis and whiskey, and sat in Grenoble's temporarily vacant *chambre* to drink. Over the next few hours he smashed bottles up against the wall, smashed the TV and video, and then flattened the lockers. He broke everything he could, collapsed, and then fell asleep in his own vomit.

I saw Spanker a few days later. He told me he was 'finished', and he certainly didn't look too good. The *cafard* (Legion madness) had got to him, he said; he needed to go *civil*. I told him that he was probably slightly mad, but that needn't preclude him from having a *belle carrière* in the Legion. This seemed to reassure him a little, and he thanked me. What I failed to tell him was that I didn't think he had anything else but the Legion.

As far as my own future went, instead of getting away early from my contract, I was made to take my *fin de contrat* leave and then return to Calvi before finishing at Aubagne. I knew it was possible to combine the end-of-contract permission with the annual leave one rarely got, to effectively reduce the contract to four years and nine months or so. But things hadn't worked out as planned. Big Bird had given his *parole* only a few weeks before and I had assurances from the company office that an early exit would not be a problem. They would see to it and it would be done. It was not and I was not surprised.

•

Among the others working as Military Police I had noticed a change. *Caporals* Monte and Gretin, from *2ème Compagnie,* and Leman had all signed on again. Even though Monte and Gretin were six months or more shy of their five years, the *capitaine* made them sign on for three years. If they didn't sign up for such a period, Grinch would transfer them to the CCS, the one company that generally remained in Calvi. The consequence of this was that they would rarely see a *tournante,* the big money-making activity for most of those who stayed. We all knew it was a form of blackmail. Having already done five years, a Legionnaire needed only sign on for one year at a time.

Gretin, a none-too-bright Portuguese, was offered the chance to go to Aubagne to resit the test to establish his level of intelligence. Any aspirations he might've had for promotion were currently limited to that of *caporal-chef* because his results were just seven from twenty points. Unfortunately for him, and like far too many Legionnaires, he was also semi-literate. Given this handicap, no matter how many times he sat the test, it would still prove difficult surely. But, as Gretin himself put it, all he wanted was '*un bon petit boulot, tranquille*' (a nice quiet little job).

This was entirely in keeping with his reasons for joining in the first place: to be fed, housed and provided with a pension at the conclusion of fifteen years' service. Why aspire to anything more? Like many of his countrymen in the Legion, he sold his body and his compliance for pay. Because there were so few good people with brains, enthusiasm and leadership ability, people like Gretin found themselves in the picture for command positions. As for the trip to Aubagne, it was understood that the necessary assistance would be provided to help reach the limited level required for *sous-officier*. It was another indictment that the French Foreign Legion compromised its already low standards to promote people because no others were available.

One afternoon I was assembling some equipment prior to going out on a Police Militaire patrol when the three recent re-signers brought their coffees over to where I was working. They stood around discussing the military life and decided it had its advantages, the best thing being that you never had to worry about where your next meal was to come from. Then they turned their attention to me, hands on slim green-clad hips, and asked if I was going to sign on again. I said that I was not; that I wanted to do other things in life. Gretin was aggressive and demanded, '*Comme quoi?*' (Like what?)

I stopped what I was doing. I knew that we now had very little in common and, these days, my vision was increasingly focused on the outside. I told them that I'd done enough in the Legion and it was time to move on. Life had so much more to offer.

All three shook their heads and swore. Gretin stuck out his chest and said, '*La vie civil? Jamais. Ils sont tous des cons.*' (Civilian life? Never. They're all idiots.) He and the other *caporals* thought it a certainty that I would be back, and the reason I'd be back was because I would surely fail. After all, that's why I joined the Legion in the first place, wasn't it?

For these three dark-eyed, dark-haired, dark-green creatures, anyone who left the Legion would fail. But they were simply projecting their own inadequacies. They had to think like this; because it was the only way they could reassure themselves that their own decisions to sign on had some rationale. And they had to hope that everyone else would fail, too.

They did not wish me well. Very few people did.

•

At 1330 on Tuesday, 4 May, at Ajaccio, on Corsica's west coast, I sat at a cafe, just up from the port. The sun was warm on my face and the first vine leaves were appearing in the overhead lattice of the stone-flagged courtyard. From the terminal a few hundred metres away, a ferry would take me to Marseilles, then Aubagne and Quartier Viénot and the end of five years.

There were two others leaving the Parachute Regiment that day, both of them men I'd known at Castelnaudary. Coleman, the former US Army officer, was a radio man and another rapid-promotion *caporal*. Dazinovic, from my own *section* in Castelnaudary, had gone on to Calvi with LeCoq, Canuk and the others straight after our instruction. Dazinovic told me he was fed up with Legion life. That may well have been so, but I knew the Croat had been given three successive periods of forty days' jail for his part in the sexual assault of a woman in Calvi. According to him, she was the wife of a *sous-officier* who had been deployed as part of the *compagnie tournante* to Djibouti. He had got to know her and then invited Locolo – the very same Spanish Legionnaire I had shared instruction with also – to join them. Apparently, the play got a little rough and noisy, and the *gendarmes* were called. Consent was no defence, and while Dazinovic was dealt with by the Legion (very leniently I thought), Locolo languished in a Corsican jail.

The day before, the three of us had passed *rapport* for the last time. I presented myself before the regiment's second in command *Lieutenant Colonel* Tomatis, who told me I had done very well and said, '*La porte est toujours ouverte*' (The door is always open). Furthermore, if I wanted to come back, I could still have a *belle carrière*. At the conclusion of the friendly interview, Tomatis handed me a regimental plaque inscribed with my name and service number and the *certificate de bonne conduite* (good conduct certificate), the necessary document to qualify for French citizenship.

Dazinovic did not receive his certificate. When I asked what he planned to do, all he said was, '*Je m'en fou.*'

28

FIN DE CONTRAT

Je ne regrette rien.
(I regret nothing.)

I arrived in Aubagne for my last week in the Legion. I spent the days being interviewed and, alternately, asked if I really did want to leave. I presented myself before three personnel officers, who variously offered me a stay overseas – Tahiti, Djibouti, wherever I wished – and a place on the *sergent* course. When I declined, they repeated, '*Tres bonne notes. Bon element. La porte est toujours ouverte.*' (Very good reports. Good element. The door is always open.) They told me if I returned within a year, I could have my stripes back and be sent off on a *sergent* course.

If days were spent being flattered, nights and my final weekend I passed on guard duty. At the CAPLE, I met one-eyed Weng, now a *caporal*, and Crocodile, the man who'd joined me on a search detail outside Bel Air years before, when three deserters were on the loose. Crocodile was also now a *caporal*. It was also good to see *Sergent-Chef* Reed, from my machine-gun course, who was not at all happy working in the transport *section*.

I even met up with Lafaible, now *Sergent* Lafaible, 13 DBLE's one-time pool guard and full-time hypochondriac. He was doing a tour as *chef de poste* at Quartier Viénot's front gate. Lafaible took me aside and begged me not to spread it around that he had deserted from Djibouti. I said there were two things he needed to know: I did not tell stories, and certainly, he had deserted. At this, he blustered and blew out his cheeks. I threatened to bash him and told him to fuck off.

On a sour note, I heard that *Adjudant* (formerly *Sergent-Chef*) Mahmood had killed himself at Fort de Nogent. According to some of the medics at the *infirmerie*, he had either AIDS or a '*maladie Guyanese*'. No one was surprised. Many men died in Guyane and on their return to France, either at their own hand or from something that they'd acquired during their two years. Even *Capitaine* Schpeck of 'shut your arses' fame died of some unexplained disease shortly after having returned from a patrol in the jungle.

We were bussed off to Lavéran hospital for X-rays, the very same hospital I had visited when I had joined and on my return from Djibouti. In the bus were a number of EVs in dirty green tracksuits. It never stopped.

Lavéran was full of broken bodies and broken minds. Legionnaires I had known over the years asked me if I remembered them. For the most part I did. They came up to me with stooped backs or legs suspended in a metal frame. Much worse was the ward where Legionnaires were kept subdued with pills.

I had heard that one of the Legionnaires I had done basic training with was there, so I paid him a visit. When I asked for the particular ward, some of the nurses frowned and waggled their index fingers at me. I ignored them and made my way along the stuffy, snot-green coloured corridors until I came to the ward.

I thought my visit might help him, but he wouldn't have cared if I was there or not. He was incapable of recognising me, or speaking. All he could do was drool spit down his chin while quietly rocking on the bed under the four webbing straps that embraced his body. I touched him on his forehead, said gentle words and imagined his eyes focused on me briefly. I was in tears and wondered at the life of a young man from Brazil, full of smiles, who had joined the Legion and ended up trapped on a bed in a hospital far from home. I could not get out of Lavéran quickly enough.

On Friday, 14 May 1993, six days short of five years, I walked out the front gate at Quartier Viénot at 1742 and caught the 1815 train to Marseilles.

For the final parade I was one of thirteen leaving the Legion. Five of these were *caporal-chef*s who had done fifteen years and received their pensions. Of the rest, there were only four who had done five years or more, the others, all French, were being released early for a variety of reasons, mainly medical.

We waited on the *place d'armes* 10 metres away from and facing the *Monument aux Morts*, the Legion's iconic memorial retrieved from Algeria in 1962. We waited almost two hours for the *Genéral de la Légion Étrangère*, *Général* Colcomb, to descend from his office.

When he did come, it was an anticlimax. His kepi sat awry on his head – perhaps he thought it was a jaunty angle. His right top button was not done up and his shirt was not properly tucked into his trousers.

The *général* stood before each of us and asked a few questions. He soon arrived before me and for the last time I recited:

'*Caporal* Mason. *Cinq ans de service.*

Quatre ans quatre mois de grade
A l'instant fin de contrat
À vos ordres, mon Général.'

Général Colcomb asked whether I had enjoyed myself. I replied with a single word, accompanied by a short, sharp turn of the head: '*Non.*'

He asked whether I regretted having joined. I looked into his eyes and said, '*Non. Je ne regrette rien.*'

He paused and asked his aide-de-camp for my record of service. '*Mais t'as bien servi!*' he exclaimed. (But you have served well!)

Of course I had, and the *général* looked at me for a moment. Then he shrugged his shoulders and said under his breath, '*Je m'en fou.*' Then louder, he concluded with: '*Bonne chance.*'

When *Général* Colcomb was through speaking with each man, he went to a position before the Legionnaires and said, '*N'oubliez jamais que vous êtes toujours Légionnaires.*' (Never forget that you are always Legionnaires.)

He then saluted, with button undone, kepi awry and shirt not quite right. It was a salute flaccid and weak. What did he care? We were lost to him.

Before we did a left turn to march off the parade ground, the darkness cast by the offices of the General Commanding the French Foreign Legion touched the *Monument aux Morts*. It would soon be in shadow, and in the going down of the sun, it would rest in silent darkness.

END NOTE

On quiet days when I am at home, I sometimes leaf through old photographs of my time in the Legion. The corners are sharp against my skin, pricking memories. Now and again the echoes of men's voices in my mind remind me of how I felt, the fears and frustrations with a system fundamentally flawed; a system that failed to live up to reasonable expectations of a well-led, well-trained military. At least, not any military I know, and I have worked with a few. I am an officer in the Australian Army Reserve and have served and worked with armies of many nations. I know what a good army is; its training, its leadership and treatment of its soldiers.

Instead, I discovered that while the French Foreign Legion has all the fierce passion, fear, fighting and fucking a man might want, there is no heart in it. It is a place of soulless, non-critical self-indulgence. Where there should be friendship, there is suspicion. Where there should be glory, there is fraud. Where there should be trust, there is betrayal. Where there is death, there are lies. Sure, life is like this, at least in small parts. But in the Legion, it is everywhere.

In the early part of the twenty-first century I read and hear French officials advocating the Legion as the model for a United Nations standing army. I also read of the men in the Legion being described as mercenaries. So many commentators write so many things that are consistently wrong about the Legion, they perpetuate a myth and a fiction.

The French Foreign Legion was fundamentally flawed when I was in its ranks, and the situation has changed little today. In a practical sense, the Legion does not reach an acceptable standard because there does not exist within its ranks a sufficient cadre of competent and professional non-commissioned officers who can capably lead men. This is because the Legion has failed to attract and retain enough men who are military-minded and committed to professionalism. Instead, the majority of men who remain in the Legion are those with little else to do, and nowhere to go, who view the Legion as a refuge where satisfactory performance is the very least they can get away with. This encourages and underpins the *Je m'en fou* attitude of the ranks and reinforces inertia, discourages initiative and derides excellence. Without a critical mass of men prepared to stay in the Legion and devote themselves to improving the non-commissioned ranks, the Legion will remain what it has been for too long.

The officers in the Legion know this. It was one of the reasons they were so keen to keep me in their ranks. The same officers knew that not enough men stay to make a significant difference to the way in which the Legion operates. And so, men who joined looking for a different life, a military life, where expectations were transparent, understood and delivered, decided with their feet, and left the Legion in droves.

In not staying, these same men undermined the Legion. They slipped through the coarse mesh of Legion expectations and left behind those who, for whatever reason, had little choice but to stay. It meant that those who stayed became *caporals* and *sergents* and drove away those who could make the Legion a better-trained and led force. It was a cycle that meant the Legion failed itself.

Contrary to what French officials say, the Legion is not a model for a United Nations force. Indeed, far from it. What the United Nations does require are forces that exercise command and control over their troops. These troops must be well trained, well led, observant of the laws of war and human rights law, and sensitive to the cultural and political environments in which they are deployed. Up to now, the United Nations experience has been mixed. The Legion is not a solution.

If the Legion is not the model for a United Nations force, nor are its men mercenaries. The word 'mercenary' can be an adjective, verb or noun. In any of the uses, it most often has pejorative or negative connotations. In the Legion context, its use is wrong. At international law, and specifically at Article 47 of Additional Protocol I to the Geneva Conventions, the definition of what is a mercenary does not include a member of the French Foreign Legion. Nor would it include a Ghurka in the British armed forces. The fact is that most people who write about French Foreign Legionnaires as mercenaries are just plain wrong. In the same way, in inaccurate or poorly researched material, they are wrong about many other aspects of the Legion.

I should know. I was in the Legion, I lived it, embraced the challenge it offered and excelled in its ranks. If courage is to seek out adventure, endure and succeed in a forbidding and difficult environment, I have demonstrated it more than enough, in the Legion and in other places.

It takes courage of a different kind to expose a past of which I was not proud. When I think back on my time I wonder if I would have done better to leave once I knew what the Legion was like. That I did not was for two reasons. The first was because I am an optimist; I believed things would change and improve. They did not. The second reason was that so many people either wanted me to or assumed I would desert. I am a fighter and I did not desert.

So at the very least, I gained an insight to myself, that even under pressure and when vulnerable, I was not going to give up or give in to other people when they expected me to. There was a price to pay, however. Sometimes my phone rings at night, or very early in the morning. These are calls from all over the world, from Finland, Germany and the UK. They are calls from men I served with in the Legion. Sometimes we will talk of things we did. Sometimes we talk very little at all, and in the space between silences I will hear gentle crying. Some men cry of the hurt done to them and of the hurt done to others.

Just as certain as the scars on my body, the Legion has marked these men. For some, it is a dark shadow where they fear to look. For others the layers of pain have made them impervious to hurt. In these and other ways, men have been marked by the Legion, perhaps damaged, certainly changed, and never to be the men they once were.

I feel a hurt too. It is not a shadow, and nor has it made me impervious to pain. Instead, it is the realisation that a young man's passion, optimism and trust can be so ill used and discarded with so little care. Perhaps this is part of growing up, part of the compromise of the innocence of youth, but I refuse to believe it is necessary. I prefer to believe that there are other places that embrace enthusiasm, harness it and use it to drive the world. Without it, there would be so little passion and creativity that the world would be a grey and very lonely place.

There are many men who recognise passion and creativity in themselves, but they are timorous. They stand at the crossroads of choice, tempted by future challenge and the rewards it might offer, but incapable of making a decision because they are paralysed by the fear of failure and shame. They cannot see that even failure brings reward. Without failure a man never knows himself, the depths of his fears and his true potential. Those who never dare to challenge or risk failure, they truly risk what every man knows and fears: that his soul will never be tempered.

And as to the hellion, the fire that drives a young man to do the extraordinary, it is a blind, capricious thing. Even so, not to heed it is to deny the self and the energy and passion of life. Had I not embraced its energy, I could not have lived. The secret I know now is to find the thing that gives direction to the fire, a thing that brings colour, not dark. Life, not death. Because the fire is an ill-directed, wandering, vagrant thing, it must be focused. Perhaps I could've done something else with five years of my life. I could've devoted myself to poetry or painting, each difficult and challenging, each with their own dark places. But I chose the Legion and I stayed.

Joining the French Foreign Legion is a journey, like attempting to cross, on your own, a never-before crossed desert, or falling in love. I have done all three and recognise you can never be sure if the journey will be of wonder, pain, or perhaps both, in differing measures. Whatever the outcome, the journey is the thing that sets some men from others. For, in a journey there is strength, and in risking a journey a man lives.

What I do know for certain is that whenever I hear a song of the Legion, the sound of men singing makes my hair stand on end and I feel a catch in my throat. Those songs bring back mixed feelings of the things I saw and did. They remind me that the journey has forever marked me as a Legionnaire.

Had I not stayed, I would not have had a diary filled with a day-to-day account of life in the French Foreign Legion. Reading its pages reminds me that an idea is not reality. Nor is an idea reality because people say it is, or because it is an idea passionately held. Perhaps learning this, just maybe, was worth five years of my life.

ACKNOWLEDGMENTS

I would like to thank those men who were posted with me at Forward Operating Base Shield, south of Sadr City, Baghdad. They included Mike Kamin, LTC Mark Schreiber United States Army, Mr Tony Lym, MAJ Joe Musacchia United States Air Force, and Captain Anthony Mancari United States Army. They read early drafts of this manuscript and were generous in their support and encouragement.

Another American I must acknowledge is Professor Douglas Porch, whose work makes him the most highly regarded writer on the French Foreign Legion.

In Australia, John Turner was enthusiastic in his support too, listening patiently to my stories, reading a very early draft and plying me with Cooper's ale. Craig Cormick was helpful with his advice and encouraged me to keep writing.

Thanks also go to Ms Sally Bird, my agent, who was thoughtful, measured and clear about her expectations of me and the likelihood of being published. One must always thank a publisher who has the courage to take on a first time author; so to Vanessa Radnidge of Hachette Australia go many thanks.

Not least, I will never forget the patience and endurance of the wounded men of 2/5 Cavalry Regiment, United States Army, who, on 25 June 2009, tolerated a tie-wearing lawyer/medic who tried to help them. It was the day of the Improvised Explosive Device, when their youth and innocence were forever lost.

I can never forget, or thank too much, Linda, without whose patience, generosity and love I would be a far lesser man.

GLOSSARY

Regiments of the French Foreign Legion:

1 REC   *1er Régiment Étranger de Cavalerie* (1st Foreign Cavalry Regiment); Orange

1 RE   *1er Régiment Étranger* (1st Foreign Regiment); Aubagne

2 REI   *2ème Régiment Étranger d'Infanterie* (2nd Foreign Infantry Regiment); Nîmes

2 REP   *2ème Régiment Étranger de Parachutistes* (2nd Foreign Parachute Regiment); Calvi, Corsica

3 REI   *3ème Régiment Étranger d'Infanterie* (3rd Foreign Infantry Regiment); Kourou, French Guyane

4 RE   *4ème Régiment Étranger* (4th Foreign Regiment); Castelnaudary

5 RE   *5ème Régiment Étranger* (5th Foreign Regiment); Papeete, Tahiti and Mururoa

6 REG   *6ème Régiment Étranger de Génie* (6th Foreign Engineers Regiment); Avignon

13 DBLE *13ème Demi-Brigade de Légion Étrangère* (13th
Foreign Legion Half-Brigade); Djibouti

DLEM *Détachement de Légion Étrangère de Mayotte*
(Detachment of the Foreign Legion at Mayotte);
Dzaoudi, Comoro

ancien – veteran or any Legionnaire who's completed instruction
and served in a Legion regiment

AND (*Armée Nationale de Djibouti*) – Republic of Djibouti's
armed services

appel – rollcall

bâtiment – building, living quarters

binome – partner

bureau de semaine – company office or term for one-week duty
therein

caisse popotte – box containing accoutrements for in-the-field
dining

CAPLE (*Compagnie Administrative des Personnels de la Légion
Étrangère*) – the Legion's administration and personnel
department, part of headquarters regiment 1 RE

capote – condom

casse-croûte – snack or morning tea break

CCS (*Compagnie de Commandement et des Services*) – company
providing administrative and infrastructure support to the
regiment

CCAS (*Compagnie de Commandement Appui et des Services*)
– The same as above, but with fire support (which would
only occur overseas)

ceinturon bleu – a Legionnaire's wide blue woollen sash

chambre – room, particularly a bedroom

chant – song

cheche – Long piece of cloth used as a scarf or headscarf

chef de corps – regimental commander (colonel)

compagnie – company

connard – fucker/bastard

con – damned idiot

corvée – cleaning duty or other menial work

couloir – corridor

CRAP (*Commandos de Recherche et d'Action dans le Profondeur*) – the Legion's special forces unit, attached to 2 REP and traditionally the first troops into any crisis zone

crétin – cretin, fool

dégage – piss off

dehors – outside

demerde – make do, improvise

dépêche/dépêchez – hurry up

disposer – to dismiss

élève – student, pupil

ENDF (Ethiopian National Defense Force) – Ethiopia's armed services

engagé volontaire – new recruit

épaulettes de tradition – red and green epaulettes worn for guard or parade

EV (*engagé volontaire*) – new recruit

FAMAS (*Fusil d'Assaut de la Manufacture d'Armes de Saint-Étienne*) – bullpup-style assault rifle favoured by the French military since its introduction in 1978

footing – running, a run

foyer – bar with shop attached

FRUD (*Front pour la Restoration de l'Unité et de la Démocratie*) – Djibouti-based Afar rebel organisation

fut fut – Legionnaire rapidly promoted to *caporal*

gamelles – mess tins, pots and pans

garde 24 – 24-hour guard duty at camp

gardez-vous – attention or standing to attention

go civil – to abandon your commitment to five years in the Legion and exercising your contractual right to leave. Often very difficult.

infirmier – medic

instruction – period of recruit training or instruction generally

jamais – never

je m'en fou – I don't care

képi blanc – iconic white hat worn by Legionnaires

malade – sick

matricule – military service number

médécin – doctor

médécin chef – regimental medical officer

monument aux morts – memorial to the dead

nyah – local woman, prostitute (Djibouti)

ordinaire – dining hall, soldiers' mess hall, refectory

parcours du combattant – combat or assault course

pass rapport – report or present oneself to an officer

pédé – homosexual

peloton – a number of Legionnaires under training, especially a promotion course, in size like a platoon

permission – leave

PI (*piquet d'intervention*) – regimental rapid response force – a duty of 24-hours

PILE (*poste d'information de la Légion Étrangère*) – Foreign Legion recruiting office

place d'armes – parade ground

plonge, la – washing-up duties

popottier – cook-come-waiter to officers and NCOs when in the field

prêt – ready

quartier – camp, base

rassemblenent – assembly, parade

repos – at-ease position or a period of rest

reveil – reveille, wake-up call

sac à dos – backpack

sac marine – duffel bag

salle – room or hall

section – literally, a section, but closer to a British/Australian platoon

SEPP (*Section d'Entretien et de Pliage des Parachutes*) – 2 REP's parachute maintenance section

selecteur de tir – lever for selecting a weapon's firing option

soldats du rang – other ranks, including *caporals*

sous-officier – non-commissioned officers, from *sergent* up to *adjudant-chef* and major

stage – course of instruction or specialist training

stagier – anyone on a course

tenue – uniform

tenue de combat – army greens

tête de noeud – dickhead

EXPLOSIVE FRONTLINE ACTION IN NORTHERN
IRELAND, TIMOR, IRAQ AND AFGHANISTAN

'an honest, insider's
account of the dark
arts of sniping and
special forces'
HERALD SUN

SAS

THE WORLD
OF AN ELITE
AUSTRALIAN
MARKSMAN

SNIPER

ROB MAYLOR with Robert Macklin

In SAS Sniper, *Rob Maylor takes us inside the closed world of
the Australian Special Forces – it's tough to get in, but the fighting
that follows is even tougher . . .*

ROYAL MARINE . . . SAS MARKSMAN . . . ELITE SOLDIER

Rob Maylor has seen action in the world's most dangerous combat
zones. From East Timor and Iraq to Afghanistan, he has been places
where no-one else wants to go.

He was there when a Black Hawk helicopter crashed, drowning two
of his mates. He was there at Australia's biggest battle in Afghanistan
when a Taliban ambush left him shockingly wounded.

He has walked for hours, sometimes days, through hostile country
until he has found the right position, sometimes more than a kilometre
away from his target, then when the moment is right he aims, and
with absolute precision, puts the bullet just where it is going to have
the most effect . . .

This is a gritty, no-holds-barred behind-the-scenes look at life on
the frontline from an elite SAS Sniper.

hachette
AUSTRALIA

If you would like to find out more about Hachette Australia,
our authors, upcoming events and new releases you can visit
our website or our social media channels:

hachette.com.au

[f] HachetteAustralia

[twitter] [instagram] [snapchat] HachetteAus